Mastering Functional Programming

Functional techniques for sequential and parallel programming with Scala

Anatolii Kmetiuk

BIRMINGHAM - MUMBAI

Mastering Functional Programming

Commissioning Editor: Aaron Lazar
Acquisition Editor: Sandeep Mishra
Content Development Editor: Manjusha Mantri
Technical Editor: Abhishek Sharma
Copy Editor: Safis Editing
Project Coordinator: Prajakta Naik
Proofreader: Safis Editing
Indexer: Mariammal Chettiyar
Graphics: Jisha Chirayil
Production Coordinator: Shantanu Zagade

First published: August 2018

Production reference: 1300818

Published by Packt Publishing Ltd.
Livery Place
35 Livery Street
Birmingham
B3 2PB, UK.

ISBN 978-1-78862-079-6

www.packtpub.com

To my father and mother, Alexander Kmetiuk and Aurelia Kmetiuk, for shaping me into the person that I've become.

`mapt.io`

Mapt is an online digital library that gives you full access to over 5,000 books and videos, as well as industry leading tools to help you plan your personal development and advance your career. For more information, please visit our website.

Why subscribe?

- Spend less time learning and more time coding with practical eBooks and videos from over 4,000 industry professionals

- Improve your learning with Skill Plans built especially for you

- Get a free eBook or video every month

- Mapt is fully searchable

- Copy and paste, print, and bookmark content

PacktPub.com

Did you know that Packt offers eBook versions of every book published, with PDF and ePub files available? You can upgrade to the eBook version at `www.PacktPub.com` and as a print book customer, you are entitled to a discount on the eBook copy. Get in touch with us at `service@packtpub.com` for more details.

At `www.PacktPub.com`, you can also read a collection of free technical articles, sign up for a range of free newsletters, and receive exclusive discounts and offers on Packt books and eBooks.

Contributors

About the author

Anatolii Kmetiuk is a Functional Programming and Data Science Freelance Developer. During his programming career, he has worked on Scala projects involving parallel computing, web APIs, SaaS, and data engineering. His areas of expertise include using applications of pure functional programming to build fault-tolerant, reactive systems, as well as parallel computing. Another area of his focus is machine learning and natural language processing.

I want to express gratitude to Marco Borst and André van Delft for the time and effort they put into reviewing this book thoroughly.

About the reviewers

Marco Borst is an independent programmer with more then 20 years of experience programming systems that yield useful applications. He teaches development teams alternative points of view regarding the applicability and limits of our functional abstractions. Stoked to be the most pragmatic person in the room, Marco shares his appreciation that, out of a multitude of daily choices to do either A or B, the least useless choice is often to do neither A nor B. It is a difficult choice to act upon. Being an engineer by education, a programmer by experience, and a communicator because nature forced him to be, Marco is inclined to share his craft with others and is positively thrilled when able to learn from others as well.

André van Delft is an independent computer science researcher in the Netherlands. Having studied mathematics and business administration, he has made a living as a consultant and scientist in various organizations. His main project is SubScript, which extends Scala with the so called Algebra of Communicating Processes, a concurrency theory from the 1980s, which he has presented at various conferences, such as Lambda Days, LambdaConf, and FLOPS. His product, SlideMight, may be the first off-the-shelf software that is partially powered with the Algebra of Communicating Processes.

Packt is searching for authors like you

If you're interested in becoming an author for Packt, please visit `authors.packtpub.com` and apply today. We have worked with thousands of developers and tech professionals, just like you, to help them share their insight with the global tech community. You can make a general application, apply for a specific hot topic that we are recruiting an author for, or submit your own idea.

Table of Contents

Preface

Functional programming languages, such as Java, Scala, and Clojure, are attracting attention as an efficient way to handle the new requirements for programming multi-processor and high-availability applications. This book will teach you functional programming with the help of Scala. The book takes a thought-leadership approach, gently introducing you to functional programming and taking you all the way to becoming a master at the paradigm. Beginning with an introduction to functional programming, the book gradually moves forward teaching you how to write declarative code, making use of functional types and values. After covering the basics, we will discuss the more advanced concepts in functional programming.

We will cover the concepts of pure functions and type classes, problems they aim to solve, and how to use them in practice. We will see how libraries can be used for purely functional programming. We will look at the broad family of libraries for functional programming. Finally, we will discuss some of the more advanced patterns in the functional programming world, such as Monad Transformers and Tagless Final. After covering the purely functional approach to programming, we will look into the subject of parallel programming. We will introduce the Actor model and how it is implemented in the modern functional languages. By the end of this book, you will have mastered the concepts entailing functional programming alongside OOP to build robust applications.

Who this book is for

If you are from an imperative and OOP background, this book will guide you through the world of functional programming, irrespective of which programming language you use.

What this book covers

Chapter 1, *The Declarative Programming Style*, covers the main idea of declarative style of abstracting away repeating algorithmic patterns and control flows so that, with one statement, it is possible to describe what otherwise would have been 10 lines of imperative code. Functional languages usually have an elaborate infrastructure to make such an approach especially relevant and usable. One good way to feel this difference is to have a look at the difference in programming with Java and Scala collections—the former employs the imperative style and latter the functional style.

Chapter 2, *Functions and Lambdas,* will start with the concept familiar to an OOP programmer—a method. We will then explore some more advanced, functional concepts specific to functional programming—things such as lambdas, currying, generic type parameters, implicit arguments, and higher-order functions. We will see how higher-order functions may be useful to abstract control flow. Finally, we will look at the concept of partial functions.

Chapter 3, *Functional Data Structures,* explains a functional collections framework. It features a hierarchy of collections data types designed for different scenarios. It then moves to other data types that are not part of the collections framework but are often used in functional programming and hence deserve our attention. The data types are Option, Either, and Try. Finally, we will see how the data structures are separated from their behavior via an implicit mechanism, which is present in some advanced languages.

Chapter 4, *The Problem of Side Effects,* is about side effects that are ubiquitous in programming. Functional programming advocates for so-called pure functions—functions that do not produce any side effects, which means you can't write a file from such a function, or contact the network. Why would functional programming advocate against functions that cause side effects? Is it possible to write a useful program using pure functions only? This chapter explores these questions.

Chapter 5, *Effect Types - Abstracting Away Side Effects,* provides solutions to the problems of working with side effects in a pure way. The solution presented by purely functional programming is to turn the side effects you encounter into functional data structures. We will explore the process of identifying side effects and turning them into such data structures. Then, we will quickly realize functions that produce side effects usually work one with another. We will hence explore how one can combine these functions using the concept of the Monad.

Chapter 6, *Effect Types in Practice,* focuses on the material of the Chapter 3, *Functional Data Structures,* from a new perspective. We will see how functional data structures have a deeper meaning to the data types-that of representing phenomena as data. A phenomenon is something that happens, such as an exception or a delay. By representing it in data we are able to shield ourselves from the effects of the phenomenon while preserving the information about it.

Chapter 7, *The Idea of the Type Classes,* explore how the Type Class pattern logically emerges from practical needs encountered when working with effect types.

Chapter 8, *Basic Type Classes and Their Usage*, outlines the most frequently encountered type classes and their family in general. After discussing the motivation for the creation of type class systems, we proceed further to examine their structure and a few basic type classes from them. Type classes such as Monad and Applicative are frequently used in functional programming, so they deserve some special attention.

Chapter 9, *Libraries for Pure Functional Programming*, discusses how to use the purely functional techniques (effect types and type classes) learned so far in order to develop server-side software. We will learn how to write concurrent, asynchronous software for responding to HTTP requests, contacting the database. We will also learn about the concurrency model modern functional programming offers.

Chapter 10, *Patterns of Advanced Functional Programming*, explores how to combine effect types to get new effect types. You will see how to leverage the power of the compiler's type system to check guarantees about the program on compile time.

Chapter 11, *Introduction to the Actor Model*, starts with examining the traditional model of concurrent programming in details. This model rises a bunch of problems such as race conditions and deadlocks, which make programming in it prone to errors that are particularly hard to debug. This chapter presents the idea of an Actor model that aims to solve these problems.

Chapter 12, *The Actor Model in Practice*, covers the fundamentals of the framework and its concepts. You will proceed to learn some of the patterns that emerge during actor-oriented programming and also see how Actors interoperate with other widespread concurrency primitives—Futures.

Chapter 13, *Use Case - A Parallel Web Crawler*, examines a larger concurrent application written with the Actor model. One good such example is a web crawler application. A web crawler is an application that collects links from websites. Starting from a given website, it collects all the links on it, follows them, and recursively collects all the links from them. This chapter will examine how to implement such a larger application.

Appendix A, *Introduction to Scala,* is a short introduction to the Scala language, which is used for examples throughout the book.

To get the most out of this book

Before reading this book, readers need to know about the concepts of object-oriented and imperative programming.

To test the code of this book, you need Docker version 18.06 or higher and Git version 2.18.0 or higher.

Download the example code files

You can download the example code files for this book from your account at `www.packtpub.com`. If you purchased this book elsewhere, you can visit `www.packtpub.com/support` and register to have the files emailed directly to you.

You can download the code files by following these steps:

1. Log in or register at `www.packtpub.com`.
2. Select the **SUPPORT** tab.
3. Click on **Code Downloads & Errata**.
4. Enter the name of the book in the **Search** box and follow the onscreen instructions.

Once the file is downloaded, please make sure that you unzip or extract the folder using the latest version of:

- WinRAR/7-Zip for Windows
- Zipeg/iZip/UnRarX for Mac
- 7-Zip/PeaZip for Linux

The code bundle for the book is also hosted on GitHub at `https://github.com/PacktPublishing/Mastering-Functional-Programming`. In case there's an update to the code, it will be updated on the existing GitHub repository.

We also have other code bundles from our rich catalog of books and videos available at `https://github.com/PacktPublishing/`. Check them out!

Download the color images

We also provide a PDF file that has color images of the screenshots/diagrams used in this book. You can download it here: https://www.packtpub.com/sites/default/files/downloads/MasteringFunctionalProgramming_ColorImages.pdf.

Conventions used

There are a number of text conventions used throughout this book.

CodeInText: Indicates code words in text, database table names, folder names, filenames, file extensions, pathnames, dummy URLs, user input, and Twitter handles. Here is an example: "The instances package contains the implementations of the type classes for basic data types that are present in the language core and the ones defined by the Cats library."

A block of code is set as follows:

```
public void drink() {
    System.out.println("You have drunk a can of soda.");
}
```

Any command-line input or output is written as follows:

```
:help
```

Bold: Indicates a new term, an important word, or words that you see onscreen. For example, words in menus or dialog boxes appear in the text like this. Here is an example: "The for comprehension is shorthand for sequentially calling flatMap. This technique is called the **Monadic flow**."

Warnings or important notes appear like this.

Tips and tricks appear like this.

Get in touch

Feedback from our readers is always welcome.

General feedback: Email feedback@packtpub.com and mention the book title in the subject of your message. If you have questions about any aspect of this book, please email us at questions@packtpub.com.

Errata: Although we have taken every care to ensure the accuracy of our content, mistakes do happen. If you have found a mistake in this book, we would be grateful if you would report this to us. Please visit www.packtpub.com/submit-errata, selecting your book, clicking on the Errata Submission Form link, and entering the details.

Piracy: If you come across any illegal copies of our works in any form on the Internet, we would be grateful if you would provide us with the location address or website name. Please contact us at copyright@packtpub.com with a link to the material.

If you are interested in becoming an author: If there is a topic that you have expertise in and you are interested in either writing or contributing to a book, please visit authors.packtpub.com.

Reviews

Please leave a review. Once you have read and used this book, why not leave a review on the site that you purchased it from? Potential readers can then see and use your unbiased opinion to make purchase decisions, we at Packt can understand what you think about our products, and our authors can see your feedback on their book. Thank you!

For more information about Packt, please visit packtpub.com.

The Declarative Programming Style

1

Declarative programming is tightly connected to functional programming. Modern functional languages prefer to express programs as algebra and not as algorithms. This means that programs in functional languages are combinations of certain primitives with operators. The technique where you express your programs by specifying what to do, but not how to do it, is referred to as declarative programming. We will explore why declarative programming appeared and where it can be used.

In this chapter, we will cover the following topics:

- Principles of declarative programming
- Declarative versus imperative collections
- Declarative programming in other languages

Technical requirements

To run the examples in this book, you will need the following software, as well as basic understanding of how to use it:

- Docker version 18.06 or higher: `https://www.docker.com/`
- Git version 2.18.0 or higher: `https://git-scm.com/`

To run the samples:

1. Clone the `https://github.com/PacktPublishing/Mastering-Functional-Programming` repository on your machine.

2. From its root, compose and run the Docker set of images specified in `docker-compose.yml`. If you are on a Linux/Mac machine, you can run `./compose.sh` to complete this step. If you are on Windows, open `compose.sh` in text editor and run each command from your terminal manually.

3. Run shell (Bash) on the Docker service called `mastering-functional-programming_backend_1`. You can complete this step by running `./start.sh` on a Linux/Mac machine from a separate terminal window. If you are on a Windows machine, run `docker exec -ti mastering_backend bash`. Then `cd Chapter1` for Chapter 1 examples, or `cd ChapterN` for Chapter N examples.

4. The `cpp` folder contains C++ sources. You can run them with `./run.sh <name-of-the-source>` from that directory.

5. The `jvm` folder contains Java and Scala sources. You can run them by running `sbt run` from that directory.

Note that it is necessary to run the examples under Docker. Some chapters run examples against a live database, which is managed by Docker, so make sure to get the above procedure working.

The codes presented in this book are available at: `https://github.com/PacktPublishing/Mastering-Functional-Programming`

Principles of declarative programming

Why declarative programming? How did it appear? To understand declarative programming, we need to first understand how it is different from imperative programming. For a long time, imperative programming has been a *de facto* industry standard. What motivated people to start switching to the functional style from the imperative style?

In imperative programming, you rely on a set of primitives that your language provides. You combine them in a certain way so as to achieve a functionality that you need. We can understand different things under primitives. For example, these can be loop control structures, or, in the case of collections, operations specific to collections, such as creating a collection and adding or removing elements from a collection.

In declarative programming, you also rely on primitives. You use them to express your program. Yet, in declarative programming, these primitives are much closer to your domain. They can be so close to your domain that the language itself can be regarded as a **domain-specific language (DSL)**. With declarative programming, you are able to create primitives as you go.

In imperative programming, you usually don't create new primitives, but rely on the ones the language provides you with. Let's go through some examples to understand the importance of declarative programming.

Example – go-to versus loops

How imperative turns into declarative is best understood by means of an example. Most likely, you already know the go-to statement. You have heard that using the go-to statement is bad practice. Why? Consider an example of a loop. It is possible to express a loop using only the go-to statement:

```cpp
#include <iostream>
using namespace std;
int main() {
    int x = 0;
    loop_start:
     x++;
    cout << x << "\n";
    if (x < 10) goto loop_start;
    return 0;
}
```

From the preceding example, imagine you need to express a while loop. You have the variable x and you need to increment it in a loop by one until it reaches 10. In modern languages such as Java, you would be able to do this using the while loop, but it is also possible to do that using the go-to statement. For example, it is possible to have a label on the increment statement. A conditional statement after it will check whether the variable reached the necessary value. If it did not, we perform a go-to on the line of code to increment a variable.

Why is `go-to` a bad style in this case? A loop is a pattern. A pattern is an arrangement of two or more logical elements in your code that repeats in different places of your program. In our case, the pattern is the loop. Why is it a pattern? First, it consists of three parts:

1. The first part is the label that is the entry point to the body of the loop—the point where you jump from the end of the loop to reiterate the loop.
2. The second part is the condition that must be true in order for the loop to reiterate.
3. The third part is the statement to reiterate the fact that it is a loop. It is the end of the body of the loop.

Besides being composed of three parts, it also describes an action that is ubiquitous in programming. The action is repeating a chunk of code more than once. The fact that loops are ubiquitous in programming needs no explanation.

If you re-implement the loop pattern each time you need it, things can go wrong. As the pattern has more than one part to it, it can be corrupted by misusing one of the parts, or you could make a mistake when arranging the parts into a whole. It is possible to forget to name the label to which to jump, or to name it incorrectly. You may also forget to define the `predicate` statement that guards the jump to the beginning of the loop. Or, you could misspell the label to which to jump in the `q` statement itself. For example, in the following code, we forgot to specify the predicate guard:

```
int main() {
  int x = 0;
  loop_start:
   x++;
  cout << x << "\n";
  goto loop_start;
  return 0;
}
```

Example – nested loop

It's pretty hard to get such a simple example wrong, but consider a nested loop. For example, you have a matrix, and you want to output it to the console. This can be done with a `nested` loop. You have a loop to iterate on with every entry of the 2D array. Another loop nested in that loop examines the row the outer loop is currently working on. It iterates on every element of that row and prints it to the console.

It is also possible to express these in terms of the `go-to` statement. So, you will have the first label to signify the entry point into the large loop, another label to signify the entry point to the small loop, and you will call the `go-to` statement at the end of each loop to jump to the beginning of the respective loop.

Let's see how to do that. First, let's define a 2D array as follows:

```
int rows = 3;
int cols = 3;
int matrix[rows][cols] = {
    { 1, 2, 3 },
    { 4, 5, 6 },
    { 7, 8, 9 }
};
```

Now, we can loop over it as follows:

```
int r = 0;
row_loop:
if (r < rows) {
 int c = 0;
  col_loop:
  if (c < cols) {
 cout << matrix[r][c] << " ";
     c++;
     goto col_loop;
  }
  cout << "\n";
  r++;
  goto row_loop;
} return 0; }
```

You can already see an increase in complexity here. For example, you can perform a `go-to` from the end of the inner loop to the beginning of the outer loop. This way, only the first item of each column receives output. The program becomes an infinite loop:

```
int r = 0;
row_loop:
if (r < rows) {
  int c = 0;
 col_loop:
 if (c < cols) {
   cout << matrix[r][c] << " ";
    c++;
   goto row_loop;
  }
 cout << "\n";
```

```
    r++;
    goto row_loop;
}
```

Don't Repeat Yourself (DRY)

One of the fundamental rules of engineering is to create abstractions for logic that repeats. The pattern of the loop is ubiquitous. You can experience it in almost any program. Hence, it is reasonable to abstract away. This is why contemporary languages, such as Java or C++, have their own built-in mechanisms for loops.

The difference it makes is that, now, the entire pattern consists of one component only, that is, the keyword that must be used with a certain syntax:

```
#include <iostream>
using namespace std;
int main() {
  int rows = 3;
  int cols = 3;
  int matrix[rows][cols] = {
    { 1, 2, 3 },
    { 4, 5, 6 },
    { 7, 8, 9 }
  };
  for (int r = 0; r < rows; r++) {
    for (int c = 0; c < cols; c++) cout << matrix[r][c] << " ";
    cout << "\n";
  }
}
```

What happened here is that we gave a name to the pattern. Every time we need this pattern, we do not implement it from scratch. We call the pattern by its name.

This calling by name is the main principle of declarative programming: implement patterns that repeat only once, give names to those patterns, and then refer to them by their name anywhere we need them.

For example, `while` or `for` loops are patterns of loops. They are abstracted away and implemented on a language level. The programmer can refer to them by their names whenever they need a loop. Now, the chance of making an error is much less likely because the compiler is aware of the pattern. It will perform a compile-time check on whether you are using the pattern properly. For example, when you use the `while` statement, the compiler will check whether you have provided a proper condition. It will perform all the jump logic for you.

So, you do not need to worry whether you jumped to the correct label, or that you forgot to jump at all. Therefore, there is no chance of you jumping from the end of the inner loop to the start of the outer loop.

What you have seen here is the transition from an imperative to a declarative style. The concept you need to understand here is that we made the programming language aware of a certain pattern. The compiler was forced to verify the correctness of the pattern at compile time. We specified the pattern once. We gave it a name. We made the programming language enforce certain constraints on the programmer that uses this name. At the same time, the programming language takes care of the implementation of the pattern, meaning that the programmer does not need to be concerned with all the algorithms that were used to implement the pattern.

So, in declarative programming, we specify what needs to be done without specifying how to do it. We notice patterns and give them names. We implement these patterns once and call them by name afterward whenever we need to use them. In fact, modern languages, such as Java, Scala, Python, or Haskell do not have the support of the `go-to` statement. It seems that the vast majority of the programs expressed with the `go-to` statement can be translated into a set of patterns, such as loops, that abstract away `go-to` statements. Programmers are encouraged to use these higher-level patterns by name, rather than implementing the logic by themselves using lower-level `go-to` primitives. Next, let's see how this idea develops further using the example of declarative collections and how they differ from imperative ones.

Declarative versus imperative collections

Another great illustration of how the declarative style works can be seen in collection frameworks. Let's compare the collection frameworks of an imperative and functional programming language, for example, Java (imperative) collections and Scala (functional) collections.

Why a collection framework? Collections are ubiquitous in any programming project. When you are dealing with a database-powered application, you are using collections. When you are writing a web crawler, you are using collections. In fact, when you are dealing with simple strings of text, you are using collections. Most modern programming languages provide you with the implementation of collection frameworks as part of their core library. That is because you will need them for almost any project.

We'll go into more depth about how imperative collections are different from declarative collections in the next chapter. However, for the purpose of an overview, let's briefly discuss one of the major differences between the imperative and declarative approaches to collections here. We can see such a difference using the example of filtering. Filtering is an ubiquitous operation that you most likely will find yourself doing pretty often, so let's see how it differs across the two approaches.

Filtering

Java is a classic example of a very imperative approach to programming. And hence, in its collections, you will encounter operations that are typical of imperative programming. For example, consider that you have an array of strings. They are the names of the employees of your company. You want to create a separate collection with only those employees whose names start with the letter 'A'. How do you do that in Java?

```
// Source collection
List<String> employees = new ArrayList<String>();
employees.add("Ann");
employees.add("John");
employees.add("Amos");
employees.add("Jack");
// Those employees with their names starting with 'A'
List<String> result = new ArrayList<String>();
for (String e: employees)
   if (e.charAt(0) == 'A') result.add(e);
    System.out.println(result);
```

First, you need to create a separate collection to store the result of your computation. So, we create a new `ArrayList` of strings. Afterward, you will need to check every employee's name to establish whether it starts with the letter 'A'. If it does, add this name to the newly created array.

What could possibly go wrong? The first issue is the very collection where you want to store your results. You need to call `result.add()` on the collection – but what if you have several collections, and you add to the wrong one? You have the freedom to add to any collection at that line of code, so it is conceivable that you add to the wrong one – not the dedicated one you have created solely for the purpose of filtering the employees.

Another thing that can go wrong here is that you can forget to write the `if` statement in the large loop. Of course, it is not very likely in such a trivial example, but remember that large projects can bloat and code bases can become large. In our example, the body of the loop has fewer than 10 lines. But what if you have a code base where the `for` loop is up to 50 lines, for example? It is not as obvious there that you won't forget to write your predicate, or to add the string to any collection at all.

The point here is that we have the same situation as in the `loop` versus `go-to` example. We have a pattern of an operation over a collection that might repeat itself in the code base. The pattern is something that is composed of more than one element, and it goes as follows. Firstly, we create a new collection to store the result of our computation. Secondly, we have the loop that iterates on every element of our collection. And finally, we have a predicate. If it is true, we save the current element into the result collection.

We can imagine the same logic executed in other contexts as well. For example, we can have a collection of numbers and want to take only those that are greater than 10. Or, we can have a list of all our website users and want to take the age of those users visiting the site over a particular year.

The particular pattern we were discussing is called the filter pattern. In Scala, every collection supports a method defined on it that abstracts away the filter pattern. This is done as follows:

```
// Source collection
val employees = List(
  "Ann"
, "John"
, "Amos"
, "Jack")
// Those employees with their names starting with 'A'
val result = employees.filter ( e => e(0) == 'A' )
println(result)
```

Notice that the operation remains the same. We need to create a new collection, then incorporate the elements from the old collection into the new collection based on some predicate. Yet, in the case of the pure Java solution, we need to perform three separate actions to get the desired result. However, in the case of the Scala declarative style, we only need to specify a single action: the name of the pattern. The pattern is implemented in the language internals, and we do not need to worry about how it is done. We have a precise specification of how it works and of what it does, and we can rely on it.

The advantage here is not only that the code becomes easier to read, and thus easier to reason about. It also increases reliability and runtime performance. The reason is that the filter pattern here is a member of the core Scala library. This means that it is well tested. It was used in a large number of other projects before. The subtle bugs that could have existed in such a situation were likely caught and fixed.

Also observe that the notion of anonymous lambdas gets introduced here. We pass one as an argument to the `filter` method. They are functions that are defined inline, without the usual tedious method syntax. Anonymous lambdas are a common feature of functional languages, as they increase your flexibility for abstracting logic.

Declarative programming in other languages

In other modern languages, such as Haskell or Python, a similar declarative functionality is also present out of the box. For example, you can perform filtering in Python—it is built into the language, and you have a special function in Haskell to perform the same filtering. Also, the functional nature of Python and Haskell makes it easy to implement the same control structure as filtering by yourself. Both Haskell and Python support the notion of the lambda function and higher-order functions, so they can be used to implement declarative control structures.

In general, you can spot whether a language is declarative programming-friendly by looking at the capabilities it provides. Some of the features you can look for are anonymous functions, functions as first-class citizens, and custom operator specifications.

Anonymous lambda gives you a great advantage because you can pass functions to other functions inline, without first defining them. This is particularly useful when specifying control structures. A function expressed in this way is, first and foremost, to specify a transformation that is supposed to transform an input into an output.

Another feature that you can look for in programming languages is support for functions as first-class citizens. This means that you are able to assign a function to a variable, refer to the function by that variable's name, and pass that variable to other functions. Treating functions as if they are ordinary variables allows you to achieve a new level of abstraction. This is because functions are transformations; they map their input values to some output values. And, if the language does not allow you to pass transformations to other transformations, this is a limitation of flexibility.

Another feature that you can expect from declarative languages is that they allow you to create custom operators; for example, the synthetic sugar available in Scala allows you to define new operators very easily, as methods in classes.

Summary

The declarative style is a style of programming where you call the operations you want to perform by name, instead of describing how to execute them in an algorithmic fashion via lower-level primitives provided by the programming language. This naturally aligns with the DRY principle. If you have a repeating operation, you want to abstract it away, and then refer to it by name later on. In other words, you need to declare that the operation has a certain name. And, whenever you want to use it, you need to declare your intent, without specifying directly how it should be fulfilled.

Modern functional programming goes hand in hand with the declarative style. Functional programming provides you with a better level of abstraction, which can be used to abstract away the repeating operations.

In the next chapter, we will see how first-class citizen support for functions can be useful for the declarative programming style.

Questions

1. What is the principle behind declarative programming?
2. What does DRY stand for?
3. Why is using `go-to` bad style?

2
Functions and Lambdas

The paradigm of functional programming has a lot of common features with the paradigm of declarative programming. One of the defining features of functional languages and declarative programming is the extensive use of functions. This chapter will discuss in more detail what functions are and their meaning in different paradigms. We will have a look at how we can use functions and what their role is in modern programming languages.

In this chapter, we will cover the following topics:

- Functions as behaviors
- Functions in functional programming
- Higher-order functions
- Lambdas
- The concept of functions in different programming languages

Functions as behavior

So what are functions? We can define them as **parameterized**, named chunks of code. This means that they are chunks of code that can be called from any other part of the program by their name. Parameterized means that you can call them with certain arguments. Different calls executed with different parameters usually lead to different results.

What is the motivation behind functions? The answer is the basic principle of engineering – abstract away that which repeats itself. In Chapter 1, The *Declarative Programming Style*, we saw something similar in the case of loops. However, loops are built-in control structures. This means they are defined at the language level. When we need to define some logic on the language-user level, and this logic repeats itself across different parts of the project, functions come into play.

We can trace functions across paradigms to as early as procedural programming. In procedural programming, functions are one of the units of abstraction. This means that functions encapsulate the logic that repeats. In object-oriented programming, we have an evolution of the understanding of functions. Functions are usually viewed in the context of an object or a class. In this context, they play the role of the behavior of an object.

For example, if you have an object called a soda machine, this object may have certain behaviors associated with it, such as inserting a coin into the machine, or pressing the button to get a can of soda from the machine.

Functions in functional programming

In imperative programming, functions are used to represent the behavior of an object. In object-oriented programming, the behavior usually implies side effects. For the purposes of this book, we can understand side effects as follows—a function is side-effecting when it modifies the environment outside its own body. For example, it can have a global variable of its parent object modified, it can write a file into the filesystem, or the function can perform some web API calls over the network.

In functional programming, the understanding of functions is quite different. In functional programming, we prise purity and referential transparency. Purity means the absence of side effects. Referential transparency means that the result value the function has computed can be substituted in place of the function call, while the semantics of the program execution will remain unchanged.

Consider the following example. You have an application that simulates a soda machine. Its behavior is that of the insertion of the coin into the soda machine and getting a soda can back from it. A soda machine consists of the data: the amount of money and soda cans present in the machine. Whenever a coin is inserted, a soda can will be sold.

How do we express this behavior in an imperative style? We can create a separate object called a soda machine and, in that object, a method to dispatch cans. Whenever this method is called, the number of coins present in it is increased by one and the number of soda cans decreases by one. Also, we want to return an object called SodaCan from the method.

In the spirit of object-oriented programming, we can represent the soda machine as an object with some internal state:

```java
public class ImperativeSodaMachine {
  private int coins = 0;
  private int cans  = 0;
  public ImperativeSodaMachine(int initialCans) {
    this.cans = initialCans;
  }
```

We can also define some behavior on this machine: the behavior of what needs to happen upon inserting a coin and getting a soda can back. If there are soda cans left in the machine, we decrease the number of soda cans by one, increase the number of coins by one, and return a soda can object to the user. If there are no cans left, we throw an exception:

```java
public SodaCan insertCoin() {
    if (cans > 0) {
      cans--;
      coins++;
      return new SodaCan();
    }
    else throw new RuntimeException("Out of soda cans!");
  }
}
```

Finally, the SodaCan object is defined as follows:

```java
public class SodaCan {
  public void drink() {
    System.out.println("You have drunk a can of soda.");
  }
}
```

The cans and the amount of money present in the soda machine are the variables of the soda machine. They don't belong to the function's body. This is why the function that changes variables that are outside its own scope constitutes a side-effecting function.

While imperative methods are conceptualized as side-effecting behaviors, functions in the functional style are conceptualized as computations that compute some value. In the functional world, side effects are not welcome. Let's express the preceding program in a purely functional way. We would have a soda machine with no behavior because the behavior is side-effecting. Side effects are generally bad in the functional world, as we will learn in subsequent chapters. Instead of that behavior, you would have a function that computes a new state of the soda machine. That is a new soda machine object from the old soda machine object. Such a soda machine object is an immutable object, which means that it only contains values that cannot be modified. This helps to eliminate side effects, since now, functions defined on the soda machine cannot modify its variables that are outside the scope of the functions. Whenever we want to get a new soda can, we would also need to compute the new state of the soda machine after the can is dispatched, and then return a soda can from this machine:

```
case class SodaMachine(cans: Int, coins: Int = 0)
def insertCoin(sm: SodaMachine): (SodaMachine, SodaCan) =
 if (sm.cans > 0) (SodaMachine(sm.cans - 1, sm.coins + 1), new SodaCan)
 else throw new RuntimeException("Out of soda cans!")
```

Expressed this way, the computation does not affect the environment outside its own scope. We no longer have the modification of some external variables, nor do we interact with the world outside the scope of the function. We just compute the result values based on the inputs to the function. This is the understanding of a function in the world of functional programming. Later on in this book, we will cover how this understanding is more beneficial than the original understanding of a method in terms of the behavior.

The absence of side effects is not the only feature of the functional style. The next feature we are going to look at is higher-order functions—functions that accept other functions as their inputs.

Higher-order functions

Another important concept that appears in functional programming is that of higher-order functions. A higher-order function is a function that accepts a function as an argument. A very trivial example of where this may be useful is control structures. For example, a `while` loop can be expressed in a functional way as a higher-order function that accepts the body of the loop and a predicate as an argument.

The body of the loop can be expressed as a function that does not accept any arguments, but computes some side effects. The way it works is that we have a function accept a `0-argument` function and a predicate, and we call the same `loop` function recursively while the predicate is true.

We can call the new control structure `whileDiy`, and it can be defined as follows:

```
@annotation.tailrec
def whileDiy(predicate: => Boolean)(body: => Unit): Unit =
  if (predicate) {
    body
    whileDiy(predicate)(body)
  }
}
```

The `whileDiy` construct accepts a predicate and a body. The predicate will be evaluated on each function call and, if it is true, we will run the body and recursively invoke the `whileDiy` construct again. Notice also that in the `@annotation.tailrec` annotation on top of the method, it indicates that the method will be called in a tail-recursive manner, which means there's no chance it will result in a `StackOverflowError`, even though it is recursive. This is because it will reuse the frame of its initial call for all subsequent recursive calls.

We can use the new construction as follows:

```
var j = 0
whileDiy (j < 5) {
  println(s"Printing from custom while loop. Iteration: $j")
  j += 1
}
```

Compare this to how the built-in `while` loop is used:

```
var i = 0
while (i < 5) {
  println(s"Printing from built-in while loop. Iteration: $i")
  i += 1
}
```

The usage is almost identical. This illustrates how higher-order functions can be used to define control structures very close to the ones built in to the language.

Understanding lambda functions

Most functional languages have a concept of a lambda function. It is an anonymous function defined inline. It can be assigned to a variable if needed. For example, consider that we need a function that accepts a cookie with user session data, in the context of a web application. Its job is to print a greeting to the user to the standard output. However, before printing, we need to decorate the user's name in a certain way. To complicate matters further, we also have a database of users who hold PhDs and, if they do, we need to refer to them as Dr. Here is how it can be done in Scala:

1. We define the dummy `Cookie` class for our example:

   ```
   case class Cookie(name: String, gender: String)
   ```

2. We define the `greeting` method. The job of the method is to extract the data from the `cookie` object, and apply the modifier to the user's name based on their gender.

3. After that, greet the user. This method does not know how exactly to modify the name. The `modifier` logic is abstracted away and we rely on the caller to specify how to do this:

   ```
   def greeting(cookie: Cookie)(modifier: (String, String) => String):
   Unit = {
       val name        = cookie.name
       val gender      = cookie.gender
       val modifiedName = modifier(name, gender)
       print(s"Hello, $modifiedName")
   }
   ```

4. Finally, this is how we can call this method:

   ```
   def isPhd(name: String): Boolean = name == "Smith"
   val cookie = Cookie("Smith", "male")
   greeting(cookie) { (name, gender) =>
     if (isPhd(name)) s"Dr $name"
     else gender match {
       case "male"   => s"Mr $name"
       case "female" => s"Mrs $name"
     }
   }
   ```

The `greeting` function accepts a string and also a function that modifies this string. Notice how, when calling this function, we specify the function that modifies the string inline. We do not define the function prior to passing it to the `greeting` function.

This is the idea behind a lambda function. You don't need to define a function before you can use it in some other higher-order function. Instead, you can define functions like that inline, using lambda syntax. Obviously, this kind of approach is especially useful in the context of higher-order functions. It allows you to use higher-order functions without first defining their arguments.

The concept of the lambda function is present in the majority of functional languages, including Scala, Haskell, and Python.

The concept of functions in different programming languages

Functions are present in many programming languages. Some of the languages have better support for purely functional styles, while others favor declarative styles. This is why, for example, using Scala over Java can give you tremendous leverage, because you can declare functions inside other functions, you can declare functions that accept other functions (higher-order functions) more easily, and you can declare anonymous lambda functions (functionality also available in Java, starting from Java 8). This greatly increases your capacity for abstraction, creating control structures, and thereby enabling your application to be expressed in a more **DRY (Don't Repeat Yourself)** way.

Summary

In this chapter, we have seen what functions are and how they have evolved from the early days of programming to today. We have seen how functions were initially treated as abstractions of common logic. After that, in object-oriented programming, they represented the behavior of certain objects. Object-oriented programmers attempted to represent everything as an object. So it is only natural that functions started to be viewed in the context of a world that consists of objects. In this context, functions are best viewed as behaviors of these objects.

In functional programming, functions can be viewed in a different context. Now, the best way to view functions is as mathematical computations. They compute some value out of its inputs, in a pure way, which means without any side effects. The idea is to view them as mathematical functions.

Functional programming is close to declarative programming, so its functions are also often tailored to the needs of that style. This way, in functional languages, there is a concept of higher-order functions, anonymous lambda functions, and partial functions. From an engineering perspective, this is useful because it greatly enhances your capability for abstraction.

In programming, data structures are ubiquitous. When adopting functional style, sooner or later you will encounter a problem of working with data structures in a functional way. In the next chapter, we will see how this problem is addressed.

Questions

1. How are functions interpreted in the context of object-oriented programming?
2. How are functions interpreted in the context of pure functional programming?
3. What are higher-order functions?
4. Why are higher-order functions useful?

3
Functional Data Structures

Programming largely deals with data manipulation. Different styles of programming will treat data structures, and data itself, differently. For example, imperative programming treats data as mutable information stored in memory. We will see how the treatment of functional programming differs from that of imperative programming.

In this chapter, we will cover the following topics:

- Collections framework
- The algebraic approach
- Effect types
- Data structures in different programming languages

Collections framework

When discussing data structures, it is only natural to start with collections. Collections are data structures that abstract away multiplicity. This means that whenever you have more than one item of a particular kind, and you want to run a number of operations on this data, you will need a proper abstraction—an abstraction that will establish the rules of the game you play when you encounter multiplicity.

It transpires that you will need to deal with abstraction of this nature in nearly every programming project. When you are dealing with strings, you frequently need to represent them as a collection of characters. Whenever you have a database application, and you have some queries in relation to this database, you need to present multiple results of these queries as collections. Whenever you are dealing with a text file, you may want to represent it as a list of lines. This happens rather frequently, for example, when dealing with configuration files. We specify our configuration entries as strings on separate lines. For example, the following is how we may represent a server connection configuration:

```
host=192.168.12.3
port=8888
username=root
password=qwerty
```

Or, for example, you may want to communicate data with a web API. Most modern web APIs communicate data in the form of JSON or XML. These are structured ways of representing data and, if you observe them closely, you will notice that they follow a pattern; for example, an XML file is composed of a tree of multiple nodes, and a JSON object may contain more than one entry.

So, whenever you are working on a programming project, it is very likely that you will need to deal with some kind of abstraction over multiplicity. You require a collections framework. Because collections are so ubiquitous, it is only natural that modern programming languages include a collection framework in their core library. This is why looking at a language's collections framework is an easy way to see the philosophy of the language and its approach to programming in general.

In this section, we will compare the collection frameworks of Java and Scala. Java represents a traditional, imperative approach to programming, and, hence, its collection framework also reflects this approach. On the other hand, Scala represents a functional, declarative approach to programming. Its collection framework is built and structured according to the philosophy of functional and declarative programming.

Imperative collections

Let's have a look at how collections are understood within the framework of an imperative programming language, while also looking at Java's abstraction of a list. Its API documentation is available at `https://docs.oracle.com/javase/8/docs/api/java/util/List.html`. This interface only has a limited number of methods defined. The first thing that we need to pay attention to here is mutability. Immediately, we see methods such as `add` and `remove`. This implies that this interface is supposed to be implemented by a mutable collection that is supposed to implement the operations that add or remove data from it. You should be aware that methods can throw an `UnsupportedOperationException`, which means that certain collections may implement this interface; however, they will not implement these two operations. Later in the book, we will see that functional programming does not welcome exceptions of this kind as they are a type of side effect and here, it is especially obvious why. One of the essential principles of object-oriented programming is polymorphism, which means that you can place an interface on top of a class and, from there, you are able to interact with this class according to this interface, without caring about the internal implementation. An interface is supposed to be a protocol of interaction with an object; it is supposed to specify which behavior it supports, and throwing an exception if a behavior is not supported is a rather clumsy move on the part of Java, since you need to bear in mind that certain behavior is not supported, even though the interface declares that it is. This further taxes the programmer's mind and, hence, it can lead to bugs.

Another peculiarity we should observe is that other methods defined here are quite low level. You have the ability to add to the collection and to remove from the collection. It is assumed that whatever you need to do with the collection, you will be able to do so with the help of these and other low-level methods that the interface provides. This is realized by writing an imperative algorithm that specifies how exactly to perform a necessary operation given the low-level primitives provided by the language. This, in turn, means that you must be skilled with algorithms to write effective Java programs, because the use of algorithms is the only option open to you.

In fact, it has long been a tradition in computer science and programming to focus extensively on algorithms. The data has been perceived as some kind of mutable information written in a certain medium, and the task of the programmer is to specify a sequence of steps to modify this data as per requirements. Hence, one of the first things people learn in computer science is sorting algorithms such as Bubble Sort.

Algorithms are certainly necessary. Under the hood of any computer program, algorithms are precisely what do the job. However, they are not the best way for humans to read, understand, and write programs. They are not the best way for humans to design programs since, due to their counter-intuitiveness, they can be error-prone.

Now, let's have a look at functional collections.

Functional collections

It's quite a different picture in functional languages. Let's have a look at the same abstraction, the List, in Scala's library. Its API documentation is available at `https://www.scala-lang.org/api/current/scala/collection/immutable/List.html`. It contains many more methods than can be found in Java's List. In contrast to the Java List interface, Scala's List abstraction is immutable. This means that once you have created a list, you are not able to modify it. All the modifications to the list can be implemented by just creating a modified copy of the list. This concept is referred to as structural sharing. This means that the objects that are members of the list are not copied, just that the structure of the list is recreated. Therefore, you do not need to worry about memory leaks because only the structure is newly created. The objects that are the members of the list are not recreated.

There is also an abundance of declarative methods – high-level primitives, for example, `filter`, `map`, and `flatMap`. In contrast to Java, these methods specify fairly high-level operations. In the previous chapter, we saw how it can be pretty tedious to define a filter operation in Java. In contrast, in Scala, it is sufficient to specify the name of the operation that you need to perform, and you don't need to worry about how this operation is implemented. This seems like the right moment to draw parallels with the `goto` statement. It is a remarkable property of modern programming languages; the programs that you can express with `goto` can also be expressed with the help of several control structures. In the same way, all collection programs can be expressed using around a dozen declarative high-level methods. You don't need to specify how to create a loop with `goto` every time you need a loop. Similarly, it is not necessary to specify collection operations such as `filter` if they can be named and implemented in a language's core library.

While Java and imperative languages focus on algorithmic reasoning, functional languages, such as Scala, focus on algebraic reasoning. This means they view data transformations as algebraic expressions. Data can be viewed as operands of some algebra, and it can be combined with other data and transformed to get new data with the help of high-level operators. Hence, programs are no longer defined algorithmically, but in terms of mathematical expressions; expressions that compute some value based on their input.

When programming in a declarative language, it is no longer necessary to be an expert in algorithms, as was the case with imperative languages such as Java. This is the case because all the algorithms that you may need are already implemented in the language's core library. Of course, when you call a declarative method, such as `filter`, on a Scala collection, an algorithm is executed under the hood. The beauty of this approach is that you do not need to be aware of this at all. You're provided with a high-level building block, and you need to express your program in terms of these building blocks. You do not need to worry about how the blocks are created.

There are a number of benefits compared to the imperative approach. You do not need to deal with algorithms that are hard to read and prone to bugs. Everything you need is already implemented on a language level. This means that the implementation is used in a number of projects based on that language. Therefore, you can be sure that what you are using is tested extensively, thereby greatly reducing your chances of writing bug-prone code.

Instead of focusing on low-level operations, you can focus on describing your program in high-level terms. Consider the example of filtering that we saw in Chapter 1, The *Declarative Programming Style*. It is much easier to read the declarative code because you see the word `filter` at once, and this single word means an entire operation. In the case of Java, we have a loop and manipulation over two collections to get the same job done, and it is not at all obvious what the code stands for. This is why declarative programs are much better to read for humans.

Let's have a look at another example – mapping. Mapping is a process of transforming a collection element-wise. This means that you take a collection as an input and generate another collection by transforming every element of the original collection in some way. For example, if you have a list of integers, you can map this list by a function that squares each individual number. If you have the numbers 1, 2, and 3 in the collection, you will get a new collection with the numbers 1, 4, and 9.

Let's do this operation in Java in an imperative way. First, let's define the collections we are going to map:

```
List<Integer> numbers = new ArrayList<Integer>();
numbers.add(1);
numbers.add(2);
numbers.add(3);
```

Next, we will create a new collection we are going to write our results to. Then, we will iterate over every element of the original collection, we will apply the required function to these, and then add them to the result collection:

```
List<Integer> result = new ArrayList<Integer>();
for (Integer n: numbers)
  result.add(n * n);
```

Now, let's look at how this is done with Scala:

```
val numbers = List(1, 2, 3)
val result  = numbers.map(n => n * n)
println(result)  // List(1, 4, 9)
```

In Scala, we simply call the built-in primitive method map on the collection we need to map. Here, we can also see the role that is played by the lambda functions here. We are able to specify that mapping function as a lambda function, as an argument to the map method. In Java, lambda functions are only supported starting from version 8, hence, this style would have been impossible in that language until recently. The general pattern here is that we often need to abstract away an entire computation. We need to embed one computation in another. This can be done with a lambda function.

Algebraic approach

Functional and declarative programming can also be very well conceptualized as an algebraic style. For our purposes, an algebraic approach can be regarded as a certain language of mathematical expressions—a language that consists of two major elements: operators and operands. Operands can be taken to mean data, the information that you want to manipulate, while operators can be taken to mean their behavior as an how this data is utilized.

Consider the expression 1 + 2. Here, numbers 1 and 2 are operands. They represent some numeric data. The + symbol is an operator that binds them together. It has certain semantics associated with it, that of adding one number to another. But it is important to remember that the symbolic structure of the expression and its semantics are two separate things. You can take the expression as specified previously and assign a different meaning to the numbers *1* and *2* and to the symbol +, and the semantics of the expression will be entirely different.

This line of reasoning can be applied to declarative programs. For example, consider the following snippet in Scala:

```
val result  = numbers.map(n => n * n)
```

It can be rewritten with the Scala infix notation as follows:

```
val result  = numbers map (n => n * n)
```

This is because Scala supports a syntactic sugar that is allowed to call Scala methods as infix operators. The point here is that you can read the map function as an operator. The operator that binds its operands together specifies what to do with them. The first operand is the collection we are mapping, while the second operand is the lambda function you are mapping it with.

The behavior of the program is expressed here as operators that bind their operands together, while the execution of the program is taken to mean a computation of some value, and not an execution of an algorithm.

One advantage here is the absence of the notion of change. In algebra, time is effectively removed from the equation. Consider the implementation of map functionality in Java. It is algorithmic, which means that you explain about it in time, as follows:

1. Take the first element of the collection.
2. Then, apply a function to this element.
3. Then, insert it into the resulting collection.
4. Repeat the same process with the second element, and then the third, and so on.

Notice the presence of time in the preceding description. You clearly have a notion of what happens first and what happens after that.

Let's have a look at the Scala implementation of that functionality. In Scala, you specify what you need the program to do as an algebraic expression, as a binding of two operators, the collection and the lambda function, by the operator map. This expression no longer has a time dimension associated with it. You simply write down a mathematical expression and leave it to your language to assign some semantics to it.

Be aware that the map function in Scala is implemented with the help of algorithms and that it probably works just like it does in Java. However, for all intents and purposes, you can forget about this in most of the programs you will be writing. You can think of this program as a different paradigm, a paradigm of symbolically expressing what you want to do.

This paradigm separates the semantics from the structure of your program. When I say structure, I mean the symbols involved in describing the program; the symbols as in the collection you are mapping, the lambda function you are mapping it by, and the map as an operator. All of these entities are referred to with the help of symbols you write. By semantics, I mean the actions performed by the computer when it processes this expression, how it understands this expression, and how it runs this expression.

Thinking about programs this way allows you to treat them as mathematical expressions and work with them as with data structures—the symbolic structures of the expressions. This is in contrast to the algorithmic approach, which is so popular in traditional imperative programming, as we have seen with the example involving Java.

The advantage here is that it is easier to use symbolic logic to explain programs that are expressed as mathematical expressions and not algorithms. Second, in a proper declarative program, there is no dimension of time, which removes a whole class of bugs. Of course, you should remember all of this is an abstraction. You can fairly say that it is an illusion. Under the hood, algorithms still matter; time still exists. However, in the declarative style, you leverage the principle of abstraction. You abstract away the time and the algorithms. This is comparable to how, when your program operates with a high-level language such as Java, you do not need to think about the byte code or the low-level processor instructions it compiles to. This low-level code still exists, it still matters, but, to all intents and purposes, you can forget about it. The same thing happens with algorithms being abstracted away with the declarative and algebraic styles.

Treating programs as mathematical expressions is facilitated by techniques that abstract away side effects. These rely on data structures specific to purely functional programming. Let's now have look at such data structures.

Effect types

Previously, we discussed collections as an example of imperative and declarative data structures. However, the functional and declarative styles also contain some data structures specific to them.

Collections abstract away multiplicity. Functional languages such as Scala, Haskell, and others bring in some other data structures that abstract away side effects. We can refer to them as effect types.

We have argued that pure algebraic and declarative approaches remove time from the equation. This is advantageous because time taxes the programmer's mind. Functional programming takes this idea further by removing side effects from your programs. They also burden the mind as you also need to take them into account and handle them properly.

Previously, we discussed an example of how a Java list interface throws exceptions. We argued that it is pretty bad because it increases the mental load on a programmer's mind, since they need to constantly keep in mind that there are cases in which an exception can be thrown and they should account for these cases. In functional programming, this is not acceptable. Functional programming aspires to remove all side effects from the equation.

We will see in detail later in the book how this is done but, for now, let's have a look at the `Try` structure.

Try

The `Try` data structure is present in one form or another in many programming languages. It may contain one of two values. One possibility is an arbitrary type of value `A`, while the second is an exception. This data structure can be returned as the result of a computation that can result in an error. This way, you no longer need to throw an exception. You can just return `Try[A]` when your method may result in an error. In Scala, the square bracket after the type name stands for type parameters, so `Try[A]` means the type `Try` with the type parameter `A`.

For instance, consider an example where we have a function that divides one number by another. However, in the event that the second number is zero, we throw an exception:

```
def division(n1: Double, n2: Double): Double =
  if (n2 == 0) throw new RuntimeException("Division by zero!")
  else n1 / n2
```

When we call the method, in certain cases it may result in an exception – a side effect we may not be aware of or have forgotten:

```
println(division(1, 0))  // throws java.lang.RuntimeException: Division
by zero!
```

The program will crash at this point. However, if we wrap it in `Try`, we can prevent the program from crashing:

```
def pureDivision(n1: Double, n2: Double): Try[Double] =
  Try { division(n1, n2) }
println(pureDivision(1, 0))  // Failure(java.lang.RuntimeException:
 Division by zero!)
```

Because the return type clearly specifies the possibility of an error, this possibility no longer needs to be kept in mind. Since an error is now represented as a data structure, it does not disrupt the program when it happens. Here, we can see a representation of phenomena as data. Representing phenomena as data is called **reification**, and we will see later in the book how important this concept is in pure functional programming.

Option

Another example of a data structure that is characteristic of functional languages is an `Option`. An `Option` can either contain a value or be empty. You can think of it as an abstraction of the notion of the null pointer in Java or C++. The advantage here is that the programmer no longer needs to remember that some methods return a null. The methods that may, or may not, result in a value will return an `Option[A]` to signify this possibility, just as in the case of `Try`.

For example, consider a method that returns the name of the user by their ID. Some IDs won't map to a user. Hence, we can model the scenario where we can't return a user that does not exist as follows:

```
def getUserName(id: Int): Option[String] =
  if (Set(1, 2, 3).contains(id)) Some(s"User-$id")
  else None
```

That is, if the user ID is 1, 2 or 3, we surmise that the user is present in the database, otherwise they are not. We explicitly include the information about whether the user is present as the `Option` type. That is, we don't just return the user's name, but also the information about whether they are present or not.

The advantage here is that you won't be able to access the user's name without first checking whether they were found or not:

```
getUserName(1) match { // "User-1"
  case Some(x) => println(x)
  case None => println("User not found")
}
```

Here, the result of `getUserName` is not a raw `String` but a `String` wrapped in an `Option`. So, we first analyze the `Option` with the pattern matching statement before obtaining the result.

The preceding example outputs `User-1` to the console. However, this example outputs `User not found`:

```
getUserName(10) match { // "User not found"
  case Some(x) => println(x)
  case None => println("User not found")
}
```

Data structures in different programming languages

From the preceding discussion, you may conclude that there is a substantial difference between a functional and comparative approach to programming. While imperative programming is focused on algorithms, declarative programming is focused on the phenomena produced by these algorithms.

Imperative programming allows you to produce phenomena with the help of algorithms. Declarative programming names the phenomena you may need and then allows you to call them by name. This abstracts away all the details of the inner workings of the phenomena.

This is reflected in the separation between the approaches to data structures in different languages. Imperative programming languages, such as C++ or Java, will have their data structures, specifically, collections, implemented in a low-level manner. Typically, they will be mutable and will have some very basic primitive methods defined therein. Whatever you want to express, you will need to express it algorithmically with the help of these primitives.

Functional programming languages, such as Scala or Haskell, will usually have immutable data structures. They focus on the phenomena and the high-level behavior you need to get things done. Examples of high-level behavior include mapping values of a certain type onto values of another type, and filtering certain values out of a collection of values.

In general, it is much easier to program with purely functional and declarative programming collections. They provide you with lots of building blocks with which to build your programs.

However, in certain circumstances, it may be desirable for you to use imperative data structures. Lower-level programming styles may be desirable if you want to craft your algorithms instead of relying on off-the-shelf implementations. The circumstances in question may be high-performance operations, for example.

In the gaming industry, if you are designing a performance-demanding game, it may be possible in certain sections of the game that you will need to write your operations yourself in order to meet performance requirements. Also, it is possible that you may need to employ such low-level approaches in the case of micro-controller programming or situations where you have limited computational resources and you need to take full advantage of what you have.

Summary

In this section, we had a look at how different programming styles define data structures and their approach to building programs using these data structures. We have seen how imperative programming relies heavily on algorithms and low-level operations. You have learned about basic mutable data structures and basic operations to mutate the data structures, as well as how to compose algorithms in your programming language of choice with the help of these data structures.

In contrast, in the declarative style, the focus shifts from algorithms to mathematical expressions. The collections data structures are usually immutable. You have a lot of high-level operations defined on these data structures. You use these operations in order to express the program, not with algorithms, but as a set of algebraic expressions.

Collections are one of the main aspects of almost any program. Hence, most of the modern programming languages support them out of the box, and, looking at the collections framework, it is possible to say what approach and philosophy that programming language follows.

In addition to collections, there are other data structures that are specific to functional programming. These data structures will be covered in detail in the later chapters of this book. For now, it is worth observing that data structures such as `Try` or `Option` are needed to abstract away side effects that may occur in your program.

Some of these functional programming-specific data structures aim at bringing side effects into the purely functional paradigm. With these structures, you can work with side effects while maintaining referential transparency. In the next chapter, we will have a look at the problem of side effects in details.

Questions

1. What is the general approach you take when writing an imperative collections-based application?
2. What is the general approach you take when writing a functional collections-based application?
3. Why is it not necessary to be trained in algorithm reasoning when dealing with functional data structures (in the majority of cases)?
4. What is the algebraic approach to programming?
5. What are the benefits of adopting an algebraic style?
6. What is the purpose of effect types such as `Option` or `Try` ?

Further reading

Learning Scala Programming by Vikash Sharma and the section entitled *Getting familiar with Scala collections* (`https://www.packtpub.com/application-development/learning-scala-programming`).

4
The Problem of Side Effects

Pure functional programming is all about removing side effects and mutations. We remove them for a reason. In this chapter, we will see how shared mutable states and side-effecting functions can cause problems and why it is best to reduce them.

The topics discussed are as follows:

- Side effects
- Mutable states
- Pure functions
- Generally encountered side effects
- Pure functional paradigms in different programming languages

Side effects

So what exactly are side effects and why should they be avoided? For this discussion, we can define a side effect as some instructions in a function's code that modify the environment outside the scope of this function. The most common example of a side effect is an exception thrown by a program. Throwing an exception is a side effect because if you don't handle it, it will disrupt the program outside the scope of this function. So the program will break at this point and will stop its execution.

Take, for example, the function of the *Soda Machine* example from the previous chapter. The function that simulates coin-insertion throws an exception if there are no soda cans in the slot machine. So if you try to call that function on an empty soda machine, your program will never proceed past the function call site, because an exception will be thrown. That is, unless you handle this exception with a `try` statement at the same call site. Note that this puts the burden of handling side effects on the client, which is probably not what we want to do.

Another side effect that you will encounter is a null returned from a function. For example, you have a database of users. You can add a function that queries the database and gets a user back given their ID:

```
case class User(name: String)
def getUser(id: Int): User =
  if (Set(1, 2, 3).contains(id)) User(s"User-$id")
  else null
```

Sometimes this function will be called with IDs of users that do not exist in the database. A traditional Java solution to the problem of data that does not exist is to return a null. Returning a null quickly creates a problem. It violates the expectation of the programmer that calls this function. The function return type is set to `User`. The programmer will rightfully expect to get an object of the `User` type out of this function. Therefore, they may try to call some of the `User` methods on that object:

```
println(getUser(1 ).name)  // User-1
println(getUser(10).name)  // NullPointerException
```

Calling a method of the `User` type on null will result in a null pointer exception unless you first verify that the object is not null.

One problem here is that side effects are not reflected anywhere in the function's signature. Moreover, their handling is not enforced by the compiler. In Java, of course, you are required to declare some exceptions thrown by the functions in their signatures. However, it has proven to be a bad design decision, and most languages do not require such a declaration. Moreover, even in Java, no declaration is made to specify that the function can return a null. Unless the programmer remembers that such side effects occur in the program, they may not handle them. So unless they handle the side effects, the program may be error-prone.

The main problem here is the extra mental load on the programmer. They are required to continually remember all the side effects that their functions may produce. Because if they don't, they will also forget to handle them properly. Thus, their code can introduce bugs. This problem is caused by the fact that the compiler does not enforce the handling of the side effects. The side effects are certain phenomena that are generated by the code at runtime. These phenomena are where local functions influence or are influenced by the outer environment without this being stated explicitly in the function type. These influences may then be generated by the function code, depending on the input values it receives at runtime. The compiler knows nothing about them. For example, the phenomenon of a function returning null, or an exception happening and the program being disrupted at that point. These things happen at runtime. At compile time, the compiler does not do any checks on whether they are appropriately treated.

Mutable states

A mutable state, to put it simply, is data that can be changed. For example, at one point in time, you may read some variable, *x*, and find that it points to some data. At another time, you may read a different value from the same variable. The value is different because the variable is mutable and another part of the program mutated it.

Let's look at why exactly the mutable state is not desirable. Imagine you have an online game. It relies on multiple threads, and the concurrency architecture of choice is the actors model. You have an actor that is supposed to track the users currently present in the game. Tracking can be implemented as a mutable collection inside the actor. Users log in and out of the game by sending messages to this actor. So, every time a message for logging in arrives at the actor, the user is added to the list of logged-in users. When users want to log out, they are removed from the list:

```
class GameState(notifications: ActorRef) extends Actor {
  val onlineUsers = collection.mutable.ListBuffer[User]()
  def receive = {
    case Connect    (u) => onlineUsers += u
    case Disconnect(u) => onlineUsers -= u
    case Round          => notifications ! RewardWinners(onlineUsers)
  }
}
```

Now, imagine you want to find the users that have reached a particular score to congratulate them via an email notification. You may want to do that at the end of each round (assuming it's a round-based game), which is modeled by another message sent to the `GameState` actor. One way to implement this is to send a list of all the users to a separate notifications actor that will do the job:

```
case Round => notifications ! RewardWinners(onlineUsers)
```

Let's imagine that the job of looking up and notifying the users takes a while to complete. We can simulate the delay via the `Thread.sleep(1000)` statement. This statement pauses the execution of the current thread at the line where it is called for 1,000 milliseconds or 1 second. Let's see how this works:

```
class NotificationsActor extends Actor {
  def receive = {
    case RewardWinners(users) =>
     Thread.sleep(1000)
    val winners = users.filter(_.score >= 100)
    if (winners.nonEmpty) winners.foreach { u =>
      println(s"User $u is rewarded!") }
    else println("No one to reward!")
```

```
        }
    }
```

The communication protocol is defined as follows:

```
sealed trait Protocol
case class    Connect (user : User      ) extends Protocol
case class    Disconnect (user : User     ) extends Protocol
case class    RewardWinners(users: Seq[User]) extends Protocol
case object   Round                     extends Protocol
```

Now, let's assume the following environment:

```
val system = ActorSystem("GameActors")
val notifications = system.actorOf(Props[NotificationsActor], name =
"notifications")
val gameState     = system.actorOf(Props(classOf[GameState],
notifications), name = "gameState")
val u1 = User("User1", 10)
val u2 = User("User2", 100)
```

We have an actor system, an actor for the game state, and an actor for notifications. Also, we have two users. The second user, User2, is a *winning* user because their score is >= 100. Consider what happens if a *winning* user with the required score logs out immediately after we complete the round:

```
gameState ! Connect(u1)
gameState ! Connect(u2)
gameState ! Round
gameState ! Disconnect(u2)
```

Such a user will not be notified. Things go wrong here because the collection we sent to the actor that takes care of notifications is mutable. It is shared between the GameState actor and NotificationActor. This means that once a user logs out, they are removed from the collection by the GameState actor, which means that it will also be removed from the collection of the NotificationActor because it is the same collection.

The preceding example demonstrates the problem of the shared mutable state in action. Again, this is extra mental load on the programmer. No longer can you reason in the scope of only one thread if you have an object shared with another thread. You must expand your scope of reasoning to all the threads that own this object. Because for all you know, the shared mutable object can be changed at any time. The actor model is supposed to help you to reason as if your program were single-threaded and no other threads existed. However, it won't help if you keep using a shared mutable state.

The traditional approach to managing a shared mutable state is to use locks and monitors. The principle behind it is that a thread that is doing modifications to an object is supposed to take a lock on some monitor so that nobody else will be able to perform a modification while this thread deals with the object. However, this does not remove the mental load from the programmer. You still need to take into account threads other than the one you are currently programming. In practice, it is tough to debug programs that involve concurrency and a shared mutable state.

Pure functions

In the previous sections, we have shown you how mutations and side effects can make the code harder to read and write. In this section, we will introduce the notion of pure functions, that is, the functions that do not produce side effects. It is central to pure functional programming. The functional paradigm dictates that you should express your program with the help of functions that do not produce any side effects. How would you model a situation where you need to throw an exception with the help of a pure function? Take the familiar *Soda Machine* example.

This is the slightly shortened version of the *Soda Machine* example we encountered in our previous discussions on side effects:

```
var cans = 0
def insertCoin(): SodaCan =
  if (cans > 0) { cans -= 1; new SodaCan }
  else throw new RuntimeException("Out of soda cans!")
println(insertCoin())
```

We can avoid throwing an exception from the function by returning a result wrapped in another data structure:

```
def insertCoin(): Try[SodaCan] = Try {
  if (cans > 0) { cans -= 1; new SodaCan }
  else throw new RuntimeException("Out of soda cans!")
}
```

In our case, we are not returning a pure result but an encapsulated result in the form of a Try of the result. The behavior of Try is to trap the possibility of an exception being thrown within its body for further handling. Try, as discussed in previous chapters, is a data structure that can contain either a value or an exception. So, if the soda machine is out of cans, we no longer throw an exception. We return the information that an error has occurred from the function.

The benefit here compared to the comparative analysis is as follows. There is no longer an unexpected side effect happening in this function. An error that can happen no longer interrupts the entire flow of the program. Moreover, the call site user of the function must handle the error to access the result. Because the result is wrapped into the data structure, we cannot access that result unless we first unwrap the data structure that it is wrapped into.

We can access the result by analyzing what exactly was returned. If it is a value, we know precisely that no error has happened. If it is an exception, we know that we need to handle it. At this point, we can say that the compiler enforces the handling of the error. The fact that the error can occur is reflected in the return type of the function. Hence, there is no longer a way to use the return value directly after it is returned. If you try to use it directly without first handling the possibility of an error, you will get a compile-time error. Because you will be trying to use the `Try` data structure as if it were the type that it wraps.

Another feature of purely functional programming is that it avoids using mutable data structures. Let's have another look at the example of the actors exchanging data with one another. What if instead of exchanging a mutable data structure we exchanged an immutable data structure? An immutable list? Check out the following:

```
class GameState(notifications: ActorRef) extends Actor {
  var onlineUsers = List[User]()
  def receive = {
    case Connect    (u) => onlineUsers :+= u
    case Disconnect(u) => onlineUsers = onlineUsers.filter(_ != u)
    case Round          => notifications ! RewardWinners(onlineUsers)
  }
}
```

As you recall, in the previous example, we had a problem with the list being modified from another thread when `NotificationActor` was trying to use it. Now, if we use an immutable list instead of a mutable list, the problem of mutation from another thread goes by itself, since immutable data structures cannot be mutated. A data structure that is immutable is automatically thread-safe. You can guarantee that nothing will mutate the data structure. Hence, you can share it freely with any other thread.

This argument can be extended by exchanging data with other methods as well. Imagine you have some mutable data structures and some `blackBox` methods:

```
val listMutable  : Seq[Int] = collection.mutable.ListBuffer[Int](1, 2, 3)
def blackBox(x: Seq[Int]): Unit = ???
blackBox(listMutable)  // Anything could happen to listMutable here,
because it is mutable
```

After these `blackBox` methods have gone forth on this data structure, how do you know what exactly is contained in it now? You can't have any guarantee of a mutable data structure unless you know exactly what happens in the black box method. Now, consider an example of an immutable list and the same situation of a black box method being called on this list:

```
val listImmutable: Seq[Int] = List(1, 2, 3)
def blackBox(x: Seq[Int]): Unit = ???
blackBox(listImmutable) // No matter what happens, listImmutable remains
the same, because it is immutable
```

Do you have any guarantee of what is contained in this list after the black box method did its job? You do because the list is immutable. Nothing can modify this list. So you can freely pass it around, not only to other threads, but also to other methods within one thread, and be confident that it is not modified.

The benefit of such an approach is that there is no longer a need to extend the scope of your reasoning beyond your current local scope. If you are calling a black box method on an immutable data structure, there is no need for you to know exactly what happens in this method. This method will never modify an immutable data structure and knowing that is enough. So, if you're working in a multithreaded environment, or if you are working only with immutable data structures, no longer do you need to worry about things such as synchronization or taking locks. You know that your immutable data structure will never be changed by any thread.

So far, we've discussed the property of purity from an intuitive perspective. Now let's look at a more scientific way of defining it—the concept of referential transparency.

Referential transparency

The concepts of immutability and lack of side effects are encompassed by the term **referential transparency**. With a referentially transparent function, you can substitute the function call with the result it returns without changing the semantics of the program.

Let's see how it works on an example. Consider another type of side effect—logging. The function returns the name of a user with a given ID, but it also writes that name into a log—the standard output, in this case:

```
def getUserName(id: Int): String = {
  val name = s"User-$id"
  println(s"LOG: Requested user: $name")
  name
}
```

```
val u = getUserName(10)
```

Can we substitute the call of the preceding function with the result it computes? Let's try:

```
val u = "User-10"
```

The semantics would not be the same in this case. The original program prints the log to the standard output. The current program does not. This is so because the standard output occurred in the function that we have replaced with the result it computed, as a side effect.

Now, let's consider another program:

```
def getUserNamePure(id: Int): (List[String], String) = {
  val name = s"User-$id"
  val log  = List(s"LOG: Requested user: $name")
  (log, name)
}
val u = getUserNamePure(10)
```

The function does the same thing, but instead of producing a side effect of logging, it includes the information that the side effect should have occurred into a list of all the messages that were supposed to be logged. Now we can return the list with the messages together with the result of the function.

Can we substitute their function call with the result it computes without losing the semantics of the program? Check out the following:

```
val u = (List("LOG: Requested user: User-10"), "User-10")
```

Now the answer is yes. The original function computed the list with all the messages it produced and returned it together with the value it computed, without actually producing any side effects. Since there were no side effects produced in the process, we can substitute the function call with its result without changing the semantics of the program. The function is referentially transparent.

As you can see from the preceding example, in a referentially transparent function, all of the side effects are reflected in the return type and are usually represented by a specific data structure. This style may look verbose and unreadable to you at first because you are returning a pair with some extra stuff from your function. However, don't forget that one of the main principles of engineering is that of abstraction. So the unreadable code you see here can be abstracted away if you have proper abstractions. This can be done without losing the benefits we have achieved. The benefits include reducing the mental load on the programmer, the ability to explain your program locally, and the ability to exclude side effects from the equation.

And such abstractions have been invented. Languages such as Scala or Haskell have excellent support for such abstractions. Later in this book, we will dive much deeper into how they work and how you can write programs with them.

Generally encountered side effects

In this section, we will talk more about the side effects commonly encountered in programs. Some of them we have already introduced, and others you may already know from your everyday programming. However, it is crucial for you to pay particular attention to such side effects, because this way, you learn to distinguish them in an ordinary program.

When writing programs (and when living our lives in general), very often, we get used to things without even paying attention to them. Certain things may be a source of headaches and problems, and the first step to resolving the problems is to name the things that cause them.

As functional programming aims to eliminate side effects, it is reasonable for us to name some of the side effects that cause pain.

Error

The first effect we will be discussing is the effect of an error. An error is produced when something goes wrong in your program. In imperative languages, it is usually modeled by an exception. An exception is a phenomenon produced by a line of the program that disrupts the execution flow of the program at that point. Usually, it propagates up the call stack, disrupting the execution at its parent call stacks too. If left unhandled, exceptions propagate to the topmost call-stack frame, and the program will crash.

Consider an example of division by zero:

```
def division(n1: Double, n2: Double): Double =
  if (n2 == 0) throw new RuntimeException("Division by zero!")
  else n1 / n2
```

We have a division function that checks whether its denominator is zero. If it is, the function throws an exception. Now, consider calling this function as follows:

```
division(1, 0)
println("This line will never be executed")
```

The execution of the main program will not progress further than the line where we tried to call the division function, the second argument of which is zero. This is because the error will happen in the function and will get propagated up the stack, eventually crashing the program.

Absence of result

Consider a situation where we have a function that is supposed to make a database query. Specifically, we have users in our database, and we want a function to retrieve a user by their ID. Now, what will happen when there is no user with a given ID in the database? Consider the following:

```
def getUser(id: Int): User =
  if (Set(1, 2, 3).contains(id)) User(s"User-$id")
  else null
```

The solution of imperative languages is a null returned from the function. In Chapter 3, *Functional Data Structures*, we saw how this is dangerous. The compiler doesn't know that null can be returned from the function. More precisely, it doesn't even know this is a possibility. The compiler allows for functions returning null and does not warn us about a possible null return value. The imperative style embraces this possibility. So we have a situation in imperative languages where potentially every function that returns an object may also return null. If we do not check that the result of that function is not null, we risk bugs. And to check the result of the function, we need to keep in mind the possibility of it returning null. And this is an extra mental load.

Delay and asynchronous computations

Imagine your program performs an HTTP call. For example, it tries to retrieve some JSON object from a web API. It can take some time; it may even take several seconds to complete.

Imagine that you want to make some competition within a function and return some value based on the result of the API request. You run into a problem here because the result of the API call was not available immediately. The fact that you need to wait for a specific long-running operation to complete is also a side effect.

You can block on this long-running operation and resume your competition once the result arrives. However, this function will also block any functions that are calling it. In the context of a performance-critical environment, this may be an issue. For example, consider a web server. It has several threads to serve all the incoming requests. If its operations take too long to complete, it will quickly run out of threads. And some requests will end up waiting for a long time in the queue for a free thread.

So, you always need to keep in mind that some of your functions are blocking and take time to return. This is an extra piece of information to keep in mind. This produces an extra mental load for you. The side effect of delayed computation causes all of this.

The solution used in modern web servers is to make your server asynchronous. This means that you never wait for a long-running operation. You specify what to do next using a callback and continue according to that callback once the result is in place. This can lead to a situation known as callback hell. The problem is that when you overuse callbacks, the execution flow of the program becomes quite obscure.

Usually, when something in the program is not apparent, this indicates a need for an abstraction. So it can be a good idea to abstract away callbacks.

Functional programming also has a means to abstract away long-running computations. With it, you can write your code as if they were returning immediately. The data type of `Future` is present both in Scala and Java, and also in many modern programming languages. It servers precisely the purpose of abstracting long-running computations.

Logging

In an example in the *Referential Transparency* section of this chapter, we saw how logging can also be a side effect. Logging can be done using a separate login framework, or it can be as simple as writing to the standard output.

Things may get tricky with logging when you work in an unfamiliar environment. For example, if it is the environment of your desktop computer, everything is simple. You run a program from your terminal, and it outputs everything to the terminal. However, what if it is a web server? Often, you need to output your log into a separate file for it to be readable afterward. Alternatively, what if you are writing a mobile application? The program runs on a separate device, and it is not always the case that a print statement causes an output to your terminal. You may need to use some system-specific logging API, native to the environment you are working in.

Now imagine you have a program that has `print` statements pretty much everywhere in it. You suddenly start to understand that some of your functions try to interact with the environment outside of its scope when logging. Specifically, the logging API particular to the environment under which you are working. Now you need to modify this logging call to match the expectations of the environment.

A function that writes to a log interacts with the environment outside its scope. This means we can treat such calls as side effects according to our definition. Since you need to pay attention to these intricacies when working in different environments, it is fair to say they contribute to your mental load.

Input-output operations

The final side effect that we'll discuss here are **input-output** (**IO**) operations to the filesystem, or to the network. We can say that these operations are side effects because they depend on the environment so much.

In the case of IO operations on the filesystem, the success of the operation depends on whether the filesystem contains the specified file or if the file is readable. When performing network operations, the operation depends on whether we have a reliable internet connection or any firewalls.

When debugging an IO program, lots of moving parts come to our attention. Do we have access to the desired filesystem? What about the ownership of the files we are trying to read or write? What about the permissions the current user has? What about filesystems of different operating systems? Linux and Windows have very different approaches to structuring their filesystems, so how do we port our application from one system to another? Do we have a reliable internet connection? Are we not behind a firewall? Do our DNS servers work correctly? Is the port we are trying to listen on available on this particular system?

It is an extra mental load on you because there are so many things you need to consider. Hence, you can treat IO as side effects and an extra mental load.

But how do we get rid of the side effects?

If you come from a purely imperative background, you may be quite confused at this point. Purely functional programming says that you need to eliminate all the side effects. But can you imagine a program without logging? And what would be the use of a web API that cannot connect to a network? If we cannot throw an exception, how do we specify the erroneous behavior of the program?

The side effects specified previously are essential to most modern applications, and it is usually not possible to imagine a reasonable program without side effects.

Therefore, it would be wrong to say that purely functional programming eliminates side effects from your program completely. Instead, it would be more precise to say that it eliminates side effects from your business logic. It pushes side effects away from the parts of your application that matter. The way it usually works with the purely functional style is that your business logic, which encompasses 90% of the code, is indeed purely functional.

You do not have all of the side effects specified previously. However, whenever the business logic needs to perform a side effect, it does not enact it directly. Instead, it creates a data structure that specifies which side effect needs to be performed, without actually performing them. Functional applications often have an entire domain-specific language to describe side effects. And whenever a piece of logic needs to execute a side effect, it expresses its need in this language. The specification of what needs to be done and the act of executing that specification are separate one from another.

Functional applications usually have a thin layer that takes care of executing the side effects expressed in the effect language of the application. The advantage of this approach is that most of the time you work on the business logic, this 90% of your code. And this code is referentially transparent and pure. Which means all of the side effects that would have typically been present in it are separated away from it. All of the mental load that we were discussing previously is gone. This means that, most of the time, you are working without any extra mental load, locally, without considering the global scope.

It is true that you also need to write the interpreter for your side effects. This is the 10% of code that the side effects expressed in the effect language of your choice. However, it is separate from your business logic. You can test your effect interpreter separately. Once it is written and in place, you can forget about it, and write your business logic in a pure way.

At this point, we are not yet diving into the details of how it is done. The purpose of this section is to give you an idea of how the problem of purity in a side-effecting application is addressed. Later in this book, we'll see precisely how functional programming facilitates this technique and what exactly it provides to write programs in this style.

The pure functional paradigm in different languages

It doesn't take any particular infrastructure to program in a purely functional style. All you need is to be able to see side effects in code, to notice when they place an extra mental load on your mind and require you to hold more things in mind at once. And of course, you need to know how to abstract them away, how to make this mental load go away. Most modern programming languages are built for engineers. This is why they provide excellent capabilities for abstraction, including imperative languages such as C or Java. This is why, if you know what to abstract and how, you should be able to abstract that in these languages. And if you know precisely how the imperative style can hurt you, you can shield yourself from the trouble.

Moreover, certain imperative programming languages provide a specific infrastructure that facilitates purely functional style directly. For example, in Java, you have the `final` keyword. A variable declared with this keyword is immutable. You're not able to modify a `final` variable in Java once it is assigned a value. Also, in Java, you have immutable collections as part of its core infrastructure.

Even though you can apply the functional style in imperative languages, it is much easier to do so in functional languages. You may encounter trouble when applying the style to imperative languages. One thing may be that all the libraries you encounter are imperative. It may be hard to write purely functional code in such conditions because you will be working inside an imperative infrastructure. It will create certain inertia that may be hard to fight. So it may not be practical to work in the functional style in imperative languages. However, it may be used as a last resort, if you are overwhelmed by complexity.

The benefit of pure functional languages, such as Scala or Haskell, is that they provide you with an excellent infrastructure to write functional code. Haskell is a language that enforces functional style. There is just no other choice of style that you can use with that language. Hence, the libraries that you will be using in this language are also purely functional. You can work in a purely functional infrastructure. Scala is a more liberal language in some sense. It is a mix of the object-oriented and functional styles. So, it is convenient to use it to make a transition between purely imperative and purely functional styles. That is because you have a choice of style. If you do not know how to implement something in a purely functional way and deadlines are approaching, you can always resort to a familiar imperative style.

This blending of the imperative and functional styles is pretty standard in modern programming languages. For example, in Python, you can encounter both styles. Some libraries are quite imperative, but there is good support for purely functional style too. Java is more conservative in this sense than Python. It appears to follow the imperative, algorithmic paradigm quite strictly, even though huge efforts have been put into making the functional style more natural to Java during the last decade or so.

All in all, the point of this section is that the functional style is not about the language. The language can provide some momentum, in the sense of its existing infrastructure and the methodology of its community. This momentum can be in either direction—either it will work for you, or against you. However, if you understand the functional approach, you should be fine programming in any language using it. But you should always be aware of where the wind blows—what the moods of its community are, what philosophy its libraries follow. You should be aware of the momentum the language provides you and whether it works for you or against you.

Summary

The traditional imperative approach relies heavily upon algorithms that are supposed to produce certain phenomena at runtime—the side effects. The compiler is usually not aware of these phenomena or is not aware of them enough. We can define the side effects for this book as instructions that modify the environment outside their immediate scope. Side effects are usually not desirable, because they put extra mental load on the programmer's mind.

Another problem with the traditional imperative style is the mutation. Mutable data structures are not thread-safe. Also, they cannot be safely passed between pieces of logic even within the same thread.

Functional programming aims to resolve these problems and reduce your mental load. This style does so by abstracting away side effects, so that you write your program without explicitly performing them or mutating anything outside your current scope.

Questions

1. What are the side effects?
2. What is mutable data?
3. What problems might side effects and mutable data cause?
4. What is a pure function?
5. What is referential transparency?
6. What are the benefits of using a purely functional style?
7. What are some generally encountered side effects?
8. Is it possible to program with a purely functional style in imperative languages such as Java?
9. What are the benefits of using a functional programming language over an imperative programming language for programming with a purely functional style?

Effect Types - Abstracting Away Side Effects

5

In the previous chapter, we saw why side effects may be a source of trouble. We also briefly discussed effect types. Effect types are a technique of functional programming that allow for the abstraction of side effects.

In this chapter, we will have a look at how this works. We will learn the philosophy behind the pattern. Also, we will see how to sequentially combine side effects trapped in effect types.

In this chapter, we will cover the following topics:

- Turning effects into data
- The sequential combination of effect types with Monads – the `map` and `flatMap` functions

Turning effects into data

It's possible to compare the process of writing programs with modeling and describing a particular reality. For example, when you are writing an application for warehouse management, you are encoding in the rules of logic the concept of an online shop, its inventory, the place where the inventory is stored, and the rules according to which this inventory can be moved in and out of the warehouse. This is the reality of the business domain for which you are writing the application. We can say that your goal as a programmer is to model your business domain, that is, to encode it using your programming language into specific logical rules—to define the way information is to be stored, transformed, and interacted with.

However, in the process of execution, programs create their own reality. The same way a warehouse, an online shop, and a user are all members of the reality of the business domain, some elements are members of the domain of program execution. The same way you can define certain phenomena as they happen in your business domain, such as inventory shortage or the users buying from your shop, you can define certain phenomena that exist in the world of writing and running a program.

Reality is what is on your mind when you are working on a certain level of abstraction. When you are working in the business-domain level, one category of thing is on your mind. However, when you are creating programs, entirely different things are on your mind. These two separate sets of concepts and phenomena can be understood as separate realities you're working in.

For example, errors are in the reality of program-execution. The errors' life cycle is also the reality of the program execution. Errors can propagate up the call stack. When they are handled, they stop propagation. They disrupt programs in places where they happen.

Delays are also the reality of program-execution. When you perform a database operation, an input-output operation, or wait for a response from a server, you deal with delays.

Concurrency, modularity, class hierarchies—all of these are elements of your programming reality. The programming reality is the concept and phenomena you are concerned with when you write your program. This reality, however, does not concern your boss, who lives in the reality of the business domain.

For simplicity, let's name the business-domain reality the first-order reality, and the programming reality the second-order reality. Such naming is because the business-domain reality is something that you are immediately concerned with. The reality of your program is something that arises in the process of solving the business-domain problems, the first-order reality.

Sometimes, a programmer focuses only on the first-order reality. They may not care about the quality of the code or how it handles the second-order reality. Their primary concern is to describe the first order reality and to solve the business task. This situation can arise from the lack of experience of a programmer, or from a lack of infrastructure that would allow them to deal with the second-order reality quickly. Under pressing deadlines, trade-offs sometimes have to be made in favor of completing the task rather than the code quality.

Why is it dangerous to ignore the programming reality? Well, because it is a reality in itself, independent of the realities that may occur in business. This reality still exists, whether you ignore or address it. And if you do not pay attention to it, it may escalate in complexity, especially in large code bases.

For example, if there are too many asynchronous computations, you may find yourself in the situation of callback hell. In the context of callbacks, it is not easy to follow the execution flow of the program. Callback hell is when your program relies on callbacks too much, to the point where it starts to be hard to track what it does.

When you are dealing with a concurrent program and multithreaded computations, if you're not careful, you may end up in a situation of race conditions. Alternatively, you may encounter deadlocks or problems with system liveliness. Without specific techniques to deal with these, such as an actor system, they may produce bugs that are particularly tricky to debug.

If you are not careful about when you throw exceptions and return nulls from methods, you can expect pretty much every method to throw an exception or return null. Abusing exceptions and nulls by itself should not lead to detrimental bugs, but this will still give you a headache.

Finally, mutation is another reality that you are going to face. In the previous chapters, we discussed how mutation can increase your mental load.

The several programming situations previously discussed demonstrate the mental load that we were talking about so extensively in the previous chapters. It is the second-order reality of how programs are run and how they are written. The programs are supposed to model the reality of their business domains. However, there is an entirely different reality that you encounter when you solve, run, or write programs. If you ignore this reality, it will overwhelm you with complexity and cause a mental overload.

Consider the following example of the division function, which we have encountered in previous chapters:

```
def imperativeDivision(n1: Double, n2: Double): Double =
  if (n2 == 0) throw new RuntimeException("Division by zero!")
  else n1 / n2
```

The first-order reality here is arithmetics. It is the business domain that we are trying to model. Precisely, we model an operation of dividing one number by another number. That's our first-order reality.

However, when we start to write the code, we quickly encounter the second-order reality. That is, the possibility of the division by zero and the necessity to handle this case in the program. Now, we move from the world of mathematics and our primary business task to the world of programming.

A naive way to handle this reality is to throw an exception in case of division by zero. However, if you do not pay enough attention to the second-order reality, it will create the mental overhead that we've already discussed. There is nothing to warn you about the possibility of an error. There's nothing to force you to handle it. Hence, you need to remember all of this yourself, which contributes to the complexity of the program you need to keep in mind. The more things you need to keep in mind, the harder it is to do this, and the more things can go wrong.

A more sophisticated programmer will think of both the first- and the second-order realities when designing their program. They will not only model the business domain; they will also design the program so that the complexity of its execution does not prevent scalability. Scalability means the size of the code base does not contribute to the complexity of the programming of individual components.

To develop a program qualitatively, programmers need specific tools and approaches. Functional programming offers one approach.

Functional programming follows the fundamental principle of engineering—abstract away what repeats. The second-order reality has repeating phenomena. So functional programming devises its own abstractions to deal with them.

Learning how to describe both realities at once is harder than learning how to describe only the first-order reality. Hence, languages such as Python are much easier to learn than, say, Java. Although Java is not a functional language, it also provides an infrastructure and a methodology to deal with the complexity of programming. At the same time, Python is focused on speed and ease of prototyping. Moreover, Java is much simpler than Scala because Scala provides even more abstractions and a means for you to control both realities of your program.

Although it is harder to learn the languages that allow for more qualitative programming, the value is well worth its price. You learn to control the effects of the second-order reality. Not only can you describe your immediate business domain, but you are also able to describe the way your program is run. The way to scalability and bug-free programming is having control over complexity.

Let's revisit the division by zero example, but take into account the second-order reality:

```
def functionalDivision(n1: Double, n2: Double): Try[Double] =
  if (n2 == 0) Failure(new RuntimeException("Division by zero!"))
  else Success(n1 / n2)
```

The first thing to notice is that the second-order reality effect of an error gets modeled with the `Try` data structure. The concept of error handling is modeled by analyzing the `Try` data structure. It is enforced by the compiler—you cannot access the result value unless you analyze the data structure for errors. Hence the complexity is reduced.

The pattern where we detect a specific phenomenon of the second-order reality and create a data structure to encapsulate (reify) it is typical in functional programming. In this book, we will be calling the data structures that reify the phenomena of the second-order reality **effect types**.

The main point of this section is to look at the side effects from a wide angle to see the general pattern behind their abstraction. If you only focus on your business domain while ignoring your program's technical reality, the latter will create a tough mental load. A sophisticated programmer focuses on both realities equally. Functional programming allows you to address them adequately.

The sequential combination of effects with Monads

Analyzing the preceding data structure was cumbersome. The code that has to do with analyzing functional data structures turns out to be pretty hard to read.

However, analyzing the data structures is a pattern in the functional world. Patterns are abstracted away in programming.

In this section, we will have a look at some common abstractions that you will deal with as a functional programmer when working with effect types.

Introducing the map function

Imagine that we need to build upon the previous example of the custom-division function to construct another function. The function is parameterized by an argument, x, and computes an expression, 2 / x + 3.

How do we express it in terms of our custom-division function? One approach is first to perform the division, then analyze its result, and if it is not an error, continue with the addition. However, if it is an error, return that error:

```
def f1(x: Double): Try[Double] =
divide(2, x) match {
  case Success(res) => res + 3
  case f: Failure   => f
}
```

The situation where we have a computation that returns an effect type, and we need to continue it with another computation that returns a raw value that is not wrapped in an effect type, is a frequent pattern in functional programming. The pattern is to analyze the structure returned by a computation, extract the result, and then apply the second computation to this result.

This pattern is encapsulated in the map method. Most effect types have the map method defined on them. Here is how the preceding example will look if implemented with the help of the map method:

```
def f1Map(x: Double): Try[Double] =
  divide(2, x).map(r => r + 3)
```

Let's try to develop an intuition for the map method. First of all, you can think of the map method as of the following higher-order function— (A => B) => (Try[A] => Try[B]). This is a higher-order function that accepts an A => B function and outputs a Try[A] => Try[B] function.

What it means is that if you have a function to convert a value of the A type into a value of the B type, you can also have a function to convert a value of the Try[B] type to a value of the Try[B] type. You can think of the map function as a lift that allows you to produce functions that work under the Try effect type from functions that work on the raw values.

Introducing the flatMap function

Another example of a function that encapsulates a pattern of functional programming is flatMap. Imagine we need to create a function that computes the following mathematical expression: (2 / x)   / y + 3. Let's try to do this with the division function that we defined previously:

```
def f2Match(x: Double, y: Double): Try[Double] =
  divide(2, x) match {
    case Success(r1) => divide(r1, y) match {
      case Success(r2) => Success(r2 + 3)
      case f@Failure(_) => f
    }
    case f@Failure(_) => f
  }
```

The code becomes spaghetti-like here. First, we analyze the result of dividing 2 by x. If successful, we would divide it by y. Then we analyze the result of that division, and if there was no error, we add 3 to the result.

Here, we can no longer use the map function because the division by y returns another try. map is a lift for a function that returns a raw value, not Try. If the logic sounds obscure to you, you are encouraged to try to implement the preceding example with the map function to see the problem.

The flatMap function exists specifically for this situation. You can think of it as of a higher-order function with the (A => Try[B]) => (Try[A] => Try[B]) signature. You can interpret it as follows. If you have a function that produces a value wrapped in the Try structure, A => Try[B], you can turn it into another function, Try[A] => Try[B], that lifts the original function's A domain to the domain of Try[A]. This means that if the original A => Try[B] function could be used on the A raw values, the new Try[A] => Try[B] function can be used on Try[A] as its input.

Let's have a look at how it can be implemented with flatMap:

```
def f2FlatMap(x: Double, y: Double): Try[Double] =
  divide(2, x).flatMap(r1 => divide(r1, y))
    .map(r2 => r2 + 3)
```

We need to extract the raw result from the Try data structure we got after computing 2/x, and we need to perform another computation on this result. This computation, the result divided by y, also produces Try. With the help of flatMap, we can lift the Int => Try[Int] computation into Try[Int] => Try[Int]. In other words, once we have computed 2/x, we can divide its result by y.

So `flatMap` is for situations when you need to continue a computation with another computation, and the continuation will produce a `Try` as its result. Compare that to the situation with the `map` function, which requires the continuation to produce a raw value. Corresponding versions of `map` and `flatMap` also exist for other effect types, such as Option or Future.

One thing can be confusing here regarding the signatures of `map` and `flatMap` that we have analyzed. The signatures are functions. They take a function as an input and return another function as an output. However, the `map` and `flatMap` methods we have called on the `Try` object do not return functions but `Try` objects. However, both of our `map` and `flatMap` signatures, as we have discussed previously, return a `Try[A] => Try[B]` function.

In the functional world, we view functions outside the context of object-oriented programming. Scala is a convenient language because it combines the object-oriented and functional approaches. So, functions such as `flatMap` or `map` are defined as methods of the `Try` class. However, in functional programming, we get a better grasp of the nature of the functions by viewing them outside the context of object-oriented programming. In functional programming, they are not viewed as members of any class. They are means to transform the data.

Imagine you have a function that is defined as a member of some `Dummy` class:

```
class Dummy(val id: Int) {
  val f: Int => String = x => s"Number: $x; Dummy: $id"
}
```

The function `f` takes some argument of type `Int` and outputs some result of type `String`. Its signature is `Int => String`. This signature is the signature of the function as it is defined inside the `Dummy` class. However, notice that since it is defined inside the `Dummy` object, the context of that object is always implied. We can use the data of the enclosing object when performing the computation inside the function.

What happens if we decide to bring this function outside the scope of the class? Will the `Int => String` signature still reflect the nature of the function? Can we even implement it that way? Consider the following:

```
// val f: Int => String = x => s"Number: $x; Dummy: $id"  // No `id` in
scope, does not compile
```

The answer is no because now we do not have the required class context. The preceding code produces a compile-time error. If we move the function outside the scope of the class, we need to define it with the `Dummy => (Int => String)` signature. That is, if we have a `Dummy` object, we can define a function from `Int` to `String`, with this object in context:

```
val f1: Dummy => (Int => String) = d => (x => s"Number: $x; Dummy:
${d.id}")
```

Note that it is also possible to have it another way, `Int => (Dummy => String)`, without compromising the semantics:

```
val f2: Int => (Dummy => String) = x => (d => s"Number: $x; Dummy:
${d.id}")
```

This idea was applied here when analyzing the `map` and `flatMap` signatures.

Summary

In this chapter, we learned about the philosophy behind side effects. We found out that in the process of solving a business-domain problem, programmers end up in a reality different from the one of their business logic. The way you write the program and the phenomena that happen at runtime constitute a reality of their own. If you ignore it, the latter reality can grow in complexity, and this results in a mental overhead.

Functional programming allows you to address the problem of the second-order reality by providing techniques to reify its phenomena into effect types and define their behavior in the language of data structures and pure functions.

Effect types lessen your mental load because they eliminate the necessity to remember all the phenomena that happen in your program, even outside the scope of the code you may currently be looking at.

Effect types also make the compiler force you to handle such phenomena. Working with effect types can quickly become quite verbose. Hence, functions such as `map` and `flatMap` exist to abstract away common scenarios that involve effect types.

Questions

1. Which realities does a programmer need to consider when writing a program?
2. How does pure functional programming address the problem of complexity in the second-order reality?
3. What are the benefits of taking the second-order reality into account in our programs?

6
Effect Types in Practice

In the previous chapters, we saw that the general pattern for abstracting away side effects is to use effect types. This pattern allows you to reduce the mental load on your mind. The pattern states that we first define an effect type and then represent every occurrence of a particular side effect with this type. In this chapter, we will see more examples of real-world effect types and when to use them.

More precisely, we will be covering the following topics:

- Future
- Either
- Reader

Future

The first effect type we will be looking at is Future. This effect is frequently encountered in a wide range of projects, even in non-functional languages. If you have substantial experience in Java regarding writing concurrent and asynchronous applications, you probably already know about this type of effect.

First, let's take a look at the phenomenon that the effect type abstracts and the motivation behind why such an effect type may be needed.

Motivation and the imperative example

Consider the following example. Say you are developing a calendar application to compose a user's daily schedule. This application allows the user to write their plans for the Future into the database. For example, if they have a meeting with somebody, they can create a separate entry in the database, specifying when and where it will take place.

They may also want to add a weather forecast integration into the app. They would like to warn their users whenever they have outdoor activities in unfavorable weather conditions. For example, an outdoor picnic party is undesirable in rainy weather. One way to help the user avoid such situations is to make the application contact a weather forecast server and see whether the weather on the given day is satisfying or not.

For any given event, this process can be done with the following algorithm:

1. Retrieve an event from the database based on its ID
2. Retrieve the date and the place of the event
3. Contact a weather forecast server and provide it with the date and place we are interested in, and retrieve the weather forecast
4. If the weather is bad, we can send a notification to the user

The preceding algorithm can be implemented as follows:

```
def weatherImperative(eventId: Int): Unit = {
  val evt = getEvent(eventId)  // Will block
  val weather = getWeather(evt.time, evt.location)  // Will block
  if (weather == "bad") notifyUser()  // Will block
}
```

The methods are defined as follows:

```
case class Event(time: Long, location: String)
def getEvent(id: Int): Event = {
  Thread.sleep(1000)  // Simulate delay
  Event(System.currentTimeMillis, "New York")
}
def getWeather(time: Long, location: String): String = {
  Thread.sleep(1000) // Simulate delay
  "bad"
}
def notifyUser(): Unit = Thread.sleep(1000) // Simulate delay
```

There is one effect that can cause trouble in the preceding example. It takes time to connect to the database, and it takes even more time to contact the weather server.

If we perform all of these operations sequentially from the application's main thread, as in the preceding example, we are risking blocking this thread. Blocking the main application thread means that the application will become unresponsive. One standard way to avoid this experience is to run all of these time-consuming computations in separate threads. However, it is quite common for asynchronous applications to specify every computation in a non-blocking manner. It is not common to have blocking methods; rather, every method is supposed to return an asynchronous primitive representing the computation immediately.

The simplest implementation of this idea in Java is to run every computation in a separate thread:

```
// Business logic methods
def notifyThread(weather: String): Thread = thread {
  if (weather == "bad") notifyUser()
}
def weatherThread(evt: Event): Thread = thread {
  val weather = getWeather(evt.time, evt.location)
  runThread(notifyThread(weather))
}
val eventThread: Thread = thread {
  val evt = getEvent(eventId)
  runThread(weatherThread(evt))
}
```

The three business logic methods get their own threads. The `thread` and `runThread` methods are defined as follows:

```
// Utility methods
def thread(op: => Unit): Thread =
new Thread(new Runnable { def run(): Unit = { op }})
def runThread(t: Thread): Unit = t.start()
```

You can run this application as follows:

```
// Run the app
runThread(eventThread)   // Prints "The user is notified"
```

Here, every subsequent computation is invoked at the end of every previous computation because the subsequent computation depends on the result of the computation that precedes it.

The code is hard to read, and the execution flow is difficult to follow. Therefore, it is smart to abstract away the sequential composition of these computations.

Abstraction and the functional example

Let's look at a functional way of writing this example. In the functional world, one abstraction to deal with asynchronous computations is Future. Future has the following signature—Future[A]. This type represents a computation that runs in a separate thread and computes some result, which in our case is A.

A common technique when dealing with Futures is to use callbacks to specify continuations of the computations. A continuation of a computation is an instruction on what to do after the computation has completed. A continuation has access to the result of the computation it continues. This is possible since it runs after the computation terminates.

In most implications of the Future data type, the callback pattern is present in one form or another. For example, in the Scala implementation of Future, you can specify the continuation of a function as a callback using the onSuccess method:

```
def weatherFuture(eventId: Int): Unit = {
  implicit val context =
ExecutionContext.fromExecutorService(Executors.newFixedThreadPool(5))
  Future { getEvent(eventId) }
  .onSuccess { case evt =>
  Future { getWeather(evt.time, evt.location) }
  .onSuccess { case weather => Future { if (weather == "bad") notifyUser }
}
}
```

In the preceding example, we can start the new Futures after the previous Futures terminate using the results they computed.

Also, note the implicit val that we defined before running the Future. It brings into scope an implicit execution context for the Future. Future is an asynchronous computation that runs in a separate thread. Which thread does it run on, precisely? How do we control how many threads there are and whether or not the threads are reused? We need a specification of a threading strategy when running Futures.

In the Scala implementation of the Future type, we are using Scala's mechanism of implicits to bring the threading context in scope. However, in other languages, you should expect that similar controls of the Futures' threading strategy will exist.

Composing Futures

A situation where we need to run one computation after another in an asynchronous manner is a frequent pattern. One way to solve this task is via callbacks, as we have seen previously. Every asynchronous computation is a separate entity and is started from a callback that's registered on another computation it depends upon.

Another way of conceptualizing such a pattern is to treat Futures as composable entities. The concept in question is the ability to compose two Futures into one. The semantics of the combined Future is a sequential execution of the second Future after the first one.

So, given a Future for contacting the database and a Future for contacting the weather forecast server, we can create a Future that combines both sequentially, with the second one being able to use the result of the first one.

The sequential composition is facilitated using the flatMap method, which we are already familiar with from the previous chapter. So, our example can be implemented as follows:

```
def weatherFutureFlatmap(eventId: Int): Future[Unit] = {
  implicit val context =
ExecutionContext.fromExecutorService(Executors.newFixedThreadPool(5))
  for {
    evt     <- Future { getEvent(eventId) }
    weather <- Future { getWeather(evt.time, evt.location) }
    _       <- Future { if (weather == "bad") notifyUser() }
  } yield ()
}
```

The for comprehension is shorthand for sequentially calling flatMap. This technique is called the **Monadic flow**, and is present in some functional languages, including Scala and Haskell. The preceding Scala code is syntactic sugar for the following:

```
def weatherFutureFlatmapDesugared(eventId: Int): Future[Unit] = {
  implicit val context =
ExecutionContext.fromExecutorService(Executors.newFixedThreadPool(5))
  Future { getEvent(eventId) }
    .flatMap { evt => Future { getWeather(evt.time, evt.location) } }
    .flatMap { weather => Future { if (weather == "bad") notifyUser() } }
}
```

flatMap generalized

In the previous chapter, we have already seen flatMap in the context of the Try type. It was conceptualized as a continuation of a computational that may result in an error. We can extrapolate this conceptualization to the case of Futures. The same way as flatMap was a conceptualization of a continuation of an error-prone computation in the case of Try, it is a continuation of an asynchronous computation in the case of Future.

The role of the flatMap function is more or less the same in the case of any effect type you deal with. It is a continuation of a computation that produces a side effect with another computation that produces the same side effect, but requires the result of the first computation to proceed.

Similarly to the way we used it in the case of Try in the previous chapter, we can also define a signature of flatMap for Futures as follows— (A => Future[B]) => (Future[A] => Future[B]). Another way to look at this flatMap function is that it is a lift. The flatMap lifts a function that produces the Future side effect and depends on some value, such as (A => Future[B]), to a function that does the same thing the original function did, but depends on the Future[A] (Future[A] => Future[B]) value. That is, the dependency is no longer available in a raw format, but is computed by another computation that produces the Future side effect.

It should be mentioned that Futures are not specific to functional programming. You can encounter them in lots of other languages, such as Java, JavaScript, Python, and many others. Asynchronous computations are so ubiquitous that it is natural that programmers devised a primitive to abstract their complexity away. However, in functional programming languages, such as Scala or Haskell, Future gets a functional twist to it, as we have seen previously.

Let's continue our exploration of side effects and what you can do with them by using an example with Either.

Either

Either is an effect that is similar to the Try effect that we encountered in the previous chapters.

If you remember, `Try` is a structure that can contain either of two values—an exception, or the result of the computation. Let's briefly recall our division by zero example from the previous chapters:

```
def functionalDivision(n1: Double, n2: Double): Try[Double] =
  if (n2 == 0) Failure(new RuntimeException("Division by zero!"))
  else Success(n1 / n2)
```

Here, in the case of success, we create a `Success` data structure. In case of failure, we need to create an exception with a specific error message.

Is it essential to create an exception here? The useful payload is the error message, after all. Exceptions are needed in cases where they are thrown with the `throw` statement. However, as we discussed in previous chapters, functional programming avoids such a side effect, rectifying it into an effect type instead. If we are not throwing an exception, then what is the point of explicitly creating and wrapping it in the `Failure` data structure? A more efficient way of doing things would be to return a raw error message such as a `String`, not an exception with this error message. However, when you look at the signature of the `Failure` data structure, you will see that it can only contain the subclasses of `Throwable`.

To be able to return a string instead of an exception in an erroneous case, we can use another data type: `Either`.

`Either` represents an alternative between two values. If `Try` is an alternative between an exception and a result, then `Either` is an alternative between two arbitrary types. It has two subclasses. So, a value with type `Either[A, B]` can be either `Right[B]` or `Left[A]`. Traditionally, the right case is reserved for the results of successful computations, and the left case is reserved for errors.

Let's take a look at how our division by zero example can be improved with this new data structure:

```
def division(n1: Double, n2: Double): Either[String, Double] =
 if (n2 == 0) Left("Division by zero!")
 else Right(n1 / n2)
 println(division(1, 0))  // Left("Division by Zero")
 println(division(2, 2))  // Right(1.0)
```

We no longer need to wrap the error message in an exception. We can return our error message directly. The result type of the function is now `Either[String, Double]`, where `String` is the way we represent an error, and `Double` is the result type.

It should be noted that the notion of an alternative can be taken further. `Either` is not the only data type that is used to abstract away alternatives. As you may have noticed, `Either` can be either of two values, but not both at the same time, or none.

Whenever you have a use case where you have two values at the same time, or when you have an empty alternative, you may want to use other effect types that are tailored specifically to this use case. Libraries for functional programming for languages such as Scala or Haskell provide such types. In Scala, for example, the library called `cats` provides the data type `Ior`, which may contain two values at the same time.

One use case where we may want to have two values at the same time is for presenting warnings. If errors can be understood as fatal occurrences that terminate a computation without producing a result, warnings are notifications that tell you that something went wrong in the computation, but that it was able to terminate successfully. In such a scenario, you may want to have a data structure that can contain both the computed value and the generated warnings at the same time.

Errors and asynchronous computations are not the only domain tackled by effect types. Now, let's take a look at how the problem of dependency injection is solved in a purely functional way. Let's take a look at the `Reader` type.

Reader

Dependency injection is a mechanism that defines how parts of your program should access other parts of the same program or external resources.

Let's consider a scenario where dependency injection becomes relevant. For example, consider you are writing an application with a database for a bank. The application will include methods for reading and writing the objects of your business domain into the database. For example, you may have a method to create a new user and a method to create a new account for them. These methods depend on the connection to the database. One way to inject this dependency is to pass the database connection object into the methods as arguments:

```
def createUser(u: User, c: Connection): Int = ???
def createAccount(a: Account, c: Connection): Int = ???
```

The preceding types are defined as follows:

```
class Connection
case class User(id: Option[Int], name: String)
case class Account(id: Option[Int], ownerId: Int, balance: Double)
```

However, this clutters the signatures of the methods. Also, other methods that call the database, such as dependent methods, get cluttered because they need the database connection object to satisfy the dependency of the methods they call. For example, imagine a business logic method that creates a new user and an account for them at the same time:

```
def registerNewUser(name: String, c: Connection): Int = {
  val uid   = createUser(User(None, name), c)
  val accId = createAccount(Account(None, uid, 0), c)
  accId
}
```

It is composed of two database calls, and since each of these calls depends on a database connection, this method must also depend on a database connection. Hence, you must provide a database connection as an argument to the business logic method. Providing the dependency as an argument is not very convenient as it brings the connection object into your focus. On the business logic layer, you want to focus on the business logic and not on the details of how the database connection works.

Functional solution

One solution that functional programming provides for the problem of dependency injection is that it can treat dependency requirement as a function defined with the dependency as an argument and then abstract this function away. If we want to do this, then first we have to define our database access methods as follows:

```
def createUserFunc   (u: User ): Connection => Int = ???
def createAccountFunc(a: Account): Connection => Int = ???
```

The approach states that whenever we have a computation that depends on some external resource, we model this dependency as a function that accepts this resource as an argument. So, when we have a method that is supposed to create a user, it does not perform the computation itself. Rather, it returns a function that performs the computation, provided you supply it with the database connection.

Here's how to express the business logic method in this setting:

```
def registerNewUserFunc(name: String): Connection => Int = { c:  Connection
=>
  val uid   = createUserFunc(User(None, name))(c)
  val accId = createAccountFunc(Account(None, uid, 0))(c)
  accId
}
```

This approach is not very different from the approach of having an extra argument in the functions. However, this is the first step of the abstraction process, and this step is to bring focus onto the effect we are abstracting.

The second step is to abstract away these functions. One way to do this is to treat the functions as effects. This effect is used so that the computation represented by this function cannot be performed unless you provide it with its dependency—the argument of the function. Consider our already familiar example that has been rewritten with the help of the Reader effect type:

```
def createUserReader   (u: User ): Reader[Connection, Int] = Reader { _ =>
0 }  // Dummy implementation, always returns 0
def createAccountReader(a: Account): Reader[Connection, Int] = Reader { _
=> 1 }  // Dummy implementation, always returns 1
def registerNewUserReader(name: String): Reader[Connection, Int] =
createUserReader(User(None, name)).flatMap { uid =>
createAccountReader(Account(None, uid, 0)) }
```

Reader can be defined as follows:

```
case class Reader[A, B](f: A => B) {
  def apply(a: A): B = f(a)
  def flatMap[C](f2: B => Reader[A, C]): Reader[A, C] =
   Reader { a => f2(f(a))(a) }
}
```

We can see that the pattern of flatMap and the effect types are repeating again. Previously, we saw the side effects of asynchronous computation and errors. All of them were represented by separate data structures—Future and Either (and Try). Now, we can see an effect of dependency. That is, the effect is that the computation is unable to be executed unless a specific resource demand is satisfied. This effect, too, is modeled by its own effect type: Reader.

As we stated previously, we provided the `flatMap` method for the `Reader` class. The meaning of this method is the same as in the cases of `Future` and `Try`. That is, to perform a continuation on a side effecting computation. This method can be used in the setting of a business logic method that relies on the `createUser` and `createAccount` methods.

Notice that `Reader`s are essentially functions. This means that you cannot run them until you provide the dependencies they require. To do so, you can call a method that is usually defined in the API of the `Reader` data structure. In our case, according to the definition of the preceding `Reader` class, this can be done as follows:

```
val reader: Reader[Connection, Int] = registerNewUserReader("John")
val accId = reader(new Connection)
println(s"Success, account id: $accId") // Success, account id: 1
```

Summary

In this chapter, we were armed with the theoretical foundations of effects, what they are, and why they are needed. We took a look at some examples of effects types which are frequently encountered in practice. We have seen how the `Future` type abstracts away asynchronous computations. We also looked at the `Either` type, which is similar to `Try`, but allows alternative representations for errors. Finally, we covered the `Reader` effect type, which abstracts away the effect of dependency. We also saw that `flatMap` is a typical pattern among effect types, which abstracts away the sequential composition of side effecting computations, and the effects of which are rectified into effect types.

In the next chapter, we'll have a look at how to generalize patterns of working with effect types.

Questions

1. What does the `Future` effect type `abstract`?
2. Why do we need the `Either` effect type if we already have the `Try` effect type?
3. How does functional programming represent dependency injection?
4. What role does the `flatMap` function play in all of the effect types we have encountered?

The Idea of the Type Classes

7

In the previous chapter, we saw the views of functional programming on data representation. In functional programming, data is most often encountered in the form of what a function returns. This result is usually a data structure that includes both the results of the function and data about the side effects that have occurred in the function. Different side effects are represented with different data structures.

We also saw how analyzing and working with these data structures can become tedious, so functional programming gives rise to patterns such as map and `flatMap`. There are many more patterns for working with effect types. The map and `flatMap` are just utility methods that are used in a specific context. However, they are general enough to repeat from one data type to another.

In this chapter, we will see how functional programming treats the behavior of data structures. We will see how things such as map and `flatMap` are organized into logical units, and show how these types represent the behavior of data structures.

We will introduce a notion of type classes, and we will cover the reasoning behind it in order to better understand this pattern.

In this chapter, we will cover the following topics:

- Rich Wrapper pattern
- The Type Class pattern
- Interpretation of the Type Class pattern
- Type Classes in different languages

Rich Wrapper pattern

In this section, we will start our journey to understand the pattern of type classes. We'll start by covering the idea of the *Rich Wrapper* pattern. The pattern is specific to Scala, but it introduces the problem of separating data from behavior, which becomes important in the Type Class pattern.

Motivation

Consider the following problem. Scala is a language built on top of JVM, so it has access to the Core Java library, and you can use the Java Core classes. You can also use any Java library in your Scala programs.

In this manner, Scala String and Array data types come from the Java Core. However, if you are familiar with Scala, you know that String and Array are more like Scala collections than Java strings and arrays. They are treated this way because Scala provides you with a set of extra methods, such as `map`, `flatMap`, and `filter`, on top of these types. So all the methods that ordinary Scala collections have are also available when working with strings and arrays. Strings are treated as collections of characters, and arrays as indexed sequences of elements.

How is it possible that in Scala we have collections methods on strings and arrays that come from Java? The answer is that Scala has a mechanism to simulate method injection into classes. We can have a class that comes from a third-party library in Scala and be able to inject additional methods into this class, without modifying its original implementation and not extending the original class via subtyping. This mechanism for method-injection is handy in the context of separating data from its behavior in the functional world.

This solution is called the **Rich Wrapper** pattern. To understand it, you need to understand the mechanism of implicit conversions that Scala has. This mechanism provides a way to make the compiler do extra work that ordinarily is done manually. The easiest way to understand the implicit conversions is with an example.

Implicit conversions

Imagine that you have two different models of the same domain. Some methods expect the domain objects of one domain, but you want to call them with the domain objects of another domain.

Concretely, imagine a web API that responds to HTTP requests with JSON. You may want to have two versions of the object that represents your users. One version is a full version of this entity. It contains the password hash and all the other data. Here is the full version is the internal representation of the entity, meant to be used on the backend and not meant to be leaked to the end user:

```
case class FullUser(name: String, id: Int, passwordHash: String)
```

Another version of this object is supposed to be sent to the end user upon their HTTP requests to the web API. We don't want to expose too much information, so we are going to return a shortened version of this object. This version does not expose any sensitive information:

```
case class ShortUser(name: String, id: Int)
```

Consider that you need to return an object from a server from a request handler. Since the backend represents users with the `FullUser` class, we'll first need to convert it into `ShortUser` using a conversion method:

```
def full2short(u: FullUser): ShortUser =
  ShortUser(u.name, u.id)
```

Consider also that the following method must be executed in order to return an object from a request handler in response to the HTTP request:

```
def respondWith(user: ShortUser): Unit = ???
```

Let's assume we have a `root` user and we need to be able to return it upon request:

```
val rootUser = FullUser("root", 0, "acbd18db4cc2f85cedef654fccc4a4d8")
```

From the preceding code snippet, we can imagine an HTTP request handler defined along the following lines:

```
val handlerExplicit: PartialFunction[String, Unit] = {
  case "/root_user" => respondWith(full2short(rootUser))
}
```

You don't want to explicitly perform the conversion from the backend representation each time you need to return this object. There may be many contexts in which you may want to do so. For example, you can associate the `User` entity with forum posts of that user or their comments when these are requested.

The concept of implicit conversions exists precisely for these situations. In Scala, you can define a method as follows:

```
implicit def full2short(u: FullUser): ShortUser =
  ShortUser(u.name, u.id)
```

Whenever we use a `FullUser` instance in a place where `ShortUser` is expected, the conversion from the full object into the short object will be done automatically by the compiler using the `implicit` method in scope. This way, you can convert one value to another implicitly, without cluttering the code with irrelevant details.

With the implicit conversion in scope, we can write the code as follows:

```
val handlerImplicit: PartialFunction[String, Unit] = {
  case "/root_user" => respondWith(rootUser)
}
```

The preceding code is equivalent to the original code where the conversion is done explicitly.

Rich Wrapper

How are implicit conversions related to the example when we need to inject methods into classes? We can treat method-injection as a conversion problem. We can use the wrapper pattern to define a class that wraps the target class (that is, accepts it as a constructor argument) and defines the methods that we need. We can then implicitly convert the original class to the wrapper whenever are we are calling any of the methods that are not initially present in the wrapper.

Consider the following example. We are calling a `filter` method on a String:

```
println("Foo".filter(_ != 'o'))  // "F"
```

This method is not a member of the `String` class, as the `String` class here is `java.lang.String`. However, Scala collections have this method. What happens next is that the compiler realizes that the object does not have this method, but it does not fail right away. Instead, the compiler starts to look for implicit conversions in scope that can convert this object into some other object that does have the required method. The mechanics here are the same as in the case when we are passing the user object to a method as an argument. The point is that the compiler expects one type but receives another type in its place.

In our case, the compiler expects the type with the `filter` method defined on it but receives a `String` type that does not have this method. Hence, it will try to convert it to the type that matches its expectations, that is, the existence of the `filter` method in the class. It turns out that we do have such a method in scope:

```
implicit def augmentString(x: String): StringOps
```

There is an implicit conversion defined in the `Predef` object in Scala that converts strings into a Rich Wrapper with all the collections methods, including `filter`. The same technique is used to inject the Scala collection methods into Java's arrays.

 This technique is not specific to Scala, although the underlying mechanism is. In one form or another, it is present in many languages. For example, in C#, you have the concept of implicit conversions and can convert one type to another implicitly. In Haskell, we have a more powerful, functional version of the same technique.

The Type Class pattern

Sometimes, the effect type that we are going to use is not known in advance. Consider the problem of logging. Logging can be performed to a list or a file. Logging to a list can be implemented using the Writer effect type.

A Writer is an abstraction of a pair of a result and a log generated by a computation. In its simplest form, a Writer can be understood as a pair of a list of strings and an arbitrary result. We can define the Writer effect type as follows:

```
case class SimpleWriter[A](log: List[String], value: A) {
  def flatMap[B](f: A => SimpleWriter[B]): SimpleWriter[B] = {
    val wb: SimpleWriter[B] = f(value)
    SimpleWriter(log ++ wb.log, wb.value)
  }
  def map[B](f: A => B): SimpleWriter[B] =
    SimpleWriter(log, f(value))
}
```

Notice that we have also defined the familiar `map` and `flatMap` methods for this effect type.

A few words should be said about how we have implemented the `flatMap` method. We are using a simplified version of the Writer type, in fact. In its simplified form, it is a data structure that contains a result and a list of strings—the log entries—in one data structure.

The `flatMap` method answers the question of how to combine sequential computations whose effect is `SimpleWriter`. So, given two such computations, one being a continuation of another (that is, the result of the previous computation parameterizes it), the question is—how do we produce the result of that continuation so that the log of the previous computation is preserved in that result?

In the preceding code snippet, you can see how the implementation of the `flatMap` method is done for the `SimpleWriter` data structure. So, first, we run the continuation with the result of the current data structure as an input. This run produces another result under the side effect of `SimpleWriter`, that is, a result with a log of the computation. After that, we produce a combined Writer with the result of the second computation and the combined logs of the first and second computations.

We can also define a companion object for this data type that contains convenience methods to lift any value to the effect type and to create an empty structure with a single log message:

```
object SimpleWriter {
  // Wraps a value into SimpleWriter
  def pure[A](value: A): SimpleWriter[A] =
    SimpleWriter(Nil, value)
  // Wraps a log message into SimpleWriter
  def log(message: String): SimpleWriter[Unit] =
    SimpleWriter(List(message), ())
}
```

Using the Writer effect type, we can use logging from an operation as follows:

```
import SimpleWriter.log
def add(a: Double, b: Double): SimpleWriter[Double] =
for {
  _ <- log(s"Adding $a to $b")
  res = a + b
  _ <- log(s"The result of the operation is $res")
} yield res
println(add(1, 2))  // SimpleWriter(List(Adding 1.0 to 2.0, The result
of the operation is 3.0),3.0
```

Logging to a file can be implemented with the help of another effect, IO. The IO type stands for an input-output effect, which means that the computation exchanges information with some external resources. We can define a dummy version of IO that just suspends a computation, as follows:

```
case class IO[A](operation: () => A) {
  def flatMap[B](f: A => IO[B]): IO[B] =
    IO.suspend { f(operation()).operation() }
  def map[B](f: A => B): IO[B] =
    IO.suspend { f(operation()) }
}
object IO {
  def suspend[A](op: => A): IO[A] = IO(() => op)
  def log(str: String): IO[Unit] =
    IO.suspend { println(s"Writing message to log file: $str") }
}
```

The preceding definition follows the same pattern as the SimpleWriter type. The log method does not actually write to any file, but simulates this operation by outputting to the terminal. With the help of this effect type, we can use logging as follows:

```
import IO.log
def addIO(a: Double, b: Double): IO[Double] =
for {
  _ <- log(s"Adding $a to $b")
  res = a + b
  _ <- log(s"The result of the operation is $res")
} yield res
addIO(1, 2).operation()
// Outputs:
// Writing message to log file: Adding 1.0 to 2.0
// Writing message to log file: The result of the operation is 3.0
```

What if we do not know beforehand where we are going to log? What if sometimes we need to log to a file and sometimes we need to log to a list? The preceding can be the case if we are working in different environments, for example, stage, test, or production. The question is: how exactly should we proceed with generalizing the preceding code so that it is effect-independent? The problem here is that the preceding two snippets differ only in the effect type they are using to log. In programming, whenever we see a pattern, it is a good idea to extract it.

One way to abstract away the effect type is as follows:

```
// Does not compile
// def add[F[_]](a: Double, b: Double): F[Double] =
//    for {
//      _ <- log(s"Adding $a to $b")
//      res = a + b
//      _ <- log(s"The result of the operation is $res")
//    } yield res
```

So, the effect type becomes an F type parameter. The function becomes parameterized on the type level. However, when we try to implement the body of the method, we will quickly run into difficulties. The preceding code does not compile because the compiler knows nothing about the F type parameter. We are calling the map and flatMap methods on this type, and the compiler has no way of knowing which methods are implemented on this type.

The solution to this problem comes in the form of the Type Class pattern. Under the Type Class pattern, the method looks as follows:

```
import Monad.Ops
def add[F[_]](a: Double, b: Double)(implicit M: Monad[F], L: Logging[F]):
F[Double] =
for {
  _ <- L.log(s"Adding $a to $b")
  res = a + b
  _ <- L.log(s"The result of the operation is $res")
} yield res
println(add[SimpleWriter](1, 2))  // SimpleWriter(List(Adding 1.0 to 2.0,
The result of the operation is 3.0),3.0)
println(add[IO](1, 2).operation())
// Outputs:
// Writing message to log file: Adding 1.0 to 2.0
// Writing message to log file: The result of the operation is 3.0
// 3.0
```

The reason we can use the map and flatMap methods here is that we now have an implicit dependency in the method's arguments list. The dependency in question is on the type class called Monad. Monad is one of the most common type classes in functional programming. One more dependency is Logging, which provides the log method, which is also a common method available for both effect types we are interested in.

Let's look at what type classes are and how they work on the example of Monad.

In the body of the function, we can use the map and flatMap functions, and the compiler can resolve them. Previously, we saw the same method-injection trick done with the help of implicit dependencies. In that case, we had an implicit conversion that converts the target type to a Rich Wrapper. In this case, a similar pattern is used. However, it is more complex. The complexity is because Rich Wrapper wrapped concrete classes, but we are now targeting abstract type variables, in our example, it is F.

Just as in the case of Rich Wrappers, the map and flatMap methods are injected into the preceding code using implicit conversions. Let's have a look at the methods and classes that enable this conversion:

```
trait Monad[F[_]] {
  def pure[A](a: A): F[A]
  def map[A, B](fa: F[A])(f: A => B): F[B]
  def flatMap[A, B](fa: F[A])(f: A => F[B]): F[B]
}
object Monad {
  implicit class Ops[F[_], A](fa: F[A])(implicit m: Monad[F]) {
    def map[B](f: A => B): F[B] = m.map(fa)(f)
    def flatMap[B](f: A => F[B]): F[B] = m.flatMap(fa)(f)
  }
  implicit val writerMonad: Monad[SimpleWriter] =
   new Monad[SimpleWriter] {
     def pure[A](a: A): SimpleWriter[A] =
       SimpleWriter.pure(a)
     def map[A, B](fa: SimpleWriter[A])(f: A => B): SimpleWriter[B] =
       fa.map(f)
     def flatMap[A, B](fa: SimpleWriter[A])(f: A => SimpleWriter[B]):
       SimpleWriter[B] = fa.flatMap(f)
  }
  implicit val ioMonad: Monad[IO] = new Monad[IO] {
    def pure[A](a: A): IO[A] =
    IO.suspend(a)
    def map[A, B](fa: IO[A])(f: A => B): IO[B] =
    fa.map(f)
    def flatMap[A, B](fa: IO[A])(f: A => IO[B]): IO[B] =
    fa.flatMap(f)
  }
}
```

In the preceding code snippet, you can see the entire code that enables the required conversion. This code implements the Type Class pattern. Let's have a look at it step by step:

```
trait Monad[F[_]] {
  def pure[A](a: A): F[A]
  def map[A, B](fa: F[A])(f: A => B): F[B]
  def flatMap[A, B](fa: F[A])(f: A => F[B]): F[B]
}
```

In the preceding code snippet, you can see the definition of the trait that contains all the methods that a particular set of effect types must implement. The concrete implementations of the trait will have the trait's type parameter set to the type for which the class is implemented. The trait consists of the declaration of all the methods that the type in question is supposed to support. Notice that all of the methods expect the object on which they are supposed to be called. This means this trait is not supposed to be implemented by the target object. Instead, the instances of this trait are supposed to be a sort of toolbox that defines certain behaviors for the type in question, without making that type extend the trait.

Next, we have a companion object of this trait. This companion object defines specific methods that are also part of the pattern:

```
implicit class Ops[F[_], A](fa: F[A])(implicit m: Monad[F]) {
  def map[B](f: A => B): F[B] = m.map(fa)(f)
  def flatMap[B](f: A => F[B]): F[B] = m.flatMap(fa)(f)
}
```

First of all, there is a Rich Wrapper, as you can see in the preceding code. The pattern works the same way as we have seen previously, in the case of wrappers for strings and arrays. However, there is one little difference. It is defined on an F[A] abstract type. In principle, it can be any effect type. It may seem at first that we are defining a set of methods for every type possible. However, there are constraints on the types for which the methods are implemented. The constraints are enforced by the implicit argument that follows a constructor of the Rich Wrapper:

```
implicit m: Monad[F]
```

So, to construct the wrapper, we need to satisfy an implicit dependency on the type class defined in the preceding code snippet. This means that for the F type to be able to use the Rich Wrapper pattern, we need to have an instance of the trait defined in the preceding code in scope implicitly for this F type. When we say *an instance of the type class for the F type*, we mean a concrete object that extends the type class trait where the type parameter is set to F.

For example, a `Monad for Writer` instance is an object whose type conforms to `Monad[Writer]`.

All the Rich Wrapper's methods mimic that of the type class and are delegated to it.

After that, we have some default implementations of the type class for certain common classes. For example, we can define ones for our Writer and IO types:

```
implicit val writerMonad: Monad[SimpleWriter] = new Monad[SimpleWriter] {
  def pure[A](a: A): SimpleWriter[A] =
  SimpleWriter.pure(a)
  def map[A, B](fa: SimpleWriter[A])(f: A => B): SimpleWriter[B] =
  fa.map(f)
  def flatMap[A, B](fa: SimpleWriter[A])(f: A => SimpleWriter[B]):
  SimpleWriter[B] = fa.flatMap(f)
}
implicit val ioMonad: Monad[IO] = new Monad[IO] {
  def pure[A](a: A): IO[A] =
  IO.suspend(a)
  def map[A, B](fa: IO[A])(f: A => B): IO[B] =
  fa.map(f)
  def flatMap[A, B](fa: IO[A])(f: A => IO[B]): IO[B] =
  fa.flatMap(f)
}
```

Note that in the preceding examples, we implement the `map` and `flatMap` methods by delegating them to the implementations owned by the `SimpleWrapper` and IO classes. This is because we have already implemented these classes with the methods in question. In the real world, it is often the case that the classes will not have the required methods. So you will write the entire implementation of them instead of delegating them to the methods owned by the classes.

Similar to the `Monad`, the `Logging` type class encapsulates the `log` method common to the two effect types:

```
trait Logging[F[_]] {
  def log(msg: String): F[Unit]
}
object Logging {
  implicit val writerLogging: Logging[SimpleWriter] =
  new Logging[SimpleWriter] {
    def log(msg: String) = SimpleWriter.log(msg)
  }
  implicit val ioLogging: Logging[IO] = new Logging[IO] {
    def log(msg: String) = IO.log(msg)
  }
}
```

It follows the same pattern as the `Monad` type class. First, the trait declares the methods the type class will have. Next, we have the companion object with some default implementations for our effect types.

Let's see how the preceding code enables the logging example to use the `flatMap` and `map` methods, and how the mechanics of implicit resolution work here.

First of all, the compiler sees that we are trying to call the `flatMap` method on an `F` type. The compiler doesn't know anything about the `F` type—it is not aware of whether it has the method in question. In an ordinary programming language, a compile-time error would have occurred at this point. However, in Scala, implicit conversions kick in. The compiler will try to convert this `F` type to something that has the required `flatMap` method. It will start the implicit lookup to find the implicit conversion that would convert an arbitrary `F` type into something that has the required method. It will find such a conversion. The conversion will be the Rich Wrapper of the `Monad` type class, as discussed previously. The compiler will see that it can convert any `F[A]` effect type into a wrapper that has the required methods. However, it will see that it is not able to do so unless it can provide the constructor of the Rich Wrapper with an implicit dependency on the type class. This type class, `Monad`, defines the `map` and `flatMap` methods for the effect types for which it is implemented. So, in other words, only the effect types for which there is an implementation of the type class in scope can be converted into this Rich Wrapper. If a type does not have an implementation of the `Monad` type class, it will not be wrapped by the Monad's Rich Wrapper, and hence it will not have the `map` and `flatMap` methods injected into it, and a compile-time error will be generated.

So, the compiler will see that it can inject the required methods implicitly, but only if it finds an implicit implementation of the necessary type class. Hence, it will try to find this implementation. If you are calling it with the Writer or IO types, it will be able to find the instances of the type class because they are defined inside the Monad companion object. The companion objects are searched for the implicit implementations of their companion classes.

Here, we have covered a few details specific to Scala—the *Rich Wrapper* pattern is more specific to Scala than anything else. However, the Type Class pattern repeats in many languages. Next, we will cover some reasoning for the type classes so that you know how to think about this pattern.

Interpretation of the Type Class pattern

Since the idea of a type class is highly abstract, it is necessary to develop an understanding of what it is and how it can be used in practice.

Injectable interfaces

One way to think about the Type Class pattern is as of a way of injecting entire interfaces into existing classes.

In ordinary imperative languages, interfaces facilitate polymorphism. They allow you to treat classes that exhibit similar behavior uniformly. So for example, if you have classes for a car, a motorcycle, and a truck, you can define an interface vehicle, and treat all these classes as instances of that interface. No longer do you care about the peculiarities of the implementations of each class, all you care about is that all of its entities can drive. That is, they exhibit one behavior typical to all of them. An interface is a way to encapsulate a common behavior. When programming to interfaces, you are grounding your programs on the assumption that a set of entities of your program exhibits a behavior that is the same in its nature, although may differ in its details for each implementation.

However, in ordinary imperative languages, such as Java, you must declare the interfaces at definition-time. This means, that once the class is defined, you are not able to make it implement additional interfaces. This fact makes you struggle with polymorphism in certain situations. For example, if you have a bunch of third-party libraries and you want the classes of this library to implement specific interfaces defined in your program, you will not be able to do that.

If you have a look at the example with the logging, we will see that the example is precisely about the polymorphism. We take a random F effect type and define the example based on the assumption that it has certain behaviors—`flatMap` and `map`. Although these behaviors may differ from effect type to effect type, their nature remains the same—the sequential composition of side-effecting computations. All we care about is that an effect type we are using supports these methods. As long as this condition is met, we don't care about other details of an effect type.

This technique is of particular help in the functional programming world. Let's recall—how did the need for `map` and `flatMap` emerge in the first place? There is a theoretical foundation for them from a mathematical perspective. However, for engineering purposes, the need for the `map` and `flatMap` methods is quite pragmatic. Functional programmers need to frequently analyze the data structures of effect types in code in order to compose pure side-effecting computations sequentially, and this quickly becomes quite tedious. So, for us to avoid the boilerplate of analyzing the data structures every time, we have abstracted away the problem of sequential composition into the `map` and `flatMap` methods.

The general pattern here is that we need to do various things with functional data structures. The `map` and `flatMap` functions define how to do sequential composition of computations. However, we may want to do much more than that. The general pattern is that we should be able to abstract away common repeating operations that we have, and we may not know beforehand all the operations we may want to support. This situation makes a case for separating data from behavior. In the modern functional programming libraries, effect types (data structures with information about the side effects of a computation) are separated from their behavior (what you can do with them). This means that the effect types contain only the data that represents the side effects. Whenever we need to do something with the effect types, we inject the required behavior into them using the Type Class pattern discussed previously. Many functional libraries are divided into two parts—the data part that describes the effect types, and the type class part that represents what you can do with the data, its behavior. The two parts are unified using the type class mechanism specific to the programming language the library is written for. For example, in Scala, the mechanism of implicit conversions powers the Type Class pattern and method-injection. The Scala compiler itself has no notion of the Type Class pattern, but you can express it effectively using the tools the language provides.

 Haskell has language-level support for type classes. In Haskell, there is a language-level separation between data and the type classes. You are not able to define any behavior on data. Haskell implements the philosophy of the separation of data and behavior at the language level. This cannot be said about Scala. In Scala, you can have ordinary OOP classes that can have both data (variables) and behavior (methods).

Toolboxes

Another useful metaphor for the Type Class pattern is that there are toolboxes that allow you to do things to your data.

Imagine yourself as a carpenter. A carpenter is a person who creates things from wood. How does one go about creating useful things from wood? They take raw wood and go to their workshop, where they have a bunch of tools to work with wood. They use hammers, saws, and so on to turn wood into tables, chairs, and other goods. If the carpenter is sophisticated, they will probably differentiate between different types of wood. For example, certain trees have robust wood, and other trees have soft wood. The same saw is more effective with one type of wood than with another. So, the carpenter has different types of saws for different types of wood. However, the fact that the carpenter needs a saw to cut the trees remains constant, no matter the type of wood.

Back in the programming world, the effect types are wood. They are the raw material of the functional programming from which you compose your program. In the raw state, they are hard to process without tools—it is hard to analyze, compose, and process effect types by hand, precisely the same way it is hard to carve goods from wood without saws and hammers.

For this reason, there are tools to process effect types. Type classes are to effect types what saws are to wood. They are tools that allow you to process your raw material.

The same saw may not apply to different types of wood. In the same way, different effect types need different implementations of one type class. For example, the Writer and IO effect types need separate implementations of the `Monad` type class. The purpose of the type class, the sequential composition, remains the same; it is the way the sequential composition is done in each case that is different. This can be compared with the fact that the purpose of sawing remains the same for a wide variety of raw material, that is, to cut wood. However, the details of how it is done vary, hence separate saws for separate types of raw material.

This is why in the Type Class pattern, we first declare what behavior must be exhibited in a trait, and only then do we implement this behavior for each type individually.

Just as a carpenter has a toolbox to process raw wood, a functional programmer has a type class to process raw effect types. And just as a carpenter has an entire workshop full of tools, a functional programmer has libraries full of type classes for different purposes. We will cover these libraries in the next chapter.

Type classes in different languages

In principle, the idea of type classes is present even in Java. For example, Java has the `Comparator` interface, which defines how to compare two arbitrary types. It defines a relationship of order on a type. The type that is used with collections defines the order in which they are sorted.

However, a language such as Java lacks a mechanism for applying that class to types conveniently. So, for example, when you are sorting a collection, you need to explicitly provide an instance of the type class to the sorting method. This is unlike Scala, where it is possible to use implicit conversions and implicit lookup for the compiler to look up the implementation of the type class by itself, so as not to clutter the code.

In Scala, the compiler is much smarter than in Java, in part due to the presence of the implicit resolution mechanism. So, when we want to inject a specific set of methods into a class, we can do so with the help of the implicit conversions. If in Java we are required to provide all the type classes explicitly, in Scala we can leave most of this work to the compiler.

In Haskell, a similar mechanism is present to perform the implicit lookup of type classes. Also, Haskell follows the separation between data and behavior. So, in general, you are not able to declare methods on data, and you are not able to define classes that have both variables and methods. This is to enforce the purely functional style of programming. In Scala, which is a mix between purely functional and object-oriented programming, you can have classes that have both variables and methods.

Talking about the implicit resolution mechanism, we should note that it is a relatively advanced feature, and not every programming language has it.

Summary

In this chapter, we introduced the idea of a type class, which is central to modern functional programming. We built up to this idea by introducing the Rich Wrapper pattern first, which facilitates type classes in Scala. A type class can be understood as a toolbox to process raw effect types. Another understanding of the Type Class pattern is that it is an injectable interface that you can inject into your classes to achieve polymorphism. Finally, we had a look at how type classes are used in languages other than Scala. In the next chapter, we will learn about the commonly used type classes and the libraries they are organized in.

Questions

1. What is the *Rich Wrapper* pattern for in Scala?
2. How is the Rich Wrapper implemented in Scala? What is the implicit conversions mechanism in Scala?
3. Explain the Type Class pattern.
4. What is the motivation behind the Type Class pattern?
5. Do imperative languages have type classes?

Basic Type Classes and Their Usage

8

In the previous chapter, we discussed the idea of the type class and how type classes are a methodology for decoupling data from behavior. We have also seen how type classes can be treated as toolboxes that abstract away certain behavior. In essence, to a functional programmer, they are what a workshop is to a carpenter.

In the previous chapters, we also saw how type classes are motivated based on the practical needs that arise during functional programming. In this chapter, we will see how an entire library of classes for functional programming arise from practical needs. We'll take a look at one such library, and we will see how typical libraries are structured and how they can be used in practice.

The following are the topics that we will be covering in this chapter:

- A motivation for organizing type classes into systems and libraries
- The `Cats` library for purely functional programming and its structure
- Type classes `Cats` defines

A motivation for organizing type classes into systems and libraries

The basic principle of engineering is abstracting away what repeats. In the previous chapters, we saw how functional programming deals with effect types extensively and encapsulates side effects into them. This is because working with them directly can be tedious. It is pretty hard to analyze these data structures in an ad hoc using only the services provided to you by your programming language of choice. Hence, patterns of working with effect types get abstracted away into type classes.

So far, we have only seen a small amount of type classes. However, the most important thing to realize is the principle behind their creation, that is, realizing how the type classes get created and what the motivation is for their existence. The motivation for creating new type classes is precisely dealing with the complexity that side effects impose on the programmer.

We have also learned that the type class pattern consists of at least two parts. The first part is a declaration of the methods that are supported by the type class, and the second part is the implementation of the type class for the effect types you are going to work with. Certain effect types are embedded into the language's core. For example, in Scala, types such as `Future`, `Option`, and `Either` are present in the language core library by default. This means that you are going to be dealing with them frequently, and this, in turn, means that you will need the implementation of the type classes whenever you deal with these effect types. Basically, this means that you are going to redefine our implantation of type classes for these types every time you need them in different projects.

Whenever some functionality repeats from project to project, it makes sense to encapsulate it into a separate library. So, the preceding discussion shows that here, we have the situation where you have functionality that repeats from project to project. The first one is the type classes themselves that we use in multiple projects. For example, Monad deals with sequential composition, and sequential composition is frequent in both the functional and non-functional worlds.

Another item that repeats from project to project is the implementation of the type classes for frequently repeating effect types.

The preceding argument can be extended a little bit to the effect types themselves. Previously, we mentioned that the core libraries of functional languages usually include support for frequently encountered effect types. However, it is possible to imagine a situation where you're going to want to define the effect types yourself. For example, you may be dealing with some new effects that you want to encapsulate, or maybe you are going to define something that is specific to your own use case, and your own project.

With that, you'll notice that certain side effects that are not members of the core library start repeating from project to project. In this case, it would be wise to encapsulate them into a separate library, too. Of course, if you are frequently dealing with the same effect types that are not present in the language core, it is also a good idea to define the type class implementations for them in the library as well.

This is because whenever you need these effect types, you will also need the type classes to work with them. So, if you are going to encapsulate the effect types into a separate library, you will also need to encapsulate the type class implementations in that library as well.

To summarize the preceding argument, we need to encapsulate three things:

- The type class definitions
- The type class implementations
- The frequently encountered effect types that are not present in the language core and the type class implementations for them

Such libraries for purely functional programming have been implemented for various programming languages. Now, let's take a look at what such a library may look like and how you can use it in practice. We will use a library called `Cats`, which comes from Scala.

The Cats library for purely functional programming

In this section, we will introduce the library that we will be using for purely functional programming in Scala. It encapsulates frequently encountered type classes, implementations of them for frequently encountered effect types, and some effect types as well.

In this section, we will dive deeper into the structure of the library, and we will see how you can use it in practice. We will be following an example of a `Monad` type class that we discussed in the previous chapters. We will see how this type class is defined in this library and how it is implemented for its data types.

The structure of the library

The library consists of the top-level package and its subpackages. The top-level package is called `cats` and is a location where basic type classes are defined:

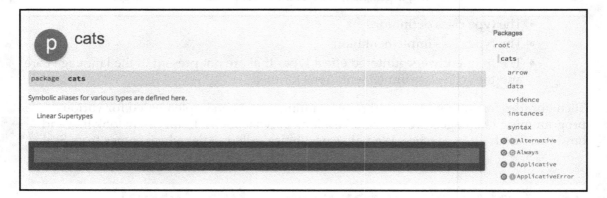

Apart from that, there are several subpackages present in the top-level package. The most important ones are `instances`, `data`, and `syntax`.

The `instances` package contains the implementations of the type classes for basic data types that are present in the language core and the ones defined by the `Cats` library. Finally, data types that are frequently encountered and absent from the language core are defined under the `data` package.

We will now take a look at each of these structural pieces in detail. We will start from the top level package, that is, `cats`.

Core

The core package, `cats`, of the library exposes the following API:

The core package contains a list of all the type classes that are defined by the library. The type classes pattern in the `Cats` implementation usually consists of a trait and its companion object.

Let's use an example of Monad to take a look at what a typical type class looks like in the context of the library:

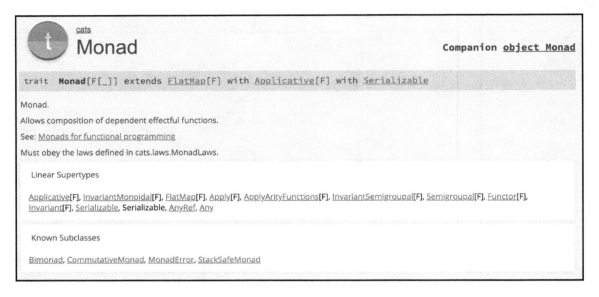

Let us now take a closer look at how the type classes in the type class hierarchy of Cats are structured.

Type class hierarchy

The first thing to notice here is that the type classes are defined in the format that we saw in the previous chapter. Another thing to notice is the hierarchy of type classes in the Cats library. So, for example, the Monad class extends the FlatMap and Applicative type classes, and if you take a look at the linear super types of the type class, you will see that the ancestors are far more numerous. Also, if you have a look at the subclasses, you will notice that a number of type classes also extend the Monad type class.

The reason for this hierarchy is that the Cats library is quite fine-grained. We previously discussed that type classes can be treated as containers for methods that you're going to use. Type classes such as Monad may define several methods at once. Therefore, it may be reasonable to have a separate type class for each of the method. Let us now discuss the abstract methods that Monad defines.

Abstract methods

Let's take a look at the *value member* section of the Scaladoc documentation of the `Monad` implementation by `Cats`. The abstract members section is the most important section of any type cause definition. A type class is a declaration of certain tools, and its concrete instances must support these tools. They are declared, but not implemented in the type class trait. So, the abstract methods defined by a type class constitute a definition of this type class.

Concretely, in the case of Monad, we have three abstract methods, as follows:

- There is a `flatMap` method, which we are already familiar with.
- The pure method is able to lift any value into an effect type of `F`.
- There is a `tailRecM` and type class. It is a tail recursive Monadic loop. The intuition for this method is as follows. Monad's `flatMap` defines a sequential composition of effectful computations. Where there is a sequence, a loop may also be desirable. A loop is a sequence of instructions that repeat over and over. Therefore, a loop is built on top of the sequential composition. If you define the sequential composition, you can use it to also define the loop. The role of `tailRecM` is to provide such a loop for the functional programming under effect types. You can think of it as a `while` loop of pure functional programming. We will discuss this method in more detail later on in the chapter.

Concrete methods

Besides abstract methods, the `Monad` type class provides a bunch of predefined concrete value members. These are implemented by default in the type class, so when you define the type class instance, you do not need to provide the implementation of these value members. Their definitions are based on the abstract value members that we saw previously. This means that every method that you encounter under concrete value members can be defined in terms of the abstract value members we saw previously.

It is very common for concrete value members to contain methods that are abstract value members in a superclass of the type class in question. Take, for example, the `map` method, which we are already familiar with. Technically, it comes as an abstract member of the `Functor` type class. However, it is possible to define a type class in terms of only `flatMap` and pure functions. These two functions are abstract members of the `Monad` class, and hence we can override the inherited `map` function with a concrete implementation of it, as follows:

```
def map[A, B](fa: F[A])(f: A => B): F[B] = fm.flatMap(fa)(x => pure(f(x)))
```

In the preceding code snippet, you can see how exactly that function can be implemented when you have `flatMap` and `pure` functions. A word of caution, that this kind of implementation based on the `flatMap` and `pure` functions is not always desirable. There are situations where you will want to have a custom implementation of the functions that can be implemented in terms of the abstract methods. In some scenarios, reusing the functionality that you already have is not always the best solution.

The intuition for this logic is as follows. We have already discussed that sequential composition in pure functional programming is facilitated by Monad. Later in this chapter, we will see a type class that has been designed for parallel composition. The operator to compose two computationals in parallel can be implemented in two ways. One way is what you would expect from real parallelism. It performs computations independently. For example, if one computation fails, the other computation will still continue and will still produce a value. However, it is possible to implement the parallel composition operator with the help of sequential composition. You may have an implementation of such a composition that just composes two computations sequentially, although you will have it named as a parallel composition operator. So, if you have a sequential composition operator such as `flatMap`, a naive parallel composition operator will be defined as a sequential composition of the computations using this sequential composition operator.

The reason we are having this discussion is that Monad inherits from the Applicative type class. The Applicative type class was designed for parallel computation. It contains a method called `ap` that is designed to compose computations in parallel. However, when we discussed the `Monad` type class in the past, we did not see this method among the abstract members. This is because it is a concrete member of the `Monad` type class, which means that it was implemented using the methods defined by Monad—the `flatMap` and the `pure` functions. In practice, it means that if you want to perform a parallel composition, you may be able to, depending on either the Monad or Applicative type class. However, if you depend on Monad, you may not get true parallelism, since its parallelism operator may be implemented in terms of sequential composition. So, it is very important to understand the mechanics of type classes and not to treat them as something magical because you might be in for an unexpected error.

Type classes have a solid mathematical foundation in the form of Category Theory. We will not be discussing the theory in this pragmatic guide to functional programming. However, in the next section, we will touch upon the mathematical nature of type classes and discuss which mathematical laws they must obey.

Laws

Type classes are defined in terms of the methods they support. When defining a type class, you do not have an idea of how exactly the methods will be implemented for every given data type. However, you do have a rough idea of what these methods will do. For example, we have a rough idea that `flatMap` is responsible for sequential composition, and `pure` corresponds to lifting a value into an effect type without doing anything else.

This kind of information regarding how the methods should behave can be encapsulated in terms of the mathematical laws that the type class must obey. In fact, the majority of type classes can be viewed from a mathematical perspective, and so there are certain laws that they must obey.

Let's take a look at the laws that Monads must obey. There are three of them, as follows:

1. **Left identity**: `pure(a).flatMap(f) == f(a)`. This means that if you have a raw value, `a`, and a function, `f`, which takes that value as an input and computes an effect type out of it, the effect of applying this function directly on `a` should be the same as if you first used the `pure` function on `a` and flatMapped the result with `f`.

2. **Right identity**: `m.flatMap(pure) == m`. This means that a pure function must lift a value into the effect type without performing any other action. The effect of this function is nil. This also means that if you are using the `flatMap` function on pure, pure must behave as an identity, meaning the effect type you flatMapped will be equal to the result of flatMapping.

3. **Associativity**: `m.flatMap(f).flatMap(g) == m.flatMap(a => f(a).flatMap(g))`. Basically, this law states that the precedence of the `flatMap` application do not matter. Think of the associativity in the context of the + operator—`(a + b) + c == a + (b + c)`.

For the majority of type classes out there, you should expect some mathematical laws to be defined. The meaning of them is that they provide certain guarantees that you can rely on when programming your software. For every concrete implementation of the `Monad` type class, the preceding mathematical laws must hold true. For any other type class, all of its implementations must obey its own laws.

Since there is a requirement for every type class implementation to obey certain laws, it is reasonable to expect that all of your implementations must be tested with respect to these laws. Since the laws are not dependent on a particular implementation of a type class and should hold true for every implementation of the type class, it is also reasonable to have the tests defined in the same library that defines the type classes.

We do this so that we do not need to redefine these tests every time. Indeed, these tests are defined in a separate module of the `Cats` library—`cats-laws`. The module defines the laws for every cats type class and provides an integration with the majority of popular test frameworks so that once you define your own implementation of a type class, you do not need to define the tests to check this implementation against the mathematical laws.

For example, this is how tests for Monad are defined:

```
implicit override def F: Monad[F]
def monadLeftIdentity[A, B](a: A, f: A => F[B]): IsEq[F[B]] =
  F.pure(a).flatMap(f) <-> f(a)
def monadRightIdentity[A](fa: F[A]): IsEq[F[A]] =
  fa.flatMap(F.pure) <-> fa
/**
 * Make sure that map and flatMap are consistent.
 */
def mapFlatMapCoherence[A, B](fa: F[A], f: A => B): IsEq[F[B]] =
  fa.flatMap(a => F.pure(f(a))) <-> fa.map(f)
lazy val tailRecMStackSafety: IsEq[F[Int]] = {
  val n = 50000
  val res = F.tailRecM(0)(i => F.pure(if (i < n) Either.left(i + 1)
    else Either.right(i)))
  res <-> F.pure(n)
}
```

Next, let us discuss how to use methods defined by `Monad` conveniently from the Scala code with `Cats`. Let us have a look at what infrastructure `Cats` provides to expose methods on effect types.

Syntax

We should mention here that the requirement to use the implicit mechanism with a *Rich Wrapper* pattern is a requirement that's specific to Scala. Scala is a language that mixes object-oriented and purely functional styles. This is why certain functional programming features such as type classes are not a part of the language and are implemented in a more generic way instead. This means that in Scala, method injection and the type class pattern are not first-class citizens. They are not defined at the language level. Instead, they leverage a more general mechanism that is defined on the class level—the implicit mechanism. Hence, in order to seamlessly use type classes in a Scala project, you need to use this mechanism so that they take effect manually.

A note should be taken that this may not be true for other functional languages. For example, Haskell has language-level support for the type class style of programming. This is why you don't need to bother with method injection. This is because the language itself does all of the necessary work for you.

However, languages such as Scala that do not have first-class citizen support for style may require you to use such a mechanism. The exact approaches to type class programming may vary from language to language. In this section, we will take a look at how this works for Scala.

We previously discussed that method injection in Scala happens with the help of the implicit mechanism and the *Rich Wrapper* pattern. Since this kind of mechanism to inject methods is defined for every type class, it makes sense to define the required Rich Wrappers in the `Cats` library together with all of the type classes. This is indeed done in the `Cats` library, in the `syntax` package, like following:

all	BitraverseOps	syntax
alternative	BitraverseSyntax	AllSyntax
applicative	CoflatMapSyntax	AllSyntaxBinCompat
applicativeError	ComonadSyntax	AllSyntaxBinCompat0
apply	ComposeSyntax	AlternativeSyntax
arrow	ContravariantMonoidalOps	ApplicativeErrorExtension
arrowChoice	ContravariantMonoidalSyntax	ApplicativeErrorExtensionOps
bifoldable	ContravariantSemigroupalSyntax	ApplicativeErrorIdOps
bifunctor	ContravariantSyntax	ApplicativeErrorOps
bitraverse	DistributiveOps	ApplicativeErrorSyntax
cartesian	DistributiveSyntax	ApplicativeIdOps
coflatMap	EitherIdOps	ApplicativeOps
comonad	EitherKOps	ApplicativeSyntax
compose	EitherKSyntax	ApplyOps
contravariant	EitherObjectOps	ApplySyntax
contravariantMonoidal	EitherOps	ArrowChoiceSyntax
contravariantSemigroupal	EitherSyntax	ArrowSyntax
distributive	EqOps	BifoldableSyntax
either	EqSyntax	BifunctorSyntax
eitherK		

The package contains a set of classes and traits. What you need to notice are the naming conventions they follow. You will see that lots of the traits and classes end in `Ops` and `Syntax`, for example, `MonadOps` or `MonadSyntax`.

Besides classes and traits, you will also notice a set of singleton objects are present in this package. The names of these objects mimic the names of the type classes they are defined for.

Let's take a look at how this mechanism works for the `Monad` type class:

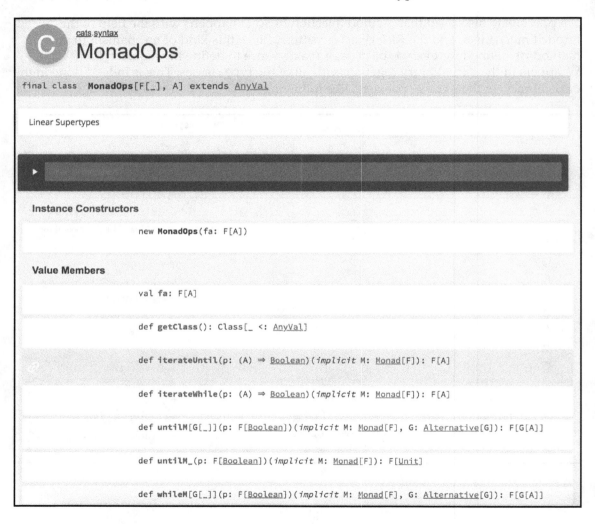

First, let's take a look at the `MonadOps` class. This is a Rich Wrapper that is supposed to be used for `Monad` method injection. It injects the methods provided by the `Monad` type class into an effect type, `f`. One thing to notice about the methods it injects is that all of them have an implicit `Monad` argument. They delegate their implementation to this type class.

However, the `MonadOps` class is not an implicit class—it is an ordinary class. We learned previously that for the *Rich Wrapper* pattern, we need an implicit conversion from an effect type to the Rich Wrapper. So, where is this conversion defined, and how is it brought into scope? To find out, let's take a look at the `MonadSyntax` trait:

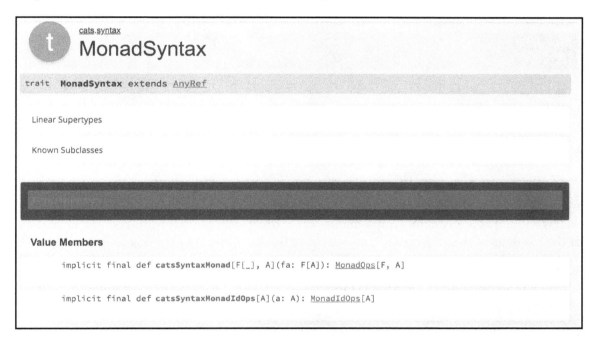

As you can see, the `MonadSyntax` contains implicit methods. These are supposed to convert any object, `F[A]`, into `MonadOps[F[A]]`. However, how do you bring the methods into scope?

For this, let's take a look at the Monad singleton:

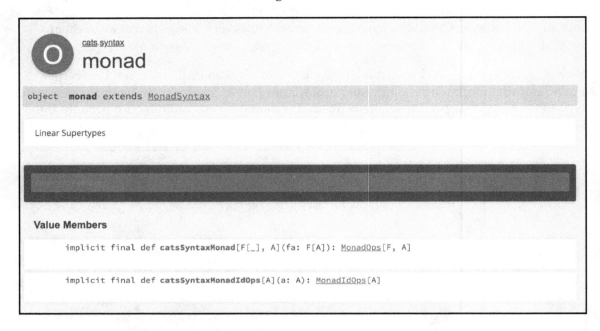

As you can see in the preceding screenshot, the singleton extends the `MonadSyntax` trait. So basically, this is a concrete implementation of the `MonadSyntax` trait. You can import all of the contents of this object, and you will have the Rich Wrapper for `MonadOps`.

Why is it implemented as a combination of a singleton and a trait? Would it not be more convenient to implement the Rich Wrapper as one singleton object that contains all of the required methods?

This can be understood if you take a look at the sheer amount of singleton objects present in the `syntax` package. If you are using a lot of type classes in a single Scala file, all of the imports for each type class can be tedious to write and track. Hence, you might want to just bring in scope the syntax for all available type classes at once, even though you will never use the majority of them.

Precisely for this reason, there is an `all` singleton object, as shown in the following screenshot:

```
cats.syntax
all

object  all extends AllSyntaxBinCompat

Linear Supertypes

AllSyntaxBinCompat, AllSyntaxBinCompat0, TrySyntax, ApplicativeErrorExtension, UnorderedTraverseSyntax, ToUnorderedTraverseOps,
AllSyntax, WriterSyntax, VectorSyntax, ValidatedSyntax, NonEmptyTraverseSyntax, ToNonEmptyTraverseOps, TraverseSyntax,
ToTraverseOps, StrongSyntax, ToStrongOps, ShowSyntax, ToShowOps, SemigroupKSyntax, ToSemigroupKOps, ReducibleSyntax,
ToReducibleOps, ProfunctorSyntax, ToProfunctorOps, ParallelSyntax, TupleParallelSyntax, OrderSyntax, PartialOrderSyntax,
OptionSyntax, MonoidSyntax, MonadSyntax, MonadErrorSyntax, ListSyntax, IorSyntax, InvariantSyntax, ToInvariantOps, HashSyntax,
GroupSyntax, SemigroupSyntax, FunctorSyntax, ToFunctorOps, FoldableSyntax, ToUnorderedFoldableOps, ToFoldableOps,
FlatMapSyntax, ToFlatMapOps, EqSyntax, EitherSyntax, EitherKSyntax, ContravariantSemigroupalSyntax, ContravariantMonoidalSyntax,
DistributiveSyntax, ToDistributiveOps, ContravariantSyntax, ToContravariantOps, ComposeSyntax, ToComposeOps, ComonadSyntax,
ToComonadOps, CoflatMapSyntax, ToCoflatMapOps, SemigroupalSyntax, BitraverseSyntax, BitraverseSyntax1, BifoldableSyntax,
ToBifoldableOps, BifunctorSyntax, ToBifunctorOps, ArrowChoiceSyntax, ToArrowChoiceOps, ArrowSyntax, ToArrowOps, ApplySyntax,
TupleSemigroupalSyntax, ApplicativeErrorSyntax, ApplicativeSyntax, AlternativeSyntax, AnyRef, Any
```

If you take a look at this object and its supertypes, you'll see that its ancestors constitute a massive list. They include all of the syntax traits defined in the package. This means that this singleton object contains all of the implicit conversion from effect types to Rich Wrappers that inject methods defined in the type classes into the effect types in question. You can import all of the contents of this object into your project and have all of these implicit conversions in scope. This is exactly why we define implicit conversions inside the trait and not inside singleton objects. If you define these implicit conversions as part of singleton objects, you will not be able to combine these singleton objects into one object, because you cannot inherit from a singleton object. However, you can inherit from multiple traits in Scala. Therefore, the reason for having traits is modularity and composability.

To summarize, the `Cats` library contains two major components:

- It contains the Rich Wrapper classes that wrap effect types and inject methods defined by the type classes into these effect types
- It contains implicit conversions from these effect types to the Rich Wrapper classes

Later in this chapter, we will see examples of how to use these capabilities in practice.

Next, let's take a look at the structure and the purpose of the `instances` package.

Instances

The `instances` package exposes the following API:

As you can see from the preceding screenshot, the `instances` package contains quite a lot of entities. As in the case of the `syntax` package, the main thing to notice here is the naming convention of these entities. First, we have a set of traits and classes. They are named as follows—the first part of the name is the name of the type for which the instances are defined, and then there's the `Instances` suffix.

There are also singleton objects, which are named after the types for which the instances are defined.

Let's take a look at what one of the instances traits looks like:

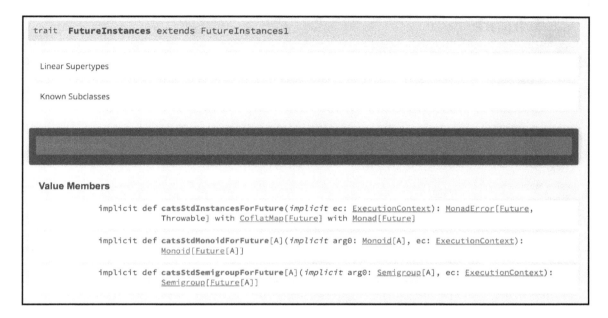

In the preceding screenshot, you can see the structure of the FutureInstances trait. All of the methods are defined as implicit methods, which means they will be brought into the implicit scope whenever the members of this trait are imported. Another important thing to notice is the result types of the methods. These result types are all some kind of type class. It is the meaning of these methods to provide the implicit implementations of various type classes for a given effect type. Also notice that the trait contains a lot of methods for various type classes, but all of them are parametrized by the Future type. All of the type classes are implemented for this effect type.

Similarly to the case of the `syntax` package, the traits are then used to create singleton objects. For example, let's take a look at the `future` singleton:

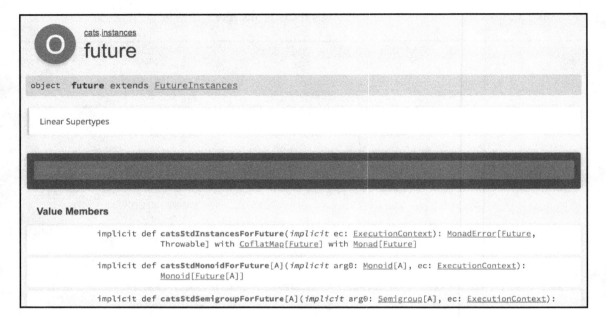

The `future` singleton object extends the `FutureInstances` trait, and the same pattern repeats for all of the other singleton objects present in the `instances` package. The reason for having the singletons extending the traits is similar to the situation with the `syntax` package:

The package also defines an `all` singleton object, which extends all of the other traits present in the package. The value of this strategy is that in order to bring the standard implementations of type classes in scope, all you need to do is import the contents of the `all` object. You do not need to import the implementation separately for every type.

Finally, let's take a look at the last essential part of the `Cats` library, that is, the `data` package.

Data

Let us now discuss the data package, which is another package you will use a lot in daily functional programming with Cats:

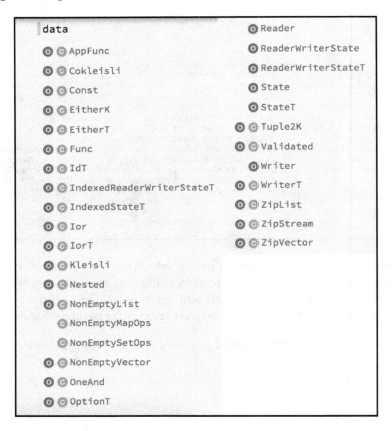

Previously, we discussed that the main utility of having a library such as cat is to abstract away the common type classes for functional programming. We have also seen that not only do the type classes get abstracted, but also all of the various kinds of supporting stuff to use them in practice efficiently. This supporting stuff includes the mechanism for syntax injection and the default implementations for commonly encountered effect types.

A final piece of the supporting infrastructure that cats provides is a set of common effect types. These are encapsulated under the data package. Under this package, you will encounter various data types that you can use to express your side effects in a purely functional way.

For example, there are data types such as `Reader`, `Writer`, and others. The effect types are often not related one to another, and you can really use each of them independently.

Infrastructure synergy

In this section, we have seen how cats defines its type classes and how it can be used in functional programming. The main points to understand about the `Cats` library are regarding the supporting infrastructure that it provides to you as a functional programmer, and how exactly to use it in practice.

The supporting infrastructure in questions provides a set of the type classes, their implementations for the commonly encountered data types, and a mechanism to inject their methods into your effect types. Also, cats provides a set of commonly encountered effect types.

The library is very modular, and you can use various parts of it independently from the rest of the library. So, it is a good strategy for beginner programmers so that they can simply start with one or two basic type classes and use the library to bring them in scope. As you gradually progress as a functional programmer, you will start to pick up and familiarize yourself with more and more type classes and chunks of this library.

In this section, we have familiarized ourselves with the general structure of the `Cats` library. In the rest of this chapter, we will familiarize ourselves with certain commonly encountered type classes. We will see how to use them in practice. We will also have a look at some of the mechanics for how the type classes are implemented.

Type classes

So far, we have performed a bird's-eye overview of the `Cats` library and its structure. In this section, we'll have a look at some individual type classes from the `Cats` library that are frequently used in real-world projects. For every such type class, will take a look at the motivation as to why it exists. We will discuss their methods and behavior in detail. We will also take a look at examples of the usage of the type class. Finally, we will take a look at the implementation of the type class for various effect types, and take a look at how the class is implemented for popular types so that you have an idea of what an implementation of the type class might look like.

Monad

Let us have a look at how you can use type classes from the Cats library on an example of Monad, the type class we are already familiar with.

In the previous sections, in order to use a Monad type class, we defined it as ad hoc. However, the Cats library provides all of the abstractions we need so that we don't need to define this type class and its syntax ourselves.

So, how do you use the Monad type class in the context of the logging example from Chapter 7, *The Idea of the Type Classes*? As you may recall, in that chapter, we took a look at an example of logging capabilities and discussed that it is a good example of the sequential composition that can be handled by Monad. So, let's take a look at how this can be done with cats:

```
import cats.Monad, cats.syntax.monad._
```

First of all, we no longer need to define the trait of Monad ourselves as well as its companion object where we normally defined the syntax for it. All we need to do is perform some imports from cats. In the preceding code, you can see that first of all we perform an import of the Monad type from the cats package, and then we import the syntax for the Monad. We have already discussed how this mechanism works in the previous section of this chapter.

After that, we can define the method from Chapter 7, *The Idea of the Type Classes*, for adding two integers and writing to the login process, as follows:

```
def add[F[_]](a: Double, b: Double)(implicit M: Monad[F], L: Logging[F]):
F[Double] =
 for {
   _ <- L.log(s"Adding $a to $b")
   res = a + b
   _ <- L.log(s"The result of the operation is $res")
 } yield res
println(add[SimpleWriter](1, 2)) // SimpleWriter(List(Adding 1.0 to
2.0, The result of the operation is 3.0),3.0)
```

Note that the definition looks exactly the same as the one from Chapter 7, *The Idea of the Type Classes*. However, the semantics is a bit different. The Monad type comes from the cats package and is not defined as ad hoc.

Also, in order to use the type class with the `SimpleWriter` effect type that we defined in `Chapter 7`, *The Idea of the Type Classes*, we still need to add an implementation of the Monad for this data type. We can do so as follows:

```
implicit val monad: Monad[SimpleWriter] = new Monad[SimpleWriter] {
  override def map[A, B](fa: SimpleWriter[A])(f: A => B):
   SimpleWriter[B] = fa.copy(value = f(fa.value))
  override def flatMap[A, B](fa: SimpleWriter[A])(f: A =>
   SimpleWriter[B]): SimpleWriter[B] = {
     val res = f(fa.value)
     SimpleWriter(fa.log ++ res.log, res.value)
  }
  override def pure[A](a: A): SimpleWriter[A] = SimpleWriter(Nil, a)

  override def tailRecM[A, B](a: A)(f: A =>
   SimpleWriter[Either[A,B]]): SimpleWriter[B] = ???
}
```

Actually, `cats` already provides a type similar to our `SimpleWriter` effect type that is intended precisely for logging. Let us now discuss how to get rid of `SimpleWriter` in favor of the capabilities `cats` provides.

Writer effect type

The Writer effect type provides us with a bit more of a generic type class than the `SimpleWriter` implementation. However, if we use it, we do not need to define the `SimplerWriter` type, as well as an implementation of the type classes for it. Since cats provides the implementation of its type classes for its data types, we don't need to worry about doing this ourselves.

As you may recall, our `SimpleWriter` object is essentially a pair. The first element of the pair is a list of strings which represents all of the logging messages that were logged by a computation. The other object of a pair is a value that was computed by the computation.

The cats implementation of the `Writer` object is essentially very similar to our simpler Writer implementation, except the first element of a pair is not a list of strings but an arbitrary type. This has a certain utility, because now you have the ability to use it for logging data structures other than lists of strings.

The `SimpleWriter` that we are using can be expressed in terms of the cats Writer if we explicitly specify the type in which the log messages are stored:

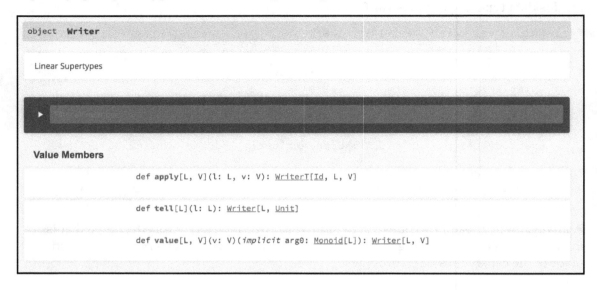

In the preceding screenshot, you can see the documentation of the Writer singleton object from the `data` package. This object can be used to write log messages into a Writer effect type. The two most important methods over here are `tell` and `value`. The `tell` method writes a message into the log and the `value` method lifts an arbitrary value into the Writer data structure with an empty log message. The Writer data type has a `Monad` instance that defines how to sequentially compose two Writers. During the sequential composition, the logs of two effect types are combined into one.

Also, if you look through the `data` package of `cats`, you will discover that there is no trait or class called Writer. The real name of the Writer data type is `WriterT`. One thing to remember about `cats` is that it aims to provide highly generic and abstract tools that can be used in a wide range of different scenarios. So, in this particular situation, the technique of Monad Transformers is used, hence why is has the strange name of `WriterT`. For the time being, you don't need to worry about the Monad Transformers, and you can use the Writer type, which is defined in `cats` in terms of `WriterT`. The Writer singleton provides a convenient set of methods to deal with it.

Since the Writer data type is a standard data type of `cats`, we can replace our custom `SimpleWriter` with the Writer that comes from `cats`, and we can also remove the Logging type class from our application altogether. The reason we do this is to standardize on the `Cats` library. This standardization makes the code more compact, eliminates redundancy, and increases reliability. We do this because we are using standard tools instead of reinventing them ad hoc.

In the code snippet, you can see an implementation of an addition method from `Chapter 7, The Idea of the Type Classes,` using the capabilities from `cats` that we discussed previously.

```
def add(a: Double, b: Double): Writer[List[String], Double] =
  for {
    _ <- Writer.tell(List(s"Adding $a to $b"))
    res = a + b
    _ <- Writer.tell(List(s"The result of the operation is $res"))
  } yield res
println(add(1, 2)) // WriterT((List(Adding 1.0 to 2.0,
  The result of the operation is 3.0),3.0))
```

The tailRecM method

Previously in this section, we touched on the `tailRecM` method briefly. It is pretty useful in certain situations, because it allows you to define loops in the context of an effect type. In this subsection, let's take a more detailed look at its signature and at how this method works:

Abstract Value Members

```
abstract def flatMap[A, B](fa: F[A])(f: (A) ⇒ F[B]): F[B]


abstract def pure[A](x: A): F[A]
    pure lifts any value into the Applicative Functor.

abstract def tailRecM[A, B](a: A)(f: (A) ⇒ F[Either[A, B]]): F[B]
    Keeps calling f until a scala.util.Right[B] is returned.
```

Let's take a look at the arguments of this method. First of all, let's take a look at the second argument of this method, the `f` function. The function takes a raw value of type `A`, and the result of this function is an effect type, which is `F[Either[A, B]]`.

Let's think about what we can do with this computation to make a loop out of it. Suppose that we start from some value, A. Suppose that we run the computation f on this value. Then, our result is of the type F[Either[A, B]]. There are two possibilities of what exactly this type will be—either F[Left[A]] or F[Right[B]]. If it is F[Left[A]], then we are able to use flatMap on F[Left[A]]; after that, we can extract A from Left, and then we can run the computation f again on that A. If it is the F[Right[B]], there is nothing left to do but return the result of the computation, that is, F[B].

So, the function passed to tailRecM will run on argument A while it produces the results of type F[Left[A]]. Once it produces F[Right[B]], this result is counted as the final result and is returned from the loop.

Basically, if we have the ability to perform a flatMap on the effect type F, we are also able to define a loop based on flatMap. However, why is it an abstract method? If all it takes to make a loop is the ability to perform flatMap, then why can we not define it as a concrete method implemented in terms of flatMap?

Well, we might want to try and do that. Consider the implementation of the Monad for our SimpleWriter example, as follows:

```
override def tailRecM[A, B](a: A)(f: A => SimpleWriter[Either[A,B]]):
  SimpleWriter[B] = f(a).flatMap {
    case Left (a1) => tailRecM(a1)(f)
    case Right(res) => pure(res)
}
```

In the preceding example, we have a tailRecM in terms of flatMap. What happens if we try an infinite loop?

```
Monad[SimpleWriter].tailRecM[Int, Unit](0) { a =>
Monad[SimpleWriter].pure(Left(a)) }
```

The preceding code results in a StackOverflowError:

```
[error] java.lang.StackOverflowError
...
[error] at jvm.TailRecM$$anon$1.tailRecM(TailRecM.scala:18)
[error] at jvm.TailRecM$$anon$1.$anonfun$tailRecM$1(TailRecM.scala:19)
[error] at jvm.SimpleWriter.flatMap(AdditionMonadic.scala:19)
[error] at jvm.TailRecM$$anon$1.tailRecM(TailRecM.scala:18)
[error] at jvm.TailRecM$$anon$1.$anonfun$tailRecM$1(TailRecM.scala:19)
[error] at jvm.SimpleWriter.flatMap(AdditionMonadic.scala:19)
[error] at jvm.TailRecM$$anon$1.tailRecM(TailRecM.scala:18)
[error] at jvm.TailRecM$$anon$1.$anonfun$tailRecM$1(TailRecM.scala:19)
[error] at jvm.SimpleWriter.flatMap(AdditionMonadic.scala:19)
```

```
[error] at jvm.TailRecM$$anon$1.tailRecM(TailRecM.scala:18)
[error] at jvm.TailRecM$$anon$1.$anonfun$tailRecM$1(TailRecM.scala:19)
[error] at jvm.SimpleWriter.flatMap(AdditionMonadic.scala:19)
...
```

This error occurs most frequently in the scenario of a recursive call where we run out of stack frames of memory that are allocated for us by the JVM.

Every time you perform a method call, a specific memory fragment is allocated by the JVM for all of the variables and parameters of that method call. This memory fragment is called a stack frame. So, if you are calling a method recursively, you will have the number of stack frames growing proportionally to the depths of your recursion. The memory you can use for the stack frames is set on the JVM level and is usually up to 1 MB, and it is fairly easy to run into its limit with a deep enough recursion.

However, there are situations when you do not need to create additional stack frames in cases of recursion. Here, we are talking about tail recursion. Basically, you are able to drop the previous stack frame of recursion if it is no longer needed. This situation arises if there is nothing else to do in the method owning the stack frame, and the result of this method is fully dependent on the result of the subsequent calls of the recursion.

Consider, for example, the following example of a factorial computation:

```
def factorial(n: Int): Int =
  if (n <= 0) 1
  else n * factorial(n - 1)
println(factorial(5)) // 120
```

In the preceding code, the factorial function is defined recursively. So, in order to compute a factorial of a number n, you first need to compute a factorial of n-1, and then multiply it by n. When we call the factorial method recursively, we can ask a question as to whether we need to do anything else in this method after the recursive call is done, or if its results are dependent only on the method that we are calling recursively. More precisely, we are talking about whether we need to do anything else after the factorial call inside the factorial function. The answer is that we need to perform one more step to complete the computation. This step is the multiplication of the result of the factorial call by the number n. So, until this step is completed, we are not able to drop the frame of the current call. However, consider the factorial method, which is defined as follows:

```
def factorialTailrec(n: Int, accumulator: Int = 1): Int =
  if (n <= 0) accumulator
  else factorialTailrec(n - 1, n * accumulator)
println(factorialTailrec(5)) // 120
```

In the preceding example, when we are calling the `factorial` method, we can ask ourselves the following question—do we have anything else to do in the method in order to complete its computation after the call to the `factorial` method? Or is the result of this method fully dependent on the result of the `factorial` method we are calling in this place? The answer is that we do not need to do anything else here.

The Scala compiler can recognize such situations and perform optimization in places where recursion can reuse the stack frames of the previous reclusive calls. This situation is called **tail recursion.** In general, such calls are much more efficient than ordinary recursion because you cannot get a Stack Overflow with them, and in general their speed is comparable to the speed of an ordinary `while` loop.

In fact, you can explicitly make a requirement on a method so that it's tail recursive in Scala, like so:

```
@annotation.tailrec
def factorialTailrec(n: Int, accumulator: Int = 1): Int =
  if (n <= 0) accumulator
  else factorialTailrec(n - 1, n * accumulator)
```

In the preceding example, the first method will not compile because it is not tail recursive while annotated with `@tailrec`. The Scala compiler will perform a check for all the methods annotated with `@tailrec` so see whether they're tail recursive.

Let's revisit our case of `tailRecM`. From the name, you can now guess that this method is supposed to be tail recursive. Now, let's recall our naive implementation of this method for `SimpleWriter`. Its execution resulted in a stack overflow exception. This is because, here, the recursion is split into several methods. So if you take a look at the stack trace output, you can see that the output is periodic. There are two methods repeating in this output—`flatMap` and `tailRecM`. The Scala compiler is not able to prove that the method is tail recursive in such a periodic recursion situation. In principle, you can think of a way to optimize recursion even in this, but Scala compiler cannot do that.

Also, let's see what happens if you try to declare the `tailRecM` method with the `@tailrec` annotation:

```
@annotation.tailrec
override def tailRecM[A, B](a: A)(f: A => SimpleWriter[Either[A,B]]):
SimpleWriter[B] =
  f(a).flatMap {
    case Left(a1) => tailRecM(a1)(f)
    case Right(res) => pure(res)
  }
```

You will see that the code stops compiling because the method is not recognized as tail recursive:

```
[error] /Users/anatolii/Projects/1mastering-
funprog/Chapter8/jvm/src/main/scala/jvm/TailRecM.scala:19:12: could not
optimize @tailrec annotated method tailRecM: it contains a recursive call
not in tail position
[error] f(a).flatMap {
[error] ^
```

The point of having this method as an abstract method is precisely because you must implement it, not in terms of `flatMap` (which would inevitably lead to periodic recursion), but in terms of a single tail recursive method. For example, in the context of `SimpleWriter`, we can come up with such an implementation such as the following:

```
@annotation.tailrec
  override def tailRecM[A, B](a: A)(f: A => SimpleWriter[Either[A,B]]):
  SimpleWriter[B] = {
    val next = f(a)
    next.value match {
      case Left (a1) => tailRecM(a1)(f)
      case Right(res) => pure(res)
    }
  }
```

In the preceding code snippet, as you can see, we have an implementation of `tailRecM` in a tail recursive manner. Notice that we are still using techniques similar to the ones that we are using in the `flatMap` function. However, these techniques are wrapped in a single method which is tail recursive.

One remark should be made, and that is that not every Monad implementation has an implementation of `tailRecM`. Frequently, you will find scenarios where `tailRecM` just throws a `NotImplementedError`:

```
override def tailRecM[A, B](a: A)(f: A => SimpleWriter[Either[A,B]]):
SimpleWriter[B] = ???
```

The `???` syntax is used in Scala to conveniently throw such an error.

So far, we have discussed a `flatMap` in the context of composition of side effecting computations. Now, let's take a look at an example of the composition of a side effecting computation with a non-side effecting computation. Let's take a look at Functor.

Functor

Another frequently encountered type class in functional programming is Functor. Functor is all about the map function in its essence. As you may recall from the previous chapters, the `map` function is very similar to `flatMap` function; however, it takes a non-side effecting computation as its argument. It is used to transform a value within the context of a effect type when this transformation is not side effecting itself.

You might want to use a Functor if you want to do something with the result of a side effecting computation without extracting it from its effect type.

As you may recall, we used an intuition of sequential composition in the case of the `flatMap` of a Monad. This intuition may not be the best one for Functor. In the case of `map`, we can use another intuition of function, changing a value under the effect type. The operation that is abstracted away in this case is one of extracting the value from an effect type. The `map` method asks you only about what you want to do with the result of a side-effecting computation, without demanding from you and information about how exactly to extract this result from the effect type.

As in the case of the `Monad` type class, we have already discussed the `map` method in detail in the previous sections, so we will not be stopping on this type class for long. All we will do is take a look at how you might want to use it with the `Cats` library.

Let's take a look at the classes defined by the `Cats` library for Functor:

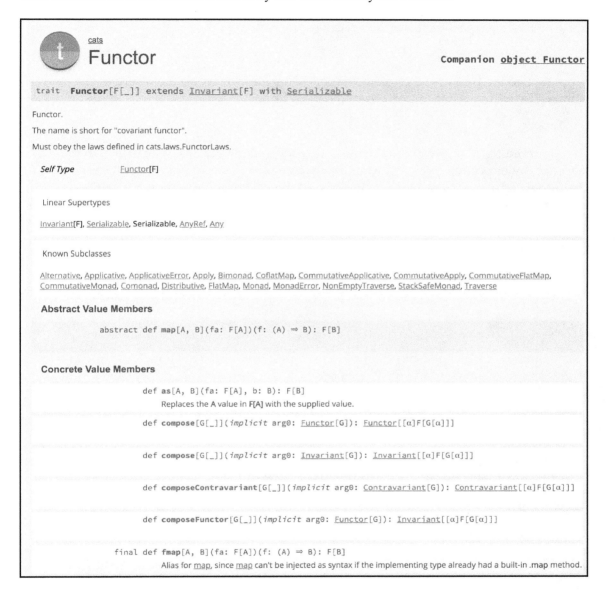

In the preceding screenshot, you can see the documentation and the definition of the Functor type class. Now, let's take a look at what its implementation may look like for our `SimpleWriter` type. First of all, let's recall the definition of the `SimpleWriter` data type:

```
case class SimpleWriter[A](log: List[String], value: A)
```

Now we need to provide an implementation of the Functor type class from the `Cats` library. We will do some imports from the `Cats` library:

```
import cats._, cats.implicits._
```

In the preceding code, we are performing an import of the Functor type from the `cats` package (by importing `cats._`). After that, we must import the syntax for this type class (by importing `cats.implicits._` imports all the syntax and instances for all the type classes). So, whenever we have an implementation of the type class in scope, we will also have the syntax for it injected.

So, let's provide the implementation of the Functor type class for `SimpleWriter`:

```
implicit val simpleWriterFunctor: Functor[SimpleWriter] =
  new Functor[SimpleWriter] {
    override def map[A, B](fa: SimpleWriter[A])(f: A => B):
      SimpleWriter[B] = fa.copy(value = f(fa.value))
  }
```

In the preceding code, you can see a simple implementation of the Functor type class for `SimpleWriter`. As you can see, all we need to do is implement the `map` method of this type class.

After that, once we have created some very simple instances of the effect type, we are able to call the `map` method on it:

```
val x = SimpleWriter(Nil, 3)
println(x.map(_ * 2)) // SimpleWriter(List(),6)
```

So, the `map` method gets injected into our effect type.

One question you might be asking is, what is the point is this? If Functor and Monad both define the `map` method, why have Functor at all? Why not have the Monad implementation for every type class where we need the `map` method and not bother with the Functor class at all? The answer is that not every effect type has the `flatMap` method implementation for it. So, an effect type might have an implementation of `map`, but it may be impossible to define a `flatMap` on it. Hence, the `Cats` library provides a fine-grained structure of its type class hierarchy so that you can use it according to your own needs.

So far, we have discussed type classes for sequential composition. Now, let's take a look at the case of parallel composition and how the Applicative type class handles it.

Applicative

Knowing how to compose computations in sequence is a basic skill that enables procedural programming to take place. This is something that we rely upon by default when we use imperative programming languages. When we write two statements in sequence, we implicitly mean that these two statements are supposed to be executed one after another.

However, sequential programming is not capable of describing all the programming situations, especially if you're working in the context of an application that is supposed to run in parallel. There may be lots of situations where you may want computations composed in parallel. This is exactly where the Applicative type class comes into play.

Motivation

Consider that we have two independent computations. Suppose we have two computations that evaluate mathematical expressions, and then we need to combine their results. Also, suppose that their computation is performed under the Either effect type. So, the main idea is that either of the two computations can fail, and if one of them fails, it is the result of interpretation being left with an error, and if it succeeds, the result is Right of some result:

```
type Fx[A] = Either[List[String], A]
def combineComputations[F[_]: Monad](f1: F[Double], f2: F[Double]):
F[Double] =
  for {
    r1 <- f1
    r2 <- f2
  } yield r1 + r2
val result = combineComputations[Fx](Monad[Fx].pure(1.0),
  Monad[Fx].pure(2.0))
  println(result) // Right(3.0)
```

In the preceding code, you can see how you can combine two such computations sequentially using the Monad type class. Here, we are using for comprehensions to compute the result of the first computation, and then the second computation.

Let's take a look at a scenario where one of these computations goes wrong:

```
val resultFirstFailed = combineComputations[Fx](
  Left(List("Division by zero")), Monad[Fx].pure(2.0))
  println(resultFirstFailed) // Left(List(Division by zero))
val resultSecondFailed = combineComputations[Fx](
  Monad[Fx].pure(1.0), Left(List("Null pointer encountered")))
  println(resultSecondFailed) // Left(List(Null pointer encountered))
```

You can see two situations and two outputs. The first one is where the first computation goes wrong and the second one is where the second computation goes from. So basically, the result of the combined computation will be `Left` if either both of the two computations fail.

What happens if both of these computations fail?

```
val resultBothFailed = combineComputations(
  Left(List("Division by zero")), Left(List("Null pointer encountered")))
  println(resultBothFailed) // Left(List(Division by zero))
```

You can see an output of the situation where both of these computations fail. An error the first computation only gets an output. This is because they are composed sequentially, and the sequence is terminated on the first error. The behavior of the Monad for `Either` is to terminate sequential composition if `Left` is encountered.

This kind of scenario may not always be desirable, especially in large applications that consist of a large amount of various modules that can fail. In such an application, for debugging purposes, you would like to collect as much information about the errors that have occurred as possible. If you're only collecting one error at a time, and you have dozens of independent computations that fail, you will have to debug them one at a time because you will not have access to the entire set of errors that have occurred. This is because only the first error encountered will be reported, even though the computations are independent on one another.

The reason why this scenarios happens is because of the very nature of the way we have composed our computations. They are composed sequentially. The nature of sequential composition is to run computations one after another, even if they are not dependent on one another's results. Since these computations run one after another, it is only natural to interrupt an entire sequence if an error has occurred in one of the links of the chain.

This solution to the preceding scenario would be to compose independent computations in parallel instead of in sequence. So, they should all be run independently one from another, and their results should be combined in some manner after they finish.

Applicative type class

We would like to define a new primitive for the preceding scenario. We can call this method `zip`:

```
type Fx[A] = Either[List[String], A]
def zip[A, B](f1: Fx[A], f2: Fx[B]): Fx[(A, B)] = (f1, f2) match {
  case (Right(r1), Right(r2)) => Right((r1, r2))
  case (Left(e1), Left(e2)) => Left(e1 ++ e2)
  case (Left(e), _) => Left(e)
  case (_, Left(e)) => Left(e)
}
```

The method will take two computations as its arguments, and it will output a combined result of two of its supplied inputs as a tuple under their common effect type.

Also notice that we are dealing with specific cases of `Left` being a list of strings. This is to combine multiple error strings for multiple failed computations into one error report.

The way it works is that if both compilations are successful, their results are combined into a pair. Otherwise, if either of these computations fails, their errors are collected in a combined list.

Given the new method, `zip`, we can express the preceding example as follows:

```
def combineComputations(f1: Fx[Double], f2: Fx[Double]): Fx[Double] =
  zip(f1, f2).map { case (r1, r2) => r1 + r2 }

val result = combineComputations(Monad[Fx].pure(1.0),
  Monad[Fx].pure(2.0))
  println(result) // Right(3.0)

val resultFirstFailed = combineComputations(
  Left(List("Division by zero")), Monad[Fx].pure(2.0))
  println(resultFirstFailed) // Left(List(Division by zero))

val resultSecondFailed = combineComputations(
  Monad[Fx].pure(1.0), Left(List("Null pointer encountered")))
  println(resultSecondFailed) // Left(List(Null pointer encountered))

val resultBothFailed = combineComputations(
  Left(List("Division by zero")), Left(List("Null pointer encountered")))
  println(resultBothFailed) // Left(List(Division by zero, Null pointer
  encountered))
```

Notice that here we're making the use of `zip` to create combined versions of two independent computations, and addressing the fact that we are using the `map` method to do something with the result of this computation.

Actually, we can express the `zip` function in terms of a more generic `ap` (short for `apply`) function. It is as follows:

```
def ap[A, B](ff: Fx[A => B])(fa: Fx[A]): Fx[B] = (ff, fa) match {
  case (Right(f), Right(a)) => Right(f(a))
  case (Left(e1), Left(e2)) => Left(e1 ++ e2)
  case (Left(e), _) => Left(e)
  case (_, Left(e)) => Left(e)
}
```

Here is how we can express the `zip` function in terms of the `ap` function:

```
def zip[A, B](f1: Fx[A], f2: Fx[B]): Fx[(A, B)] =
  ap[B, (A, B)](ap[A, B => (A, B)](Right { (a: A) => (b: B) => (a, b)
}) (f1))(f2)
```

The actual meaning of the `ap` function is a more generic way to express the combination of two independent computations running together. The trick is that the first computation results in some function, `F[A => B]`, and the second computation is raw computation, `F[A]`. The point about this function and why it is different from the `zip` function in a qualitative way is as follows. Intervention is composition plus execution. It composes some value lifted into effect type `F`, together with a computation, `A => B`, that works on this value, which is also lifted into the context `F`. Since at composition time we already deal with effect types, we already have the independent computations finished. Compare that to the case of `flatMap`, where one of the arguments is a function, `A => F[B]`, that outputs an effect type. So, in the case of `flatMap`, one of the competitions is a function that is going to be executed. It is the responsibility of `flatMap` to execute it and obtain the result `F[B]`. This cannot be said about `ap`, which already has access to the results that the effect types computed—`F[A => B]` and `F[A]`. Hence, there is independence of computations. Since one of the values of the computed effect types is a function, `A => B`, it is not only a composition in terms of zipping into a pair, but also an execution that's similar to mapping.

Actually, the `ap` function comes from the `Apply` type class, which is an ancestor of Applicative:

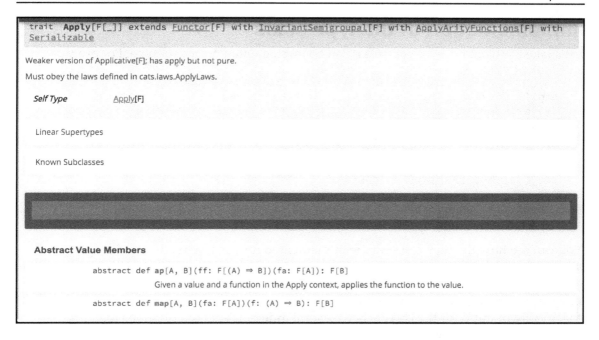

```
trait Apply[F[_]] extends Functor[F] with InvariantSemigroupal[F] with ApplyArityFunctions[F] with
Serializable
```

Weaker version of Applicative[F]; has apply but not pure.

Must obey the laws defined in cats.laws.ApplyLaws.

| *Self Type* | Apply[F] |

Linear Supertypes

Known Subclasses

Abstract Value Members

```
abstract def ap[A, B](ff: F[(A) ⇒ B])(fa: F[A]): F[B]
```
      Given a value and a function in the Apply context, applies the function to the value.

```
abstract def map[A, B](fa: F[A])(f: (A) ⇒ B): F[B]
```

However, you will encounter Applicative versions of the type class that extend the `Apply` type class more frequently. The only difference between these type classes is that Applicative also has the `pure` function, which is used to lift a raw value, a, into the same effect type, `F`.

Applicative also has a bunch of useful concrete methods defined in terms of `ap`. There is also some nice syntactic sugar support that `cats` provides for you so that you can use Applicative in your projects in an intuitive way. For example, you can perform a `map` on two values at once, as follows:

```
def combineComputations(f1: Fx[Double], f2: Fx[Double]): Fx[Double] =
  (f1, f2).mapN { case (r1, r2) => r1 + r2 }
```

We can use the syntactic sugar that `cats` injects in tuples in order to easily work with such kind of cases of parallel computation. So, you can just unite two effect types under a tuple and map them with the Applicative type class in scope.

Implementation of the type class

Let's take a look at how the type class can be implemented for a data type. For example, let's look at `Either`:

```
implicit val applicative: Applicative[Fx] = new Applicative[Fx] {
  override def ap[A, B](ff: Fx[A => B])(fa: Fx[A]): Fx[B] = (ff, fa)
  match {
    case (Right(f), Right(a)) => Right(f(a))
    case (Left(e1), Left(e2)) => Left(e1 ++ e2)
    case (Left(e), _) => Left(e)
    case (_, Left(e)) => Left(e)
  }
  override def pure[A](a: A): Fx[A] = Right(a)
}
```

You can see how the type class can be implemented for `Either` with `Left` being `List[String]`. So, as you can see, if two computations are successful, that is, they are `Right`, we simply combine them. However, if at least one of them is `Left`, we combine the `Left` side of both computations into a single `Left[List[String]]`. This is done specifically in mind for the cases where several independent computations may produce errors that you might want to combine under a single data structure.

You have probably noticed that we are using a pretty specific case of `Either`—the one where `Left` is always a `List[String]`. We have done this because we need a way to combine the `Left` sides of two computations into one, and we are not able to combine generic types. The preceding example can be generalized further to the arbitrary version of the type of `Left`, `Either[L, A]`. This can be done with the help of the `Monoid` type class, which we will learn about next. So, let's take a look at this type class and see where it can be useful.

Monoid

Monoid is another popular type class that you will frequently encounter in practice. Basically, it defines how to combine two data types.

As an example of Monoid, let's take a look at the implementation of an Applicative type class for the `Either` data type. In the previous section, we were forced to use a specific version of `Either`, the one with `Left` set to a list of strings. This was done precisely because we know how to combine two lists of strings, but we do not know how to combine any two generic types.

If we define the signature of this preceding Applicative as follows, then we will not be able to provide a decent implementation of this function because we will not be able to combine two generic types:

```
implicit def applicative[L]: Applicative[Either[L, ?]]
```

If you tried to write an implementation of this function, it would look something like the following:

```
override def ap[A, B](ff: Either[L, A => B])(fa: Either[L, A]):
Either[L, B] = (ff, fa) match {
  case (Right(f), Right(a)) => Right(f(a))
  case (Left(e1), Left(e2)) => Left(e1 |+| e2)
  case (Left(e), _) => Left(e)
  case (_, Left(e)) => Left(e)
}
```

We are using a special operator, |+|, in order to describe the operation of combining two data types we know nothing about. However, since we know nothing about the data types we are trying to combine, the code will not compile. We cannot simply combine two arbitrary data types because the compiler does not know how to do that.

This situation can be changed if we make the Applicative type class implicitly depend on another type class that does know how to implicitly combine these two data types. Meet Monoid:

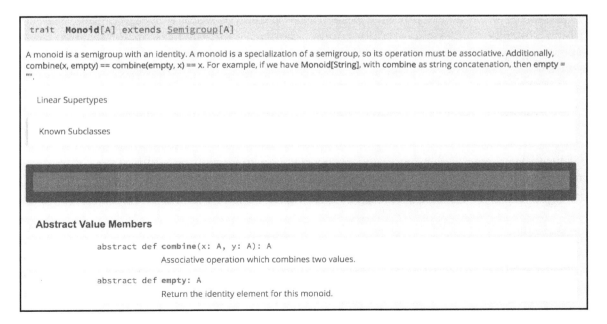

```
trait Monoid[A] extends Semigroup[A]
```

A monoid is a semigroup with an identity. A monoid is a specialization of a semigroup, so its operation must be associative. Additionally, combine(x, empty) == combine(empty, x) == x. For example, if we have Monoid[String], with combine as string concatenation, then empty = "".

Linear Supertypes

Known Subclasses

Abstract Value Members

```
abstract def combine(x: A, y: A): A
```
Associative operation which combines two values.

```
abstract def empty: A
```
Return the identity element for this monoid.

The Monoid type class extends `Semigroup`. `Semigroup` is a mathematical structure of from. It is a type class that is defined as follows:

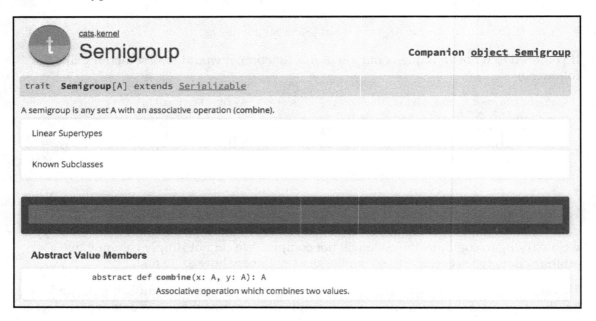

Basically, `Semigroup` is defined in the context of abstract algebra and Set Theory. Given a set, a `Semigroup` is a structure on this set that defines an operator that can combine two arbitrary elements of a set to produce another element of the same set. So, for any two elements of a set, you are able to combine them using this operator to produce another element that also belongs to this set. In the language of programming, `Semigroup` is a type class that can be defined, as shown in the preceding screenshot.

In the preceding screenshot, you can see that `Semigroup` defines a single method called `combined`. It takes two arguments of type `A` and returns another value of type `A`.

An intuitive way to understand `Semigroup` is to have a look at the addition operation on integers:

```
implicit val semigroupInt: Semigroup[Int] = new Semigroup[Int] {
  override def combine(a: Int, b: Int) = a + b
}
```

In addition operation on integers, + is an operator that can be used to combine any two arbitrary integers to obtain another integer. Hence, the operation of addition forms a Semigroup on the set of all possible integers. The Semigroup type class in cats generalizes this idea to any arbitrary type, A.

Looking back at our Monoid example, we can see that it extends a Semigroup and adds another method to it, which is called empty. Monoid must obey certain laws. One of these laws is that the empty element must be an identity with respect to the combined operation. This means that the following equalities must hold true:

```
combine(a, empty) == combine(empty, a) == a
```

So basically, if you try to combine an empty identity element with any other element of set A, you will get that same element as a result.

An intuitive way to understand this point is to have a look at the operation of the addition of integers:

```
implicit def monoidInt: Monoid[Int] = new Monoid[Int] {
  override def combine(a: Int, b: Int) = a + b
  override def empty = 0
}
```

You can see an implementation of the Monoid for integers. If we take the operation to be an addition, then 0 is an empty element. Indeed, if you add 0 to any other integer, you will get this integer as a result. 0 is an identity element with respect to the addition operation.

This remark, *with respect to the addition operation*, is really important to notice. For example, 0 is not an identity element with respect to multiplication. In fact, if you multiply 0 by any other element, you will get 0 and not that other element. Speaking of multiplication, we can define a Monoid for integers with the operation of multiplication and the identity element being one, as follows:

```
implicit def monoidIntMult: Monoid[Int] = new Monoid[Int] {
  override def combine(a: Int, b: Int) = a * b
  override def empty = 1
}
```

Actually, cats defines some nice syntactic sugar for Monoids. Given the preceding definition of that Monoid for integers for the multiplication operation, we can use it as follows:

```
println(2 |+| 3) // 6
```

You can see how you can use an infix operator, |+|, in Scala to combine two elements. The preceding code is equivalent to the following:

```
println(2 combine 3) // 6
```

This is a common practice in cats in order to define such kinds of symbolic operators for frequently encountered operators. Let us have a look at how Applicative can be implemented for Either with Monoid as its dependency.

 Another library for functional programming, ScalaZ, is more aggressive than cats with respect to operator usage, and hence it can be more difficult to understand for a beginner. cats is more friendly in this respect. The reason symbolic operators are less friendly is because their meaning is not immediately obvious from the name. For example, the preceding operator, |+|, can be pretty ambiguous for somebody who is looking at it for the first time. However, the combine method gives you a very solid idea of what it does.

Implementation for Either

Now that we have familiarized ourselves with Monoid and had a look at how it is used in the context of simple types such as integer, let's take a look at our previous example, the example of Either with a generic type of Left—Either[L, A]. How can we define the Applicative instance for a generic Left type? Previously, we saw that the body of the ap function for a generic Left type is not very different from the body of this function for the list. The only problem was that we didn't know how to combine two arbitrary types.

This combination sounds like exactly the task for Monoid. So, if we bring the implicit dependency on Monoid into scope, we can define the ap and Applicative type class for the Either type as follows:

```
implicit def applicative[L: Monoid]: Applicative[Either[L, ?]] =
new Applicative[Either[L, ?]] {
  override def ap[A, B](ff: Either[L, A => B])(fa: Either[L, A]):
  Either[L, B] = (ff, fa) match {
    case (Right(f), Right(a)) => Right(f(a))
    case (Left(e1), Left(e2)) => Left(e1 |+| e2)
    case (Left(e), _) => Left(e)
    case (_, Left(e)) => Left(e)
  }
  override def pure[A](a: A): Either[L, A] = Right(a)
}
```

You can see an implicit implementation of the Applicative type class that is also dependent on an implicit implementation of the Monoid type class for the Left type of Either. So, what happens is that the Applicative type class will be implicitly resolved, but only if it's possible to implicitly resolve the Monoid for the Left type's value. If there is no implicit implementation of Monoid for Left in scope, we will not be able to generate Applicative. This makes sense, because the body of Applicative depends on the functionality provided by Monoid in order to define its own functionality.

The only thing to notice about the body of the ap function is that it now uses the |+| operator in order to combine the left elements if both computations result in an error.

One peculiarity to notice about Monoid is that it is said it is defined not for an effective, but for an ordinary type. So, if you look at the signature of Monoid again, it is of the kind Monoid[A], not the kind of Monoid[F[A]]. So far, we have only encountered the type classes that work on effect types, that is, the types of the kind F[A].

What is the reason for the existence of type classes that work on raw types and not effect types? To answer this question, let's remember what the motivation for the existence of ordinary type classes that we are familiar with so far was. The main motivation for their existence was that certain operations with effect types were not convenient to accomplish. We had the need to abstract certain operations with effect types. We needed an abstraction to define tools that work on the effect types.

Effect types are usually data structures, and it is pretty hard to work with them ad hoc. You are not usually able to work with them using the capabilities built into your language conveniently. Hence, we encountered difficulties working with these data types on every corner if we did not have a toolset defined for them. Hence, the need for type classes manifests itself mostly for effect types.

Ordinary types like A are usually not as hard to work with as data structures. Hence, the need for tools and for abstractions over these data types is less obvious than for the effect types. However, as we saw previously, there are situations where type classes can be useful for raw types as well. The reason we had to define a separate type class Monoid for a raw type is in the fact that we needed to generalize the feature that the type must be composable.

Also notice that we can hardly do that using any other technique than type classes. An ordinary approach of object-oriented programming to the problem of making sure a datatype exposes certain functionality is interfaces. Interfaces must be declared at definition time of the class implementing them. So, for example, there is no single interface to specify that lists, integers, and strings are composable with another with the same method.

The only way to specify such an exposure of certain functionality is to define an interface as ad hoc. But ordinary object-oriented programming does not provide you with the capability to inject interfaces into already implemented classes. This cannot be said about type classes. With type classes, whenever you want to capture that a type exposes a certain functionality, you can define a type class as ad hoc. You can also define in which way exactly a class exhibits this functionality by defining and implementing this type class for this particular class. Notice exactly when it is done. This operation can be done in any part of the program. So, whenever you need to make it explicit that a type exhibits certain functionality and has this functionality in common with other types, you are able to do so by defining a type class that captures this functionality.

This kind of extensibility provides you with a greater level of flexibility that is hard to achieve with ordinary object-oriented programming techniques such as, for example, those in Java. In fact, it can be argued that it is sufficient for the programmer to drop the object-oriented style of interfaces altogether and resort to only using the type classes. In the style of programming Haskell is based on, there is a strict separation of data and behavior.

MonoidK

Previously, we saw the version of Monoid that works on all types. A version of Monoid also exists that operates on effect types, that is, on the types of the kind of `F[A]`. This type class is called `MonoidK`:

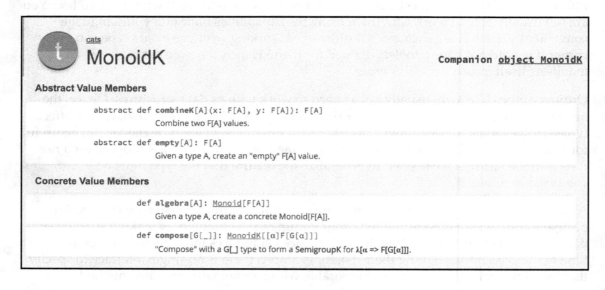

So, as you can see, the method is defined for an effect type, and instead of the `combined` method that works on two types, A, MonoidK defines a method called `combineK`, which works on values of type `F[A]`. Also notice that this method is parametrized by the type A on the method level and not on the level of the type class itself, which means that you can have the single type class defined for some effect type, `F[_]`, and you can use it for arbitrary A in the context of `F[A]`.

This example can be useful when combining lists. While it is not really an effect type, because a `List` is a data structure that does not encapsulate any side effects, it is still a type of the form `F[A]`. We can imagine an implementation of `combinedK` for it as follows:

```
implicit val listMonoid: MonoidK[List] = new MonoidK[List] {
  override def combineK[A](a1: List[A], a2: List[A]): List[A] =
    a1 ++ a2
  override def empty[A] = Nil
}
```

So, in the preceding code, we are able to implement the method in a manner that is independent of type A because the behavior of the combination of two lists is independent of the type of the elements that are contained in them. This combination is just a concatenation of the elements of one list with the elements of another list to form one combined list.

Also notice the `algebra` method here. This method can be used to obtain a `Monoid` instance from the `MonoidK` instance. This can be useful in cases where you need a `Monoid` instance, but you only have `MonoidK`.

Traverse

Previously, we learned about the Applicative type class. We argued that the main utility of the Applicative type class is that it allows us to combine two independent computations in parallel. No longer are we bound by the `flatMap` function that performs sequential composition, so that if one computation fails then no other computation is ever performed. In the Applicative scenario, all of the computations are performed, despite the fact that some of them can fail.

However, Applicative is only able to combine two independent computations. There are also methods to combine up to 22 computations into tuples. However, what if we need to combine an arbitrary amount of computations? The usual generalization for multiplicity is collections. Tuples are just special cases of collections. So, if there is a type class for combining independent computations into tuples, there must be a type class for combining independent computations into collections.

To illustrate this scenario, consider our example we we're working with in Applicative case. What if we have an arbitrary list of mathematical expressions computed under the parallel operator, and we have a function that is supposed to combine them by summing them up? What might such a function look like?

```
type Fx[A] = Either[List[String], A]
def combineComputations(f1: List[Fx[Double]]): Fx[Double] =
  (f1, f2).mapN { case (r1, r2) => r1 + r2 }
```

So, the preceding function takes a list of the results of the computations, and its job is to produce a combined result of all of the computations. This result will be of the type `Either[List[String], List[Double]]` type, which means that we also need to aggregate all of the errors that happened in all of the computationals we are trying to combine. How would we go about it in the case of Applicative?

What we need to do is take the first element of the list, combine it with the second element of the list using the `ap` function, add the results together to obtain an `Either` as a result, and combine this result with the third element, and so on.

In fact, there is a type class to perform just that. Meet the `Traverse` type class:

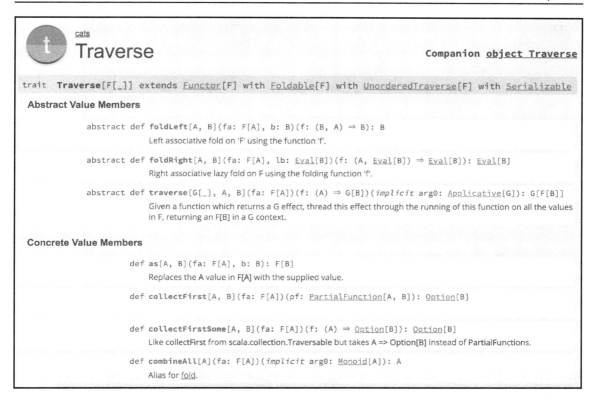

cats
Traverse

Companion **object Traverse**

trait **Traverse**[F[_]] extends Functor[F] with Foldable[F] with UnorderedTraverse[F] with Serializable

Abstract Value Members

abstract def **foldLeft**[A, B](fa: F[A], b: B)(f: (B, A) ⇒ B): B
  Left associative fold on 'F' using the function 'f'.

abstract def **foldRight**[A, B](fa: F[A], lb: Eval[B])(f: (A, Eval[B]) ⇒ Eval[B]): Eval[B]
  Right associative lazy fold on F using the folding function 'f'.

abstract def **traverse**[G[_], A, B](fa: F[A])(f: (A) ⇒ G[B])(*implicit* arg0: Applicative[G]): G[F[B]]
  Given a function which returns a G effect, thread this effect through the running of this function on all the values
  in F, returning an F[B] in a G context.

Concrete Value Members

def **as**[A, B](fa: F[A], b: B): F[B]
  Replaces the A value in F[A] with the supplied value.

def **collectFirst**[A, B](fa: F[A])(pf: PartialFunction[A, B]): Option[B]

def **collectFirstSome**[A, B](fa: F[A])(f: (A) ⇒ Option[B]): Option[B]
  Like collectFirst from scala.collection.Traversable but takes A => Option[B] instead of PartialFunctions.

def **combineAll**[A](fa: F[A])(*implicit* arg0: Monoid[A]): A
  Alias for fold.

The main point of interest of the `Traverse` type class is the `traverse` method. Let's take a look at its signature:

```
abstract def traverse[G[_], A, B](fa: F[A])(f: (A) ⇒ G[B])(implicit arg0:
Applicative[G]): G[F[B]]
```

The signature of this method is very abstract. So, let's give all the types involved a little bit more context. In the preceding signature, consider that type F is a collection type. Consider that type G is an effect type.

This means that traverse takes a collection as its first argument—a collection of some arbitrary raw elements, A. The second argument is similar to what we saw in `flatMap`. It is a side effecting computation that works on the elements of the collection we saw as the first argument. So, the idea is that you have a collection of some elements, A, and a computation that you can run on these elements, A. However, this computation is side effecting. The side effects from this computation are wrapped into the effect type G.

What would happen if you ran such a computation on every element of the collection? What would happen if you map collection F with the help of this operation?

The result type that you would expect to get is this: F[G[B]]. So, you will get a collection of effect types that are the results of the computation that you've run on every element of the original collection.

Returning to our example of Either that we need to combine together, we would get the following result:

```
List[Either[List[String], A]]
```

However, we are not looking for this. We are looking to obtain a list of all the results of our computation under the effect type Either. In the case of Applicative, the ap method was taking the results of side effecting computations and combining them under their common effect type. So, in the case of ap and zip based on it, we had the following results:

```
Either[List[String], (A, A)]
```

Here, in our generalized case, the role of tuple is replaced by List. Therefore, we are aiming for the following:

```
Either[List[String], List[A]]
```

Now, let's return to our traverse function. Let's take a look at its result type. The result of this function is G[F[B]]. G is an effect type. F is a collection type. So, all of the results of the computations are combined into a single collection under an effect type, G. This is precisely what we were aiming at in the case of Either.

So, this makes Traverse a more generic case of Applicative that can be used for situations where you do not know how many computations you are going to combine ahead of time.

A word of caution here. We have also discussed that the type F is a collection type and that the type G is an effect type. You should remember that this constraint is not encoded into a type class itself. We have imposed this constraint in order to be able to develop an intuition for the type class. So, potentially, you might come up with some more advanced uses of the Traverse type class that go beyond this collection. However, in your projects, you will be using it in the context of collections the most frequently.

Let's take a look at what our example might look like with the help of Traverse:

```
def combineComputationsFold(f1: List[Fx[Double]]): Fx[Double] =
  f1.traverse(identity).map { lst =>
  lst.foldLeft(0D) { (runningSum, next) => runningSum + next } }
```

```
val samples: List[Fx[Double]] =
  (1 to 5).toList.map { x => Right(x.toDouble) }

val samplesErr: List[Fx[Double]] =
  (1 to 5).toList.map {
    case x if x % 2 == 0 => Left(List(s"$x is not a multiple of 2"))
    case x => Right(x.toDouble)
  }

println(combineComputationsFold(samples)) // Right(15.0)
println(combineComputationsFold(samplesErr)) // Left(List(2 is not a
 multiple of 2, 4 is not a multiple of 2))
```

We can further enhance this example if we use the `combineAll` method from the `Traverse` type class:

```
def combineComputations(f1: List[Fx[Double]]): Fx[Double] =
  f1.traverse(identity).map(_.combineAll)

println(combineComputations(samples)) // Right(15.0)
println(combineComputations(samplesErr)) // Left(List(2 is not a
 multiple of 2, 4 is not a multiple of 2))
```

The examples are introduced in the context of the following type classes that are defined:

```
type Fx[A] = Either[List[String], A]
implicit val applicative: Applicative[Fx] = new Applicative[Fx] {
  override def ap[A, B](ff: Fx[A => B])(fa: Fx[A]): Fx[B] = (ff, fa)
  match {
    case (Right(f), Right(a)) => Right(f(a))
    case (Left(e1), Left(e2)) => Left(e1 ++ e2)
    case (Left(e), _) => Left(e)
    case (_, Left(e)) => Left(e)
  }
  override def pure[A](a: A): Fx[A] = Right(a)
}
implicit val monoidDouble: Monoid[Double] = new Monoid[Double] {
  def combine(x1: Double, x2: Double): Double = x1 + x2
  def empty: Double = 0
}
```

`combinedAll` works on some collection, `F[A]`, and produces the result `A` out of this collection, given `Monoid[A]` in scope. The Monoid defines how to combine two elements, `A`, into one element, `A`. `F[A]` is a collection of elements, `A`. So, given a collection of elements, `A`, `combineAll` is capable of combining all of the elements and computing a single result, `A`, with the help of the Monoid in scope that defines a binary composition operation.

One thing to notice here is that the type classes of `cats` form an ecosystem and frequently depend one on another. In order to obtain an instance of a certain type class for a certain type, you might discover that it is implicitly dependent on an instance of another type class. For other type classes, you can discover that some of its methods are dependent on some other type class implicitly, just like in the case of `combineAll` depending on Monoid.

This connection can be used to the advantage of a learner of purely functional programming. This kind of ecosystem means that you can start very small. You can start by using one or two type classes that you understand. Since the `Cats` library forms an ecosystem of dependent type classes, you will encounter situations where your familiar type classes will depend on type classes that you still do not know. Therefore, you will need to learn about the other type classes.

Other things that we need to notice about the type classes that we have learned about so far is that they are pretty generic and language independent. What it encodes is the relationships and the transformations between types. This can be encoded in any language of your choosing. For example, in Haskell, the language is built around the idea of type classes. So, if you look at Haskell, you will find that it also contain the type classes that we have covered in this chapter. As a matter of fact, there is an entire mathematical theory that deals with these concepts and defines the type classes that we have covered, called the **category theory**. That means that we could have discussed type classes from a mathematical perspective without touching programming at all. Therefore, the concepts of the type classes are language independent and have a solid mathematical foundation. We have extensively covered a library that is specific to Scala, but the concepts that we have covered are language independent. In one form or another, they are implemented in all of the languages that support purely functional styles.

Summary

In this chapter, we had an in-depth look at the system of type classes used in purely functional programming. We take a look at the library, that is, a standard library for purely functional programming. We had our first look at the structure of the library and we found out that it is composed of separate models for the type classes, the syntax, and the effect types.

Then, we had an in-depth look at some type classes that are defined by the library. We saw the motivation for their existence, as well as their implementation and usage details. One thing to remember about all of the type classes is that they are not Scala specific. In fact, there is an entire mathematical theory that deals with them in a manner that is independent from any programming language at all. This is called category theory. So, if you know the concepts from one programming language, we are able to use them in any programming language that supports the functional style.

Cats provides us with effective functional programming tools. However, we need higher-level libraries to write industrial-grade software such as web application backends. In the next chapter, we will see more advanced functional libraries that build on the basic ones.

Questions

1. What is the motivation to organize type classes into libraries?
2. What methods does Traverse define?
3. Which real-world scenario would we use Traverse in?
4. What methods does Monad define?
5. Which real-world scenario would we use Monad in?
6. What is the structure of the Cats library?

Libraries for Pure Functional Programming $\mathbf{9}$

In the previous chapter, we discussed the purely functional style with the help of essential libraries such as `cats`. This library performs quite well on tasks of purely functional programming, but in practice, that is not quite enough for comfortable programming.

If you take a look at conventional imperative languages such as Java, you will see that they usually have a lot of libraries and infrastructure for performing specific tasks. Moreover, it is also possible to argue that the choice of programming language is primarily driven by the infrastructure it provides.

This way, for example, Python is a de facto standard for machine learning, because it provides an elaborate set of scientific libraries to perform scientific computing, and R is a de facto standard for statistical computing. Companies often choose Scala because it provides access to Spark and Akka libraries for machine learning and distributed computing.

Hence, when talking about a particular programming style, it is of great importance to also mention that it is an infrastructure that is developed around the staff. In this chapter, we will cover this infrastructure by looking at a bunch of other libraries that exist for purely functional programming in Scala with `cats`.

The following topics will be covered in this chapter:

- The Cats effect
- Server-side programming

We will start this chapter by looking at the concurrency library for `cats`.

Cats effect

The Cats effect is a library for concurrent programming in `cats`. Its main feature is a bunch of type classes, data types, and concurrency primitives to describe concurrent programming in Scala with `cats`.

The concurrency primitives support among other things:

- Resource management—think try-with-resources.
- Seamless composition of parallel computations.
- Communication between parallel computations.

We will start discussing the library by looking at its central concurrency primitive, IO, and some capabilities of Cats that we will need in the process of discussing it.

ProductR

Before diving deep into the library and discussing its features, we need to mention a particular operator that is frequently used throughout this library. We have already discussed the Applicative type class, and that it is useful for parallel composition.

An operator from this type class that is frequently used in `cats` is a so-called right product operator.

The operator in question takes two computations, performs a product between them, and takes only the right-hand result. Particularly in the Cats effect, the operator is frequently used to specify that one event should happen after another.

It also has a symbolic form, which looks like this: `*>`.

IO – the concurrence data type

The primary data type that the Cats effect offers is IO. This is a data type that defines a computation that is to be performed at some point in the future. For example, you can have the following expression:

```
object HelloWorld extends App {
  val hello = IO { println("Hello") }
  val world = IO { println("World") }
  (hello *> world).unsafeRunSync
}
```

Crucial detail to notice about IO is that it is precisely a description of the computation. Here, `cats` supports a so-called computation as a value paradigm. Computation as a value dictates that you should not evaluate your competition straight away, but you should store the descriptions of these computations. This way, you will be able to evaluate them at any point in the future.

This approach has a number of benefits, and this is what we are going to discuss next.

Referential transparency

The first benefit Cats has is referential transparency. In the preceding example, the computation to print hello world to the command line will not be evaluated right away. It is side effecting, and the fact that we do not evaluate it right away means it is referentially transparent. You can evaluate the computation as follows:

```
(hello *> world).unsafeRunSync
```

IO has a bunch of methods, the names of which are prepended with the `unsafe` word.

Unsafe methods are generally what their prefix says, `unsafe`. This means that they may block, produce side effects, throw exceptions, and do other things that may cause you a headache. Following the description of the IO type in the documentation itself, you should only call such a method once, ideally at the end of your program.

So, basically, the main idea is that you describe your entire program in terms of the IO primitive, using the conveniences provided by this primitive by the Cats effect library. Once your entire application is described, you can run the application.

Inversion of control

Since a computation expressed in terms of IO is not executed immediately but is merely stored as a description of a computation, it is possible to execute the computation against different execution strategies. For example, you may want to run the computation against various concurrent backends, each with its own concurrency strategies. You may want to run a competition synchronously or asynchronously. Later in this chapter, we will see how exactly this is done.

Asynchrony with IO

The central domain of the application of the Cats effect is asynchronous programming. Asynchronous programming is an event-driven style of programming, where you do not waste threads and other resources on blocking, waiting for some event to happen.

Consider, for example, that you have a web server that handles incoming HTTP requests. It has a pool of threads that are used by the server to handle each request. Now, the handlers themselves may require some blocking operations. For example, contacting a database for contacting an external HTTP API can be a potentially blocking operation. This is because the database or an HTTP API does not respond immediately as a rule. This means that if a request handler needs to contact such a resource, it will need to wait for the service to reply.

If such waiting is done naively, by blocking an entire thread and reviving it once the request is available, we have a situation where we waste threads. If such a server comes under a high load, there is a danger that all of the threads will be blocked for the majority of the time. Blocking means that they do not do anything and are just waiting for a response from a resource. Since they are not doing anything, these threads could have well been used to handle other requests that possibly do not require such kinds of blocking.

Precisely for this reason, current server-side programming is aimed toward asynchronous processing, which means that if a handler needs to contact some potentially blocking resource, it contacts it. However, once it has nothing else to do, it is supposed to release its thread. It will continue the computation once the response it is waiting for is available.

This kind of strategy allows for very lightweight concurrent modules that do not waste threads. This also ensures that the threads are busy with useful work most of the time, and not with blocking.

However, this model requires dedicated libraries and server-side technologies that are specifically built with asynchrony in mind. The Cats effect precisely aims to meet such asynchronous requirements.

Now, let's take a look at some examples which demonstrate in practice how blocking differs from asynchrony and how Cats facilitates asynchrony. You will also learn a bunch of Cats effect APIs in the process of looking at these examples.

Blocking example

First, let's take a look at the API behind creating an asynchronous IO action:

```
def apply[A](body: ⇒ A): IO[A]

Suspends a synchronous side effect in IO.

Any exceptions thrown by the effect will be caught and sequenced into the IO.
```

So, you can supply an arbitrary task into an `apply` method of IO, and this will construct the description of this task.

We can model blocking of a computation by using the `Thread.sleep` Java API under the IO apply method as follows:

```
IO { Thread.sleep(1000) }
```

Notice that the preceding example will block its thread. IO may be just a description of a computation. However, the computations are supposed to get executed at some point. In the JVM world, any computation runs on a thread. In the preceding example, we are using the Java `Thread.sleep` API to explicitly say that we need to block a thread the computation is running on for one second, or 1,000 milliseconds.

With the help of the preceding primitive, let's compose an infinite computation that will be easy for us to trace and study. If we have a long-running computation that outputs something to the command line in equal periods of time, we can easily see whether and how the computation is progressing. Typically, such an infinite computation would be possible in terms of a loop. In functional programming, a loop can be created in terms of Monad's `tailRecM`:

```
def taskHeavy(prefix: String): IO[Nothing] =
  Monad[IO].tailRecM(0) { i => for {
    _ <- IO { println(s"${Thread.currentThread.getName}; $prefix: $i") }
    _ <- IO { Thread.sleep(1000) }
  } yield Left(i + 1) }
```

In the preceding code, you can see a Monadic infinite loop that utilizes IO to describe an infinite computation. First of all, the computation will output the name of the current thread, the name of the current task, and the number that will be incremented from iteration to iteration.

The thread output can be useful to trace which thread the computation is running on. This information can be used to see how threads in a given thread pool are allocated. The prefix is necessary to distinguish one task from another in case we want to run several such computations at once. We will do this in order to see how such a task performs in a concurrency setting.

Testing out such a blocking task in concurrent environment models requires an HTTP server under a high load. There, you also have a multitude of tasks of the same nature running concurrently. The preceding example models a situation where a handler task blocks the underlying thread.

Finally, the identifier number is used to identify the progress of a given task so that we can see how evenly the tasks progress and whether any task is getting choked.

Since, in the preceding example, we were motivated by the ability to test tasks in the concurrency settings, next, we will talk briefly about the concurrency environment we are going to run the tasks.

Concurrency infrastructure

The concurrency environment is represented by an execution context, which is a Scala class. The official documentation defines it as follows:

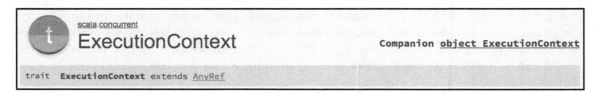

It is a standard Scala class with a single method to run a Java `Runnable`:

```
abstract def execute(runnable: Runnable): Unit

        Runs a block of code on this execution context.

        runnable    the task to execute
```

An execution context is necessary whenever we are dealing with concurrency primitives in Scala, such as Future. The Cats effect also relies on this type to describe its own execution environment. We can construct an execution context and specify the number of threads available in its thread pool as follows:

```
implicit val ec: ExecutionContext =
  ExecutionContext.fromExecutor(Executors.newFixedThreadPool(2))
```

In the preceding code, we are using the fromExecutor method of the ExecutionContext class, which is defined as follows:

```
def fromExecutor(e: Executor): ExecutionContextExecutor

  Creates an ExecutionContext from the given Executor with the default reporter.

  e         the Executor to use. If null, a new Executor is created with default configuration.
  returns   the ExecutionContext using the given Executor
```

This method uses the Java API to construct the execution context. In our concrete preceding example, we are constructing an execution contact that possesses a fixed thread pool that has two threads.

Another motivating factor for our example was running multiple instances of the same concurrently. Next, we will be looking at the API to provide this functionality.

Running tasks in bunches

We can define a function to run an arbitrary IO task on a given execution context in multiple instances, as follows:

```
def bunch(n: Int)(gen: String => IO[Nothing]): IO[List[Fiber[IO, Nothing]]]
  =
  (1 to n).toList.map(i => s"Task $i").traverse(gen(_).start)
```

The bunch function takes the number of tasks we need to launch concurrently as the first argument. As a second argument, it takes a function gen to construct tasks. The function takes a string as its first argument, which is the name of the task. In the conditions where we have the same task to run in multiple instances, it is crucial to distinguish them somehow. Therefore, we need to provide the name to the generator function.

To understand the output type of the function, let's take a look at the body of the function.

First of all, the body constructs a list of n elements. The intention is to use the list to specify the loop to create the tasks. We then create the required number of tasks by using the map function on the list we have created:

```
(1 to n).toList.map(i => s"Task $i")
```

Next, we are using the traverse function, which does something to each task we have just created. Let's take a look at what happens inside the traverse function to see how parallelism is achieved in the Cats effect:

```
.traverse(gen(_).start)
```

The main point of interest is the start function. Let's take a look at how it is defined:

---

final def **start**: IO[Fiber[IO, A]]

Start execution of the source suspended in the IO context.

This can be used for non-deterministic / concurrent execution. The following code is more or less equivalent with **parMap2** (minus the behavior on error handling and cancelation):

```
def par2[A, B](ioa: IO[A], iob: IO[B]): IO[(A, B)] =
  for {
    fa <- ioa.start
    fb <- iob.start
     a <- fa.join
     b <- fb.join
  } yield (a, b)
```

Note in such a case usage of **parMapN** (via **cats.Parallel**) is still recommended because of behavior on error and cancelation — consider in the example above what would happen if the first task finishes in error. In that case the second task doesn't get cancelled, which creates a potential memory leak.

IMPORTANT — this operation does not start with an asynchronous boundary. But you can use IO.shift to force an async boundary just before start.

The function in question produces a so-called Fiber under the IO primitive. Let's take a look at how Fiber is defined and what it is all about:

cats.effect
Fiber
Companion object Fiber

trait **Fiber**[F[_], A] extends AnyRef

Fiber represents the (pure) result of an Async data type (e.g. IO) being started concurrently and that can be either joined or cancelled.

You can think of fibers as being lightweight threads, a fiber being a concurrency primitive for doing cooperative multi-tasking.

It defines the following API:

Abstract Value Members
abstract def **cancel**: F[Unit] Triggers the cancellation of the fiber. Returns a new task that will complete when the cancellation is sent (but not when it is observed or acted upon). Note that if the background process that's evaluating the result of the underlying fiber is already complete, then there's nothing to cancel.
abstract def **join**: F[A] Returns a new task that will await for the completion of the underlying fiber, (asynchronously) blocking the current run-loop until that result is available.

Usually, waiting in an IO-based Monadic flow blocks execution. Of course, that blocking is done asynchronously. However, if you're calling the `start` method on an IO, it will not block the Monadic flow. Instead, it will return immediately with a `Fiber` object.

Think of a `Fiber` object as a remote control unit for the underlying alpha complication. It defines two methods, `cancel` and `join`. These two methods can be used to communicate with the underlying computation. The `cancel` method cancels the competition, and the `join` method blocks the current Monadic flow until an underlying IO computation finishes. `join` returns the value of this computation in the Monadic floor.

Also, notice that these `cancel` and `join` methods are all returning an IO primitive. This means that you can use this method from a Monadic flow.

So, why are we using the `start` method from our bunch example?

```
gen(_).start
```

Remember, our tasks are infinite. We have defined them has an infinite loop that blocks every second. The job of traverse is to evaluate all of the tasks supplied to it and return a combined task under a single effect type, in this case, IO. However, our tasks cannot be evaluated to some concrete result since they are infinite. Hence, we will perform the start call on every task in order to specify that we do not need the task's result itself; we can only be satisfied with the remote control unit for this task. This way, the traverse method will not wait for any single task to finish, but will start all of them asynchronously on the execution context we discussed previously.

Heavy load with blocking

Now, imagine that our `taskHeavy` is a handler for an HTTP server. The server is undergoing a heavy load and has `1000` ongoing requests. This means that we need to create `1000` tasks to handle them. With the `bunch` method, we can define such handling as follows:

```
(IO.shift *> bunch(1000)(taskHeavy)).unsafeRunSync
```

Notice that we have encountered another new primitive in this example. It is a `shift` method that's defined on the IO data type. It is defined as follows:

```
def shift(implicit timer: Timer[IO]): IO[Unit]
```

Asynchronous boundary described as an effectful **IO**, managed by the provided Timer.

This operation can be used in **flatMap** chains to "shift" the continuation of the run-loop to another thread or call stack.

For example we can introduce an asynchronous boundary in the **flatMap** chain before a certain task:

```
IO.shift.flatMap(_ => task)
```

Or using Cats syntax:

```
import cats.syntax.all._

IO.shift *> task
```

Or we can specify an asynchronous boundary *after* the evaluation of a certain task:

```
task.flatMap(a => IO.shift.map(_ => a))
```

Or using Cats syntax:

```
task <* IO.shift
```

The `shift` method is an instruction for the execution to get shifted to an `ExecutionContext`, which is present as an implicit dependency in scope. Here, we implicitly depend on a `Timer` object and not an `ExecutionContext`.
The `ExecutionContext` can be used to derive a `Timer` object using an implicit method that is a part of the IO API:

```
implicit def timer(implicit ec: ExecutionContext): Timer[IO]
```

> Returns a Timer instance for IO, built from a Scala **ExecutionContext**.
>
> N.B. this is the JVM-specific version. On top of JavaScript the implementation needs no **ExecutionContext**.
>
> ec   is the execution context used for actual execution tasks (e.g. bind continuations)
>
> *Definition Classes* IOTimerRef

Since we have an `ExecutionContext` in the implicit scope, we can call the `shift` method to shift the execution of the current IO computation to the thread pool with have defined. Also notice the `*>` operator here, which we discussed previously in this chapter. It says that the second competition should be executed after the first one, which is the shift to a concurrent context. We also ran the example in place to see how it goes with the help of `unsafeRunSync`. The output of the program is as follows:

```
                                       1. bash
[info] Application root not yet started
[info] Starting application root in the background ...
root Starting jvm.AsynchronyHeavy.main()
[success] Total time: 3 s, completed Aug 4, 2018 4:27:40 PM
sbt:jvm> root pool-1-thread-2; Task 1: 0
root pool-1-thread-1; Task 2: 0
root pool-1-thread-2; Task 1: 1
root pool-1-thread-1; Task 2: 1
root pool-1-thread-2; Task 1: 2
root pool-1-thread-1; Task 2: 2
root pool-1-thread-2; Task 1: 3
root pool-1-thread-1; Task 2: 3
root pool-1-thread-2; Task 1: 4
root pool-1-thread-1; Task 2: 4
root pool-1-thread-2; Task 1: 5
root pool-1-thread-1; Task 2: 5
root pool-1-thread-2; Task 1: 6
root pool-1-thread-1; Task 2: 6
root pool-1-thread-2; Task 1: 7
root pool-1-thread-1; Task 2: 7
root pool-1-thread-2; Task 1: 8
root pool-1-thread-1; Task 2: 8
root pool-1-thread-2; Task 1: 9
root pool-1-thread-1; Task 2: 9
root pool-1-thread-2; Task 1: 10
root pool-1-thread-1; Task 2: 10
root pool-1-thread-2; Task 1: 11
root pool-1-thread-1; Task 2: 11
root ... killing ...
MacBook-Pro-Anatolii:jvm anatolii$
```

The first thing to notice here is that both of the threads we have in our `ExecutionContext` are used to process the tasks. You can see that by looking at the name of the threads output by the task. It changes from task to task. However, also take note that it is only the first two tasks that get the chance to be executed. This is because we are using a blocking call to `Thread.sleep` to specify and delay our execution. So, in the setting of the infinite handling tasks, such as a server, it would only be able to handle two requests at a time. In a setting where you need to handle `1000` requests, this is inadequate.

Now, let's see how we can benefit from asynchrony to specify lightweight concurrency primitives to handle that volume of requests.

Synchronous tasks

You can asynchronously define the preceding computation as follows:

```
def taskLight(prefix: String): IO[Nothing] =
  Monad[IO].tailRecM(0) { i => for {
    _ <- IO { println(s"${Thread.currentThread.getName}; $prefix: $i") }
    _ <- IO.sleep(1 second)
  } yield Left(i + 1) }
```

Notice that this method is defined similarly to the previous task. However, we no longer block the thread. Instead, we are using a built-in IO primitive called `sleep`. `sleep` is a non-blocking primitive, meaning that it does not block the underlying thread. That is, it is a description of the `sleep` operation. Remember, all of the computations happening defined in terms of IO are descriptions of computations and not computations themselves. So, you can define a `sleep` operation as you please. Hence, it is reasonable to define this operation in an unblocking manner so that the underlying thread gets released when this `sleep` operation is encountered, and the computation is resumed when the execution environment receives a signal stating that the `sleep` operation was terminated successfully. A similar principle is used in all asynchronous computations. We can run this task as follows:

```
(IO.shift *> bunch(1000)(taskLight)).unsafeRunSync
```

The output of the program is as follows:

```
                                           1. bash
root pool-1-thread-2; Task 974: 2
root pool-1-thread-1; Task 975: 2
root pool-1-thread-2; Task 976: 2
root pool-1-thread-1; Task 977: 2
root pool-1-thread-2; Task 978: 2
root pool-1-thread-1; Task 979: 2
root pool-1-thread-2; Task 980: 2
root pool-1-thread-1; Task 982: 2
root pool-1-thread-2; Task 981: 2
root pool-1-thread-1; Task 983: 2
root pool-1-thread-2; Task 972: 2
root pool-1-thread-1; Task 984: 2
root pool-1-thread-2; Task 985: 2
root pool-1-thread-1; Task 986: 2
root pool-1-thread-2; Task 987: 2
root pool-1-thread-1; Task 988: 2
root pool-1-thread-2; Task 989: 2
root pool-1-thread-1; Task 990: 2
root pool-1-thread-2; Task 991: 2
root pool-1-thread-1; Task 992: 2
root pool-1-thread-2; Task 993: 2
root pool-1-thread-1; Task 994: 2
root pool-1-thread-2; Task 995: 2
root pool-1-thread-1; Task 996: 2
root pool-1-thread-2; Task 997: 2
root pool-1-thread-1; Task 999: 2
root pool-1-thread-2; Task 998: 2
root pool-1-thread-1; Task 1000: 2
root ... killing ...
MacBook-Pro-Anatolii:jvm anatolii$
```

Notice how all of the `1000` tasks get enough resources to get executed. This is because each of these tasks releases the underlying thread once they do not need it anymore. Hence, even with two threads, we are able to handle 1,000 tasks at once successfully. So, computations described asynchronously are quite lightweight and can be used in systems that are designed for high loads. Next, let's take a look at how you can create an asynchronous IO primitive yourself.

Constructing asynchronous tasks

IO provides an API that allows you to transform an existing computation based on callbacks into an asynchronous IO. This can be used to port existing computation to IO in an asynchronous manner.

Suppose you have the following computation:

```
def taskHeavy(name: String): Int = {
  Thread.sleep(1000)
  println(s"${Thread.currentThread.getName}: " +
    s"$name: Computed!")
  42
}
```

Like we saw previously, it is blocking a thread as it uses `Thread.sleep` to block the computation. The entire point of the computation is that it does not return immediately.

Now, let's take a look at how you can asynchronously run the computation:

```
def sync(name: String): IO[Int] =
  IO { taskHeavy(name) }
```

Here, we are using an already familiar way to lift a synchronous computation into an IO data type. We have already seen the consequences of doing so in our previous example. This time, since our computation is not infinite, let's take a look at the time difference of handling this computation versus an asynchronous competition we are about to construct from it. To do so, we will need a benchmarking capability:

```
def benchmark[A](io: IO[A]): IO[(A, Long)] =
  for {
    tStart <- Timer[IO].clockMonotonic(SECONDS)
    res <- io
    tEnd <- Timer[IO].clockMonotonic(SECONDS)
  } yield (res, tEnd - tStart)
```

In the preceding code, we are constructing a benchmarking capability that will run IO and will report on how long it took to run the computation.

The first thing to notice here is how computation as a value strategy that IO implies can be beneficial to augment computations. Here, the benchmark method accepts an IO that is not yet evaluated. It is just a description of a computation. Next, it wraps this computation in a capability to measure time, and, finally, it returns the result of the computation, together with the benchmark.

Also, notice how we are using the `Timer` data type here. We have already briefly touched on the `Timer` class in the context of the execution context of the IO primitive. The `Timer` class happens to be an execution context that IO uses to manage its threading:

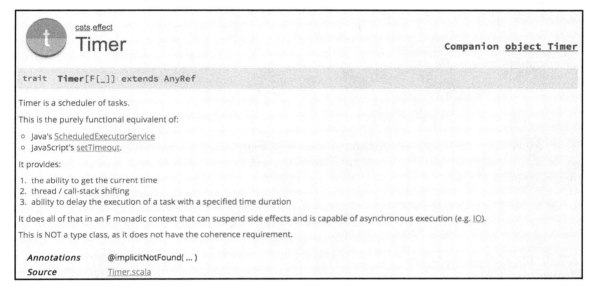

`Timer` defines the following abstract methods:

Abstract Value Members

abstract def **clockMonotonic**(unit: TimeUnit): F[Long]
> Returns a monotonic clock measurement, if supported by the underlying platform.

abstract def **clockRealTime**(unit: TimeUnit): F[Long]
> Returns the current time, as a Unix timestamp (number of time units since the Unix epoch), suspended in F[_].

abstract def **shift**: F[Unit]
> Asynchronous boundary described as an effectful F[_] that can be used in **flatMap** chains to "shift" the continuation of the run-loop to another thread or call stack.

abstract def **sleep**(duration: FiniteDuration): F[Unit]
> Creates a new task that will sleep for the given duration, emitting a tick when that time span is over.

We are already familiar with the `shift` method. It can be used to shift the execution context of a given IO flow into this `Timer`. Remember that `Timer` can be constructed from a standard Scala `ExecutionContext`. Other methods that `Timer` defines are needed for time measurement. One of them is `clockMonotonic`, which we are using for our preceding benchmark.

Finally, we may want to define a `benchmarkFlush` method to report the measurements to the command line as follows:

```
def benchmarkFlush[A](io: IO[A]): IO[Unit] =
  benchmark(io).map { case (res, time) =>
    println(s"Computed result $res in $time seconds") }
```

Next, we will try and run our synchronous example concurrently in multiple instances while measuring its time. But first of all, we will need a `bunch` function to launch multiple instances of this task:

```
def bunch(n: Int)(gen: String => IO[Int]): IO[List[Int]] =
  (1 to n).toList.map(i => s"Task $i").traverse(gen(_).start)
    .flatMap(_.traverse(_.join))
```

The first part of this function is similar to the one we had in the previous example. However, we have this function slightly extended with the following appendix:

```
.flatMap(_.traverse(_.join))
```

Remember that the original version of our bunch function started computations asynchronously from its `traverse` method. The result was a list of `Fibers` that we were not interested in. In the task of benchmarking, we are interested in the time when all the computations terminate. Hence, we would like to use the `join` method of the `Fibers` that are returned to create a combined IO data type that succeeds when all of the computations succeed. Notice that we still need the `start` capability for the tasks to be started asynchronously and not sequentially. If you don't use the `start` method from the `traverse` method here, tasks we are trying to start in the bunch will be executed synchronously, and we need parallel execution to utilize our shared thread pool.

Next, we can run the synchronous example in a `bunch` under the benchmark, as follows:

```
benchmarkFlush(IO.shift *> bunch(10)(sync)).unsafeRunSync
```

The output of the preceding program is as follows:

```
1. java
[1]  jvm.AsynchronyHeavy
[2]  jvm.AsynchronyLight
[3]  jvm.Bracket
[4]  jvm.FibersCancelled
[5]  jvm.FibersParallel
[6]  jvm.FibersSequential
[7]  jvm.HelloWorld
[8]  jvm.ProductRight
[9]  jvm.SequentialTraverse
[10] jvm.SyncVsAsyncAsync
[11] jvm.SyncVsAsyncSync

Enter number: 11

[info] Application root not yet started
[info] Starting application root in the background ...
root Starting jvm.SyncVsAsyncSync.main()
[success] Total time: 7 s, completed Aug 4, 2018 4:30:30 PM
sbt:jvm> root pool-1-thread-2: Task 1: Computed!
root pool-1-thread-1: Task 2: Computed!
root pool-1-thread-1: Task 4: Computed!
root pool-1-thread-2: Task 3: Computed!
root pool-1-thread-1: Task 5: Computed!
root pool-1-thread-2: Task 6: Computed!
root pool-1-thread-1: Task 7: Computed!
root pool-1-thread-2: Task 8: Computed!
root pool-1-thread-1: Task 9: Computed!
root pool-1-thread-2: Task 10: Computed!
root Computed result List(42, 42, 42, 42, 42, 42, 42, 42, 42, 42) in 5 seconds
```

It took us five seconds to compute 10 tasks. This is because each of the tasks blocks the underlying thread for one second, and we have two threats in our execution context.

Next, we'll take a look at how to define an asynchronous version of the same task.

Asynchronous API

First of all, we need to remark what exactly we mean by the word asynchronous. We mean asynchronous with respect to the thread pool that the IO data type is executed on. We assume that we have no control of the task itself, and we are not able to redefine it. In fact, we do not care about how it is implemented; all we care about is the precise moment when it terminates. The task here is to prevent the threads of this precise IO execution from blocking.

To achieve this, we can use the `IO.async` method:

```
def async[A](k: ((Either[Throwable, A]) ⇒ Unit) ⇒ Unit): IO[A]
```

Suspends an asynchronous side effect in IO.

The given function will be invoked during evaluation of the IO to "schedule" the asynchronous callback, where the callback is the parameter passed to that function. Only the *first* invocation of the callback will be effective! All subsequent invocations will be silently dropped.

This method has a somewhat tricky signature. So, first, let's take a look in brief at what it does. Given a particular computation, it provides a callback with which it can notify the IO task to be constructed. The IO task returned from the `async` method will be considered completed once the underlying computation calls the callback provided to it.

The benefit of this approach is that the IO does not care about where or how the computational runs. It only cares about when it is completed.

So, the `async` method is a function, the argument to which is another function with the following signature:

```
Either[Throwable, A]) ⇒ Unit
```

It is a callback that an underlying computation will call on its completion. It is provided to the user of the `async` method by IO, and acts as a notification stating that the IO should be considered completed.

Next, let's take a look at how this method can be used to create asynchronous computations.

Asynchronous example

We can redefine our previous example in terms of `async` as follows:

```
def async(name: String): IO[Int] =
  IO.async { cb =>
    new Thread(new Runnable { override def run =
      cb { Right(taskHeavy(name)) } }).start()
  }
```

So, here, we are using the `IO.async` primitive to lift our computation into an asynchronous context. First of all, this `async` method gives us a callback as an input. We are supposed to call this callback once we are done with our computation.

Next, we dispatch our heavy computation to some other execution context. In our case, it is merely starting another thread that does not belong to the thread pool on which we are executing our IO. Many scenarios are possible here, especially in the context of purely asynchronous computations, that is, the ones that do not use blocking at all. For example, you could imagine registering a callback on another asynchronous action from `async`. This can be useful, for example, for GUI programming. However, in this example, using a separate thread will suffice. The only thing to keep in mind is that threads are heavyweight primitives. Although we are not blocking the IO thread pool, we are still creating threads, and we are still blocking them. This can drain the resources of the system.

Next, we can run our computation as follows:

```
benchmarkFlush(IO.shift *> bunch(10)(async)).unsafeRunSync
```

The output is as follows:

```
                                    1. java
[2] jvm.AsynchronyLight
[3] jvm.Bracket
[4] jvm.FibersCancelled
[5] jvm.FibersParallel
[6] jvm.FibersSequantial
[7] jvm.HelloWorld
[8] jvm.ProductRight
[9] jvm.SequentialTraverse
[10] jvm.SyncVsAsyncAsync
[11] jvm.SyncVsAsyncSync

Enter number: 10

[info] Stopping application root (by killing the forked JVM) ...
[info] Starting application root in the background ...
root Starting jvm.SyncVsAsyncAsync.main()
root ... finished with exit code 143
[success] Total time: 3 s, completed Aug 4, 2018 4:38:45 PM
sbt:jvm> root Thread-0: Task 1: Computed!
root Thread-3: Task 4: Computed!
root Thread-1: Task 2: Computed!
root Thread-2: Task 3: Computed!
root Thread-4: Task 5: Computed!
root Thread-5: Task 6: Computed!
root Thread-6: Task 7: Computed!
root Thread-8: Task 9: Computed!
root Thread-9: Task 10: Computed!
root Thread-7: Task 8: Computed!
root Computed result List(42, 42, 42, 42, 42, 42, 42, 42, 42, 42) in 2 seconds
```

Notice that we were able to compute the operation in two seconds. This is because the IO tasks are no longer blocking the underlying execution thread pull the IO is executed on. So, once one IO goes to sleep, it releases its thread.

Next, we will pay a little bit more attention to `Fibers` and how you can utilize them for concurrent programming.

Fibers

As we previously discussed, Fibers are essentially remote control units for IO. Let's see how this can be used in practice to run operations in parallel.

The computation

Suppose that you have some long-running competition. Suppose that the computation in question has the task of finding a sum of numbers on a specific range. The computation is long-running because the invocation must pause for half a second from number to number:

```
def sum(from: Int, to: Int): IO[Int] =
  Monad[IO].tailRecM((from, 0)) { case (i, runningTotal) =>
    if (i == to) IO.pure( Right(runningTotal + i) )
    else if (i > to) IO.pure( Right(runningTotal) )
    else for {
      _ <- IO { println(s"${Thread.currentThread.getName}: " +
        s"Running total from $from to $to, currently at $i: $runningTotal")
    }
      _ <- IO.sleep(500 milliseconds)
    } yield Left((i + 1, runningTotal + i)) }
```

We are defining our competition in terms of a Monadic loop. In the body of the flow of the loop, we have two terminal cases. The first terminal case is when the current number is equal to the upper bound of our range. In that case, the result is the running total plus that number.

Another terminal case is when the number is greater than the upper range of the loop. In principle, this situation should never arise, but it is still a good idea to guard against it to prevent infinite loops. In this scenario, we return the running total without adding the current number.

Also notice the `pure` method, which is used in these non-terminal cases. It is defined as follows:

```
def pure[A](a: A): IO[A]
```

Suspends a pure value in IO.

This should *only* be used if the value in question has "already" been computed! In other words, something like **IO.pure(readLine)** is most definitely not the right thing to do! However, **IO.pure(42)** is correct and will be more efficient (when evaluated) than **IO(42)**, due to avoiding the allocation of extra thunks.

It lifts a value into the IO context without doing anything else with it.

Finally, we have a non-terminal case of the Monadic loop:

```
else for {
  _ <- IO { println(s"${Thread.currentThread.getName}: " +
    s"Running total from $from to $to, currently at $i: $runningTotal") }
  _ <- IO.sleep(500 milliseconds)
} yield Left((i + 1, runningTotal + i))
```

We have some debugging output stating the current thread and the current status of the computation. Then, we block the execution asynchronously by using the `IO.sleep` primitive.

Finally, we return with a new state of the computation, that is, the next number, and the updated running total.

The computation is long-running because it will pause for half a second on each number.

Next, let's see what happens if we want to combine the results of two such computations.

IO combination without Fibers

Consider that we need to compute a sum of two ranges, and then sum the results. A naive way to combine is as follows:

```
def sequential: IO[Int] =
  for {
    s1 <- sum(1 , 10)
    s2 <- sum(10, 20)
  } yield s1 + s2
```

In the preceding code, we combine our computations using the Monadic flow. Let's see what happens if we try and run the competition under a benchmark function:

```
benchmarkFlush(sequential).unsafeRunSync
```

The result of the preceding execution is as follows:

First, notice that the first range gets computed first. The second range does not even start until the first range finishes. Also notice how both of the threads of the thread pool get utilized in the process of computation. This can be considered a waste of threads and resources since we could use both of the threads to compute sums in parallel. However, we are doing so sequentially here.

We may argue that the preceding scenario occurs because we are using the Monadic flow. As you may recall, Monads define sequential composition. It is not possible to start the next computation until the previous computation finishes. Also, we know that Applicative is used for cases of parallelism. Can we apply the `traverse` function to compute all of our computations in parallel? Let's try:

```
def sequentialTraverse: IO[Int] =
  List(sum(1, 10), sum(10, 20)).traverse(identity).map(_.sum)
```

Now, the computations are independent one from another. What happens if we run them?

```
benchmarkFlush(sequentialTraverse).unsafeRunSync
```

The output looks precisely the same as it did in the preceding sequential example, which means that the default implementation of Applicative for IO runs the computations one by one, even though they are independent.

How can the situation be remedied with the help of Fibers? Let's take a look at how we can launch the computations in parallel with Fibers.

IO combination with Fibers

Previously, we briefly touched on the topic of Fibers. They are remote control units for underlying computations. We know that on any IO, we can call a `start` method, and that will cause it to run asynchronously, which means that it will not block the current execution flow of the IO effect type. Also, you know that we can later block on a Fiber in order to obtain the result. Notice that, here, we are blocking with respect to the Monadic flow. It is precisely the Monadic flow that is getting blocked, that is, the execution of the Monadic instructions gets suspended. The underlying thread IO used to run is not blocked by anything.

Let's see how we can implement our sum example with the help of Fibers:

```
def parallel: IO[Int] =
  for {
    f1 <- sum(1 , 10).start
    f2 <- sum(10, 20).start
    s1 <- f1.join
    s2 <- f2.join
  } yield s1 + s2
```

Our sum instructions are executed asynchronously with respect to the Monadic flow, which means that the Monadic flow application will not wait for either of the two sums to finish and will proceed directly through the first two instructions without blocking. The result is that both of the computations get submitted for execution and will be executed in parallel.

After that, we can block on the Fibers to obtain the results. We can run the application as follows:

```
benchmarkFlush(parallel).unsafeRunSync
```

The output is as follows:

```
1. java
[11] jvm.SyncVsAsyncSync

Enter number: 5

[info] Stopping application root (by killing the forked JVM) ...
[info] Starting application root in the background ...
root ... finished with exit code 143
root Starting jvm.FibersParallel.main()
[success] Total time: 3 s, completed Aug 4, 2018 4:33:43 PM
sbt:jvm> root pool-1-thread-1: Running total from 1 to 10, currently at 1: 0
root pool-1-thread-2: Running total from 10 to 20, currently at 10: 0
root pool-1-thread-1: Running total from 1 to 10, currently at 2: 1
root pool-1-thread-1: Running total from 10 to 20, currently at 11: 10
root pool-1-thread-1: Running total from 1 to 10, currently at 3: 3
root pool-1-thread-2: Running total from 10 to 20, currently at 12: 21
root pool-1-thread-2: Running total from 10 to 20, currently at 13: 33
root pool-1-thread-1: Running total from 1 to 10, currently at 4: 6
root pool-1-thread-2: Running total from 10 to 20, currently at 14: 46
root pool-1-thread-1: Running total from 1 to 10, currently at 5: 10
root pool-1-thread-2: Running total from 10 to 20, currently at 15: 60
root pool-1-thread-1: Running total from 1 to 10, currently at 6: 15
root pool-1-thread-2: Running total from 10 to 20, currently at 16: 75
root pool-1-thread-1: Running total from 1 to 10, currently at 7: 21
root pool-1-thread-2: Running total from 10 to 20, currently at 17: 91
root pool-1-thread-1: Running total from 1 to 10, currently at 8: 28
root pool-1-thread-2: Running total from 10 to 20, currently at 18: 108
root pool-1-thread-1: Running total from 1 to 10, currently at 9: 36
root pool-1-thread-1: Running total from 10 to 20, currently at 19: 126
root Computed result 220 in 5 seconds
```

Now, both of the tasks are executed concurrently. The time needed to compute the tasks is reduced by a factor of 2.

Next, let's take a look at another capability of Fibers, namely to cancel the underlying computation.

Canceling Fibers

Suppose we have one range shorter than another, and we would like to cancel the longer range computation when the first one is completed. You can do this with Fibers as follows:

```
def cancelled: IO[Int] =
  for {
    f1 <- sum(1 , 5 ).start
    f2 <- sum(10, 20).start
    res <- f1.join
    _ <- f2.cancel
  } yield res
```

We can run it as follows:

```
benchmarkFlush(cancelled).unsafeRunSync
```

And the result of the execution is as follows:

```
                              1. java
[1] jvm.AsynchronyHeavy
[2] jvm.AsynchronyLight
[3] jvm.Bracket
[4] jvm.FibersCancelled
[5] jvm.FibersParallel
[6] jvm.FibersSequantial
[7] jvm.HelloWorld
[8] jvm.ProductRight
[9] jvm.SequentialTraverse
[10] jvm.SyncVsAsyncAsync
[11] jvm.SyncVsAsyncSync

Enter number: 4

[info] Stopping application root (by killing the forked JVM) ...
root ... finished with exit code 143
[info] Starting application root in the background ...
root Starting jvm.FibersCancelled.main()
[success] Total time: 3 s, completed Aug 4, 2018 4:34:52 PM
sbt:jvm> root pool-1-thread-1: Running total from 1 to 5, currently at 1: 0
root pool-1-thread-2: Running total from 10 to 20, currently at 10: 0
root pool-1-thread-2: Running total from 1 to 5, currently at 2: 1
root pool-1-thread-1: Running total from 10 to 20, currently at 11: 10
root pool-1-thread-2: Running total from 10 to 20, currently at 12: 21
root pool-1-thread-1: Running total from 1 to 5, currently at 3: 3
root pool-1-thread-2: Running total from 10 to 20, currently at 13: 33
root pool-1-thread-1: Running total from 1 to 5, currently at 4: 6
root pool-1-thread-2: Running total from 10 to 20, currently at 14: 46
root Computed result 15 in 2 seconds
```

Notice that the second range gets cancelled once the first range finishes its execution.

In this chapter, we have discussed the currency capabilities of the Cats effects library in detail. It is the primary objective of the library. However, it has a bunch of other useful methods and primitives. So, next, we will take a look at one of these primitives—the `bracket` primitive—which is a try-with-resources for Cats.

Bracket

Often, we encounter a situation where we need to access a resource that we need to close afterwards. This can be a file reference, a database session, a HTTP connection, or something else. The Cats effect has a dedicated primitive to allow you to work with such resources securely. In Java, there is a dedicated statement for handling resources, which is try-with-resources. Scala does not have a similar statement. However, the situation changes with the `bracket` method, which is defined on the IO primitive:

```
final def bracket[B](use: (A) ⇒ IO[B])(release: (A) ⇒ IO[Unit]): IO[B]
```

Returns an IO action that treats the source task as the acquisition of a resource, which is then exploited by the **use** function and then **released**.

The **bracket** operation is the equivalent of the **try {} catch {} finally {}** statements from mainstream languages.

The **bracket** operation installs the necessary exception handler to release the resource in the event of an exception being raised during the computation, or in case of cancelation.

If an exception is raised, then **bracket** will re-raise the exception *after* performing the **release**. If the resulting task gets cancelled, then **bracket** will still perform the **release**, but the yielded task will be non-terminating (equivalent with IO.never).

As it says in the documentation, the `bracket` primitive makes the underlying execution engine treat the result of this IO as a resource to be closed. With the `bracket` function, you can pass two arguments. The first one specifies what you wanted to do with the underlying process. It is very much like the argument to the `flatMap` function. The second function is the specification of how to close the underlying resource. This second function will be called after the computation is finished, no matter how it finished. It could have finished with an error or canceled, however, the cleanup function will be called in any situation. This prevents memory leaks that can be a problem in the situation of a high-performance environment.

Let's take a look at how we can use it as an example. First of all, we need a closable resource, the closed status of which we can easily check. We can define it as follows:

```
class DBSession {
  var closed = false
  def runStatement(stat: String): IO[List[String]] = {
    val computation = IO {
      if (stat.contains("user")) List("John", "Ann")
      else if (stat.contains("post")) List("Post1", "Post2")
      else Nil
    }
    if (!closed) computation
    else IO.raiseError { new RuntimeException("Connection is closed") }
  }
  def close(): Unit = closed = true
  def isClosed = closed
}
```

In the preceding code, we have defined a database session connection. It has a `closed` flag which prevents any statements to be run against this session when it is set. Next, we have the `runStatement` method, which performs some execution logic to model a statement run against a database.

This `runStatement` method deserves special attention because it demonstrates the power of treating computations as values. First of all, you can see that we define the computation logic in the `computation` value.

Afterwards, we check whether the `closed` flag is set. If it isn't, we return the computation as usual. However, if it is, we return an error. The error method is defined as follows:

```
def raiseError[A](e: Throwable): IO[A]

    Constructs an IO which sequences the specified exception.

    If this IO is run using unsafeRunSync or unsafeRunTimed, the exception will be thrown. This exception
    can be "caught" (or rather, materialized into value-space) using the attempt method.

    See also        IO#attempt
```

It terminates the ongoing IO computation due to a failure.

Next, let's define a few helper methods with which we are going to test our bracket primitive:

```
def dbSession: IO[DBSession] = IO { new DBSession }

def selectUsers(db: DBSession): IO[List[String]] =
  dbSession.flatMap(_.runStatement("select * from user"))
```

In the preceding code, we have a function to create a database, and a function to query users from this database connection. Everything is done under the IO data type.

Next, let's create a setup that will allow us to see whether a connection was closed or not. We can do so by creating a Monadic flow under the bracket primitive, and from the flow, we are going to leak the reference to our session to a variable outside the flow that we are going to check afterward:

```
var sessIntercept: DBSession = null
val computation: IO[Unit] =
  dbSession.bracket(sess => for {
    users <- selectUsers(sess)

    _ = println(s"Users:\n${users.mkString("\n")}")
    _ = sessIntercept = sess
  } yield ())(sess => IO { sess.close() })

println(s"Session intercept before execution: $sessIntercept")
computation.unsafeRunSync
println(s"Session intercept after execution: $sessIntercept")
println(s"Session intercept closed status: ${sessIntercept.isClosed}")
```

So, in the preceding code, we are using the bracket from the computation value. We are on the Monadic flow inside this bracket, and as a part of this Monadic flow, we are selecting the users to verify that our program works correctly. Finally, we leak the resource to a variable outside the flow. The cleanup function is defined as closing the session.

The result of running the preceding computation is as follows:

```
                                    1. java
[warn] Multiple main classes detected.  Run 'show discoveredMainClasses' to see the list

Multiple main classes detected, select one to run:

 [1] jvm.AsynchronyHeavy
 [2] jvm.AsynchronyLight
 [3] jvm.Bracket
 [4] jvm.FibersCancelled
 [5] jvm.FibersParallel
 [6] jvm.FibersSequantial
 [7] jvm.HelloWorld
 [8] jvm.ProductRight
 [9] jvm.SequentialTraverse
 [10] jvm.SyncVsAsyncAsync
 [11] jvm.SyncVsAsyncSync

Enter number: 3

[info] Application root not yet started
root Starting jvm.Bracket.main()
[info] Starting application root in the background ...
[success] Total time: 10 s, completed Aug 4, 2018 4:38:00 PM
sbt:jvm> root Session intercept before execution: null
root Users:
root John
root Ann
root Session intercept after execution: jvm.Bracket$DBSession@5c5a1b69
root Session intercept closed status: true
root ... finished with exit code 0
```

Together with the asynchronous capabilities of IO, bracket provides you with a great
primitive that can be used in an asynchronous environment where you would like to guard
against memory leaks.

Server-side programming

One large domain for applying functional programming is server-side programming.
Server-side programming refers to web applications that constantly run on a server, and
have the ability to communicate with the outer world. Such an application will typically
listen on a port for incoming HTTP requests. After a request arrives, it will perform some
work on the server, and reply back to the requesting client with the result of the
computation.

Applications of such systems are wide. Everything from regular websites to mobile applications to **Software as a Service** (**SaaS**) systems are made as web applications. Also, once you have a web application that constantly runs on a server, communicates with the outer world via a well-defined protocol, and performs some computations, you can have a multitude of clients for such an application. For example, you may have an HTML-based frontend, together with a mobile application, together with integration with third-party applications via API.

Scala and the Cats infrastructure happens to have great support for server-side programming. They contain all the primitives that you will need to accept HTTP requests, map them to your domain model objects, communicate with the database, and reply back to the client. In this section, we will see how exactly it is done.

But first of all, let's get a brief overview of the general architecture of server-side applications, as well as specify the application we are going to be using as an example for this chapter.

The architecture of a server-side application

First of all, a server application includes a server. A server is an application that will constantly run on the given machine and listen to a given HTTP port for incoming connections. The incoming connections are typically HTTP connections that follow a certain protocol.

Communication protocol

A popular way to structure a communication protocol of a web application is to follow the RESTful paradigm of communication.

Since the application listens for HTTP requests, it is reasonable that these requests are made to a certain path. For example, a typical HTTP request contains the following headers:

```
GET http://localhost:8888/order HTTP/1.0
User-Agent: Mozilla/5.0 (Windows NT 6.3; WOW64; rv:39.0) Gecko/20100101
Firefox/39.0
Pragma: no-cache
Content-Length: 19
Host: localhost:8888
```

So, as you can see, the request contains a destination string or a so-called path, together with HTTP headers. You can reason about the resources the server exposes as entities that have certain behaviors and data defined on them. The RESTful paradigm dictates that the capabilities the server side exposes via HTTP must have the paths and HTTP methods reflect the resources and their behavior that is to be performed.

For example, consider that you have a server that manages a forum. We will have users and forum posts. Regarding the behaviors, over time, we will want to create new posts and users, list existing posts and users, and modify and delete them.

These behaviors can be exposed via the HTTP RESTful API as follows:

```
POST /user
POST /post
GET /user
GET /post
PUT /user
PUT /post
DELETE /user/{id}
DELETE /post/{id]
```

So, the HTTP methods reflect the nature of the behavior to be performed by the server. The paths reflect the nature of resources involved in the given behavior.

The client must frequently send extra information to the server. The server is supposed to reply to the client with a certain result. This request and response data must follow a certain format that is understandable to both the client and the server. Furthermore, since a web application can be exposed not only to one client but to a multitude of potential third-party clients, it is necessary that such a protocol must be standardized. The same way as the HTTP protocol is a standard protocol which a multitude of independent parties understand and implement, the same way the requests and responses protocol must also be supported by a multitude of independent parties. This is because they will need some libraries to encode and decode this request, and we do not want an overhead for them so that they can implement them themselves.

So, a standard way to encode the requests and responses is to use JSON or XML. In this example, we will be using JSON because it has much better support than XML in Scala. Furthermore, the Cats family of libraries includes capabilities to work with JSON easily.

The communication protocol is only a small part of what is involved in the server architecture. Next, we will briefly discuss which components a server is composed of.

The software architecture of a server

The first component that any server must have is an application that is capable of listening to HTTP requests and responding to them. Such a component is called an HTTP server software. Besides that, most servers need some persistence component—a database. Next, the server will need a way to communicate with the database. So, we need the database access layer.

Finally, an orchestration solution is necessary for the preceding components to play well together, which means that we need an easy capability to bootstrap both the server and the database, and a way to define the communication between them. It is important that the orchestration is well-defined and is reproducible, with minimal setup on a variety of different environments. This is important because you do not want to write the server once for one platform and not be able to port it easily to other platforms.

The preceding components are the basic components for any server-side software. Of course, more complex server-side applications involve much more complex architectures; however, for the purposes of our example, this will suffice.

Now, let's discuss the example we are going to use to demonstrate server-side programming with the cats and Typelevel libraries.

Example specification

The example in question will be an online store. So, we will have the entities for the customers, the goods, and we will have an ability to describe orders that the customers make.

We will store all of these entities in a database, and we will expose the functionality to create new users and new orders, and to list existing orders and goods via an HTTP interface.

Next, let's take a look at how this architecture can be put into practice. We will be discussing the architecture as a whole, and we will be introducing various functional programming libraries in the process. This will facilitate an integrated view of how server-side programming can be done with Cats.

Please keep in mind that we will not be going in-depth into any of the libraries we are going to discuss, as this would deserve its own book. Also, we have already mentioned that cat is on the leading edge of functional programming technology, which means that the library develops quickly, and the in-depth information that we could have covered would have become obsolete very soon. However, the general architectural principles will probably stay the same for a substantial time to come.

Orchestration and infrastructure

First of all, we will be talking about our infrastructure and the software we will use to implement our architecture.

There will be two separate components to our server-side software. First of all, it is Scala-based server-side software, and second of all, it is a Postgres-based database.

These two components are orchestrated together via Docker.

Although the topics discussed in this subsection do not deal with functional programming, it is necessary to understand the big picture in order to understand which setting the functional server will operate in.

Docker

We will define all of the components involved in other software as Docker services in a `docker-compose` file.

Docker-compose

The file as a whole will look as follows:

```
version: '3'
services:
  postgres:
    container_name: mastering_postgres
    build: postgres
    ports:
      - 5432:5432
  backend:
    container_name: mastering_backend
    build: .
    ports:
      - 8888:8888
    volumes:
```

```
        - ./_volumes/ivy2:/root/.ivy2
        - ./_volumes/sbt-boot:/root/.sbt/boot
        - ./_volumes/coursier:/root/.cache
        - .:/root/examples
      environment:
        - POSTGRES_HOST=postgres
        - POSTGRES_PORT=5432
      stdin_open: true
      tty: true
```

The file consists of two services—the Postgres service and the backend service. The Postgres service is defined as follows:

```
postgres:
  container_name: mastering_postgres
  build: postgres
  ports:
    - 5432:5432
```

This service defines a container named `mastering_postgres`. The `build` directive specifies that we want to build the contents of the `Postgres` folder, which is located in the current folder, to a separate Docker image. The port's directive specifies which ports the container will expose. The container in question will run the database, so we need to expose the ports that the database will be running on. Basically, it is a mapping from the ports of the container to the ports of the host machine.

The second service is defined as follows:

```
backend:
  container_name: mastering_backend
  build: .
  ports:
    - 8888:8888
  volumes:
    - ./_volumes/ivy2:/root/.ivy2
    - ./_volumes/sbt-boot:/root/.sbt/boot
    - ./_volumes/coursier:/root/.cache
    - .:/root/examples
  environment:
    - POSTGRES_HOST=postgres
    - POSTGRES_PORT=5432
  stdin_open: true
  tty: true
```

It also provides the name of its container, and it specifies that we want to build the contents of the current folder into a separate image. Docker will look for a `Dockerfile` in the provided directory and will build it into a separate image. Next, since this container will host an HTTP server, we also need to perform the port mapping so that we can listen to HTTP connection of the host machine from the container.

After that, we have the `volumes` array. This array specifies the directories on the local machine to be mounted to the directories on the container. In the current example, we mount a set of directories of the container that are responsible for caching. The first entry is an `ivy2` cache that is used by Scala and SBT to store their dependencies. After that, we also mount the SBT root folder, which hosts the SBT installation. Finally, we mount the cache folder, which is another location where SBT stores its dependencies.

We perform these mounts of the cache directories so that the container remembers what it fetched from invocation to invocation. So, you will not need to wait for the application to fetch its dependencies every time you restart the Docker container because all of the dependencies will be stored on the host machine under the directories that we have mounted.

Finally, we mount the current directory to the examples directory under the container. This is done so that we can access the Scala sources from the container. So, we will be able to run the application from the context of the Docker container, which means that we will be able to access all of the infrastructure defined by the `docker-compose` file.

Finally, we have an `environment` array. This array specifies the environmental variables set the container will be initialized with. We have the variables that specify the host and port of the Postgres database. We will use these environmental variables in the Scala sources to specify the location of the database.

Finally, we have two technical entries in the file:

```
stdin_open: true
tty: true
```

These are related to the ability to access the running Docker container from the command line. So, we should be able to open a command line on a running Docker container due to these two entries. Basically, they specify how the Docker container should allocate and treat a console device. If you are interested more in this or any other of the Docker entries, please consult the Docker documentation.

Next, let's discuss the two Dockerfiles corresponding to the two services we have defined in `docker-compose`.

Dockerfiles

Dockerfiles contain the descriptions of how a particular image must be built. We have two images: one is for the database, and the other one is for the backend. Let's start with the database image first:

```
FROM postgres:latest
ADD ./*.sql /docker-entrypoint-initdb.d/
```

The Docker file only contains two lines of code. First of all, we inherit from an existing image of Postgres. Second, we copy all of the SQL files from the current directory to a special directory in the Docker image. This is a standard initialization procedure described in the documentation of the Postgres image we inherit from. The main idea is to initialize the database with a schema that we are going to use. Our schema is as follows:

```
CREATE TABLE customer (
   id serial NOT NULL,
   "name" varchar NOT NULL,
   CONSTRAINT customer_pk PRIMARY KEY (id),
   CONSTRAINT customer_un UNIQUE (name)
)
WITH (
   OIDS=FALSE
) ;
CREATE UNIQUE INDEX customer_name_idx ON public.customer USING btree (name)
;

CREATE TABLE good (
   id serial NOT NULL,
   "name" varchar NOT NULL,
   price float4 NOT NULL,
   stock int4 NOT NULL DEFAULT 0,
   CONSTRAINT good_pk PRIMARY KEY (id)
)
WITH (
   OIDS=FALSE
) ;

CREATE TABLE "order" (
   id serial NOT NULL,
   customer int4 NOT NULL,
   good int4 NOT NULL,
   CONSTRAINT store_order_pk PRIMARY KEY (id),
   CONSTRAINT order_customer_fk FOREIGN KEY (customer) REFERENCES
customer(id) ON DELETE CASCADE,
   CONSTRAINT order_good_fk FOREIGN KEY (good) REFERENCES good(id) ON DELETE
CASCADE
```

```
)
WITH (
  OIDS=FALSE
) ;

INSERT INTO good (id, name, price, stock) VALUES(1, 'MacBook Pro 15''',
2500, 15);
INSERT INTO good (id, name, price, stock) VALUES(2, 'iPhone 10', 1000, 10);
INSERT INTO good (id, name, price, stock) VALUES(3, 'MacBook Air', 900, 3);
INSERT INTO good (id, name, price, stock) VALUES(4, 'Samsung Galaxy S5',
500, 8);
INSERT INTO good (id, name, price, stock) VALUES(5, 'Panasonic Camera',
120, 34);
```

We also have three tables. First, we have a table for customers and goods. Both customers and goods have an ID that uniquely identifies them. Also, goods has some goods-specific parameters, such as the price and the stock count. Finally, we have a table that will link customers to goods as orders.

After that, we will populate our database with some sample goods that we are going to run our test queries on.

Next, let's take a look at our backend image:

```
FROM hseeberger/scala-sbt

RUN mkdir -p /root/.sbt/1.0/plugins
RUN echo "\
addSbtPlugin(\"io.get-coursier\" % \"sbt-coursier\" % \"1.0.0-RC12-1\")\n\
addSbtPlugin(\"io.spray\" % \"sbt-revolver\" % \"0.9.0\" )\n\
" > /root/.sbt/1.0/plugins/plugins.sbt

WORKDIR /root/examples
```

The image inherits from a standard Scala SBT image so that we are going to have Scala and SBT in scope. After that, we define some SBT plugins that we are going to use. The first one is to speed up downloading the dependencies, and the second one is used to start the server in a separate JVM. We are going to start a server in a separate JVM because, in this way, we will retain the possibility to manage the server, and start and restart it from the SBT console.

Finally, we set the working directory to our examples directory.

You will find the instructions on how to run the Dockerfile in the README file of the examples repository.

Now that we are familiar with the architecture of the components involved, let's start by taking a more detailed look at how the backend software is constructed using Scala.

Backend architecture

The backend is composed of three separate layers. We have a model layer for the model of our business domain, the database access later, and the server layer itself. Let's take a look at these layers in turn and see how they can be implemented with Typelevel libraries.

Model

The model is represented by a single Scala file. It contains case classes that model our database. Notice that here, we are using plain Scala case classes without any other augmentations. If you are familiar with libraries for the Java-like Hibernate, you will know that there is an entire class of libraries for so-called **object-relational mapping** (ORM). These libraries intend to provide a seamless mapping of object-oriented concepts to the database schema. The main idea is to be able to manage the database, query it, and update it without the need to perform SQL statements explicitly. Such libraries aim to provide you with an object-oriented API that allows performing these operations while abstracting the underlying SQL engine.

Such libraries proved to be a bad idea because of the leaking abstractions. There are corner cases that these kinds of ORM libraries are not able to handle well. These libraries may not allow you to perform certain functionality that's native to a given database.

In modern functional programming, object-relational mapping is considered a bad practice. The current consensus seems to be that executing plain old SQL statements is the best way to model interaction with the database. So, unlike object-relational mapping libraries, we are not required to modify our domain model specifically to match the needs of the object-relational framework we are working under. We are not required to implement an interface from our model classes. We are able to define our domain model in terms of plain old case classes.

Database layer

A database layer is implemented in terms of the Doobie library. Each entity has a separate Scala file, where there is a singleton object, which has all of the methods that we need for the purposes of this application. For example, let's take a look at the API that the `customer` object exposes:

```
object customer extends CustomerDbHelpers {
  def create(c: Customer): IO[Int] = ???
  def findByName(name: String): IO[Option[Customer]] = ???
  def list: IO[List[Customer]] = ???
  def get(id: Int): IO[Customer] = ???
  def update(c: Customer): IO[Int] = ???
  def delete(id: Int): IO[Int] = ???
}

trait CustomerDbHelpers {
  val selectCustomerSql = fr"select * from customer"  // to be explained
further in the chapter
}
```

So, we have several database access methods, and each of them returns an IO—precisely the same IO we were learning about in the previous section. The Doobie library we are going to have a look at in this section integrates nicely with the Cats effect, and we are able to leverage the IO in order to communicate with the database.

Now, let's take a look at how one such method is implemented in terms of Doobie, and what the model of operation of Doobie is:

```
def create(c: Customer): IO[Int] =
  sql"""
    insert into customer (name)
    values (${c.name})
  """
  .update.withUniqueGeneratedKeys[Int]("id").transact(tr)
```

Here, we have several things going on. First, we have an SQL statement under a string interpolator that Doobie provides. Now, in Scala, you are able to define custom string interpolators that have a form of a certain keyword, written just before the string literal. In our case, such a keyword is `sql`. The main idea of string interpolators is that, on compile time, they are going to transform a string in a certain way, possibly producing an entirely different object.

First, let's find out what exactly the string interpolator is doing to the string. To do so, we will consult the documentation:

```
final val sql: fr0.type
```

So, `sql` is an alias for `fr0` and is defined as follows:

```
object fr0 extends ProductArgs

        Interpolator for a statement fragment that can contain interpolated values. Unlike fr no attempt is made to
        be helpful with respect to whitespace.
```

This object has two methods to it:

```
macro def applyDynamic(method: String)(args: Any*): Any


    def applyProduct[A](a: A)(implicit arg0: util.param.Param[A]): util.fragment.Fragment
```

Notice that one of these methods is a macro definition. The macro definition is a special method in Scala, which is invoked at compile time. It is used for metaprogramming in Scala. String interpolators are usually implemented in terms of macros.

Now, macro transforms a string into a `Fragment` object. A fragment is a model of an SQL statement under a string interpolator. Notice that, in the preceding screenshot, the string interpolator also gives us external variables to be used in SQL statements, as follows:

```
values (${c.name})
```

Interpolation is done by the dedicated Doobie macro. It interpolates the variables in a secure way so that you do not need to worry about escaping the variables that you are inserting into an SQL query—this way, you don't get an SQL injection. Doobie performs the escapes for you.

One thing to notice about the technique employed by Doobie here is that your SQL code to interact with the database is defined as a string. However, this string is processed at compile time. This provides you with a measure of type safety and compiler assistance at compile time.

Now, let's take a look at the fragment definition:

doobie.util.fragment

Fragment

Companion **object Fragment**

`sealed trait` **Fragment** `extends AnyRef`

A statement fragment, which may include interpolated values. Fragments can be composed by concatenation, which maintains the correct offset and mappings for interpolated values. Once constructed a **Fragment** is opaque; it has no externally observable properties. Fragments are eventually used to construct a Query0 or Update0.

Fragment has the following API exposed:

```
def ++(fb: Fragment): Fragment
```
    Concatenate this fragment with another, yielding a larger fragment.

```
def execWith[B](fa: doobie.PreparedStatementIO[B]): doobie.ConnectionIO[B]
```
    Construct a program in ConnectionIO that constructs and prepares a PreparedStatement, with further handling delegated to the provided program.

```
def query[B](implicit arg0: Read[B], h: doobie.LogHandler = LogHandler.nop):
    doobie.Query0[B]
```
    Construct a Query0 from this fragment, with asserted row type **B**.

```
def queryWithLogHandler[B](h: doobie.LogHandler)(implicit cb: Read[B]): doobie.Query0[B]
```
    Construct a Query0 from this fragment, with asserted row type **B** and the given **LogHandler**.

```
def stripMargin: Fragment
```

```
def stripMargin(marginChar: Char): Fragment
```

```
def toString(): String
```

```
def update(implicit h: doobie.LogHandler = LogHandler.nop): doobie.Update0
```
    Construct an Update0 from this fragment.

```
def updateWithLogHandler(h: doobie.LogHandler): doobie.Update0
```
    Construct an Update0 from this fragment with the given **LogHandler**.

For our purposes, the following two methods are of particular importance:

```
def query[B](implicit arg0: Read[B], h: doobie.LogHandler = LogHandler.nop):
    doobie.Query0[B]
    Construct a Query0 from this fragment, with asserted row type B.
```

The preceding method is used for query operations, such as selecting from the database.

The following method is used for update operations, such as making modifications to the database:

```
def update(implicit h: doobie.LogHandler = LogHandler.nop): doobie.Update0
    Construct an Update0 from this fragment.
```

A fragment is a model of the statement that you have passed to the string interpolator. However, this model does not store the information about which exact operation you want to perform against the database. So, to specify this kind of operation, you call the update or query methods on Fragment. An update method is used for insert and update operations, and the query method is used for select operations.

In our example, we are calling the update method because we perform an insert query. Next, an Update0 object is generated from the fragment:

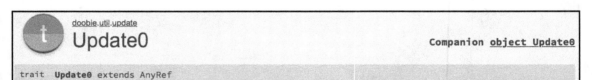

It exposes the following API:

Diagnostics

    abstract def **analysis:** <u>doobie.ConnectionIO[Analysis]</u>

        Program to construct an analysis of this query's SQL statement and asserted parameter types.

    abstract val **pos:** Option[<u>Pos</u>]

        An optional **Pos** indicating the source location where this **Query** was constructed.

    abstract val **sql:** String

        The SQL string.

Execution

    abstract def **run:** <u>doobie.ConnectionIO</u>[Int]

        Program to execute the update and yield a count of affected rows.

    abstract def **withGeneratedKeysWithChunkSize**[K](columns: String*)(chunkSize: Int)(*implicit* arg0: <u>Read</u>[K]): Stream[<u>doobie.ConnectionIO</u>, K]

        Construct a stream that performs the update, yielding generated keys of readable type **K**, identified by the specified columns, given a **chunkSize**.

    abstract def **withUniqueGeneratedKeys**[K](columns: String*)(*implicit* arg0: <u>Read</u>[K]): <u>doobie.ConnectionIO</u>[K]

        Construct a program that performs the update, yielding a single set of generated keys of readable type **K**, identified by the specified columns.

    def **withGeneratedKeys**[K](columns: String*)(*implicit* arg0: <u>Read</u>[K]): Stream[<u>doobie.ConnectionIO</u>, K]

        Construct a stream that performs the update, yielding generated keys of readable type **K**, identified by the specified columns.

Note that its API is divided into two sections. First, there is the diagnostics section. Since Doobie constructs an internal model of your query, it allows you to run certain tests on it to check whether your parameters passed to the query are of correct types and whether the query itself is composed correctly. We also have the execution API. The execution API is what you use in order to run the query.

Notice that all of the methods from the execution category return a type under the ConnectionIO effect type. ConnectionIO is essentially a so-called free object. If a fragment and Update0 are models of the SQL query you are about to run, the free object of ConnectionIO models the precise steps the program needs to take against the database to run this query. The free object is a concept that comes from abstract algebra. Essentially, the idea is to model the computation under the free object without actually running it. The idea is precisely the same as with the IO effect type that we looked at in the previous section. That type is also a free object.

Notice that we are calling the `UniqueGeneratedKeys` method in our example. The method is aware that the underlying database will generate a primary key for the insert operation we are about to perform. In our case, the primary key is an integer, and we are passing a type parameter of integer to the method.

If you have a look at the `ConnectionIO` definition, you will see that it is a `Free` Monad:

```
type ConnectionIO[A] = Free[ConnectionOp, A]
```

So, the underlying implementation of DB operations is done using the free Monad library, which is also a part of the Cats infrastructure. As we have previously said, we will not go into detail about these auxiliary libraries and ideas since, by themselves, they deserve a separate book. So, here, the main catch to make is that the Doobie library starts from constructing a model of your SQL query and provides you with an API to gradually transform it into the model of the computation to be performed against your database. Everywhere, the paradigm of computation as a value is maintained, and nothing is run until explicitly instructed to.

We are able to run the `ConnectionIO` under the given effect type using the `transact` operation on it. This operation is injected via a Rich Wrapper, which is defined as follows:

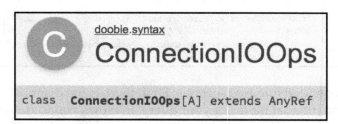

The following constructor is used to construct the wrapper:

```
Instance Constructors

          new ConnectionIOOps(ma: free.connection.ConnectionIO[A])
```

It exposes only a single method:

```
def transact[M[_]](xa: util.transactor.Transactor[M])(implicit arg0: Monad[M]): M[A]
```

Essentially, the method is tasked by running the computation under a certain effect type when given a transactor for the database. Now, the transactor for the database is a driver that knows how to communicate with the underlying database. Notice that so far, Doobie exposes the database-independent API, which is expected of this kind of library. So, the information that is database-specific is stored under the Transactor object, which must be implemented for your database in order for you to run database queries against that database.

Also notice that the effect type that we are passing to the transact method has a type parameter. This parameter specifies the effect type under which we are going to run our computation. Remember that ConnectionIO is just a description of the computation to be performed. In order to perform it, we need to specify which effect type we are going to perform it under.

In our example, we are using the tr variable as the transactor. So, let's take a look at how it is defined to understand the semantics of our example:

```
implicit lazy val tr: Transactor[IO] =
  Transactor.fromDriverManager[IO](
  "org.postgresql.Driver"
  ,
s"jdbc:postgresql://${sys.env("POSTGRES_HOST")}:${sys.env("POSTGRES_PORT")}
/postgres"
  , "postgres", "")
```

Here, we are using the built-in Doobie method to construct the transactor, given the full class name of the database driver for the database that we are going to use. In our case, we are using Postgres, and we are passing the fully qualified name of the Postgres driver to the driver manager construction API.

The next argument to the driver manager construction method is the address of the database we are going to connect to. Here, we are connecting to a Postgres database, and we are reading its host and port from the environmental variables. Remember that, when we were discussing the Docker orchestration of the backend and the database, we discussed that the backend has environmental variables populated from the `docker-compose` file. These variables specify where the database resides for the backend to connect to it.

After the connection string, we have a login and password for the database. In our case, login and password are standard connection strings for the Docker Postgres image that we are using.

Also, notice that our transactor is constructed for the effects type of IO. This means that when we are going to run the query against this transactor, the result will be an IO.

Let's recall what IO is. It is a description of the computation to take place. However, `ConnectionIO` is also a description of a computation that is going to take place. So, when we are executing the `transact` statement on the `ConnectionIO`, we are not actually running it as a computation but translating it from one free language to another. We are translating it from `ConnectionIO` to IO. This kind of translation from one free language to another is quite common in purely functional programming. A useful intuition for when it may be useful may be that of high-level programming languages versus low-level programming languages. When you compile a language such as Scala or Java, a translation happens from the high-level language to the low-level language of the bytecode.

For humans, it is more convenient to program in a high-level language, but for the machines, it is more convenient to consume a low-level language. Hence, before we actually run the program, we must first translate it from a high-level language to a low-level language.

Something along these lines can also be said about translating from one free effect type to another free effect type. Essentially, when aiming to specify all of our computations as values, we will sooner or later encounter a situation when certain tasks can be easily described using one, higher level language. However, it is more convenient to run them when they are expressed in a lower level language. So, the translation takes place from a higher level language to a lower level language.

In our example, we are performing their translation from `ConnectionIO`, which is a domain-specific language for describing interactions with a database, to the IO language, which is a general purpose low-level language that can describe any input-output operation.

Therefore, our create method of the `customer` object outputs as IO, which we can later run when we need their results.

Now, let's take a look at the additional methods that we have already mentioned are members of the `customer` object. First of all, let's take a look at the `list` method that is supposed to list all of the customers that are present in the database:

```
def list: IO[List[Customer]] =
  selectCustomerSql.query[Customer].to[List].transact(tr)
```

The `selectCustomerSql` variable is defined as follows:

```
val selectCustomerSql = fr"select * from customer"
```

We define this query in a separate variable since we are going to reuse it in other queries, as we will see a little bit later. Notice how we are using the other string interpolators that are available as part of Doobie:

```
final val sql: fr0.type
```
Alternative name for the **fr0** interpolator.

```
object fr extends ProductArgs
```
Interpolator for a statement fragment that can contain interpolated values. When inserted into the final SQL statement this fragment will be followed by a space. This is normally what you want, and it makes it easier to concatenate fragments because you don't need to think about intervening whitespace. If you do not want this behavior, use **fr0**.

```
object fr0 extends ProductArgs
```
Interpolator for a statement fragment that can contain interpolated values. Unlike **fr** no attempt is made to be helpful with respect to whitespace.

As you can see from the documentation, Doobie provides you with several ways to specify fragments as string interpolators. The main difference is whether or not they have a trailing whitespace after them. Such a trailing whitespace may be very useful if you want to compose your fragments with other fragments later. To make sure that you don't need to worry about the separating two fragments you are going to concatenate with a whitespace, there is a default string interpolator which injects the white space for you. We will see how this is useful later.

Returning to our `list` example, as you can see, we are running the query method on a fragment. This is to be contrasted with the `update` method on the `create` method of the `customer` object. We are performing a `select` query, and so we are going to run the `query` method.

The method generates a `Query` object. An interesting thing to notice here is that Doobie can automatically convert the result from the raw data returned from the database to the data type of your choice. So, we provide the `Customer` type as the type parameter to the query, and Doobie is able to automatically infer a way to convert the results to this type. In general, such conversions are supported out of the box for case classes, tuples, and primitive types. This is accomplished at compile time metaprogramming, via macros and type-level computations. This useful feature from Doobie places allows it to pose a direct competition to traditional object-relational mapping libraries because you are able to map your results to your domain model at no additional cost.

The `Query0` object produced by the `query` method is defined as follows:

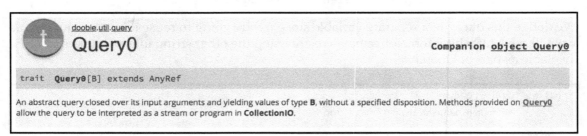

Let's take a look at its API. It consists of two parts we are interested in. First, the **Diagnostics** part:

Diagnostics
abstract def **analysis**: <u>doobie.ConnectionIO[Analysis]</u>
Program to construct an analysis of this query's SQL statement and asserted parameter and column types.
abstract def **outputAnalysis**: <u>doobie.ConnectionIO[Analysis]</u>
Program to construct an analysis of this query's SQL statement and result set column types.
abstract def **pos**: Option[<u>Pos</u>]
An optional **Pos** indicating the source location where this **Query** was constructed.
abstract def **sql**: String
The SQL string.

Next, the **Results** part:

```
Results

       abstract def accumulate[F[_]](implicit arg0: Alternative[F]): doobie.ConnectionIO[F[B]]
                    Program in ConnectionIO yielding an F[B] accumulated via MonadPlus append.

       abstract def nel: doobie.ConnectionIO[NonEmptyList[B]]
                    Program in ConnectionIO yielding a NonEmptyList[B] and raising an exception if the resultset does not have
                    at least one row.

       abstract def option: doobie.ConnectionIO[Option[B]]
                    Program in ConnectionIO yielding an optional B and raising an exception if the resultset has more than one
                    row.

       abstract def streamWithChunkSize(n: Int): Stream[doobie.ConnectionIO, B]
                    Stream with given chunk factor, with effect type ConnectionIO yielding elements of type B.

       abstract def to[F[_]](implicit cbf: CanBuildFrom[Nothing, B, F[B]]): doobie.ConnectionIO[F[B]]
                    Program in ConnectionIO yielding an F[B] accumulated via the provided CanBuildFrom.

       abstract def unique: doobie.ConnectionIO[B]
                    Program in ConnectionIO yielding a unique B and raising an exception if the resultset does not have exactly
                    one row.

             def stream: Stream[doobie.ConnectionIO, B]
                    Stream with default chunk factor, with effect type ConnectionIO yielding elements of type B.

             def sink(f: (B) ⇒ doobie.ConnectionIO[Unit]): doobie.ConnectionIO[Unit]
                    Convenience method, equivalent to stream.evalMap(f).compile.drain.
```

As with the case of `Update`, the API is separated into diagnostics and results sections. It is the results section that is most interesting to us here. Notice that it contains various methods specifying which kind of result you are expecting to retrieve from your database query. For example, the `option` method is to be called when you expect that the query may be returned empty. The `unique` method is to be called when you expect one and only one result from the query. Finally, the `to` method is to be called whenever you would like to convert your result to some collection. Actually, as you can see, there is no restriction that you can only build a collection from the given result here. As long as your result type conforms to the `F[_]` type form, you should be able to build whatever you want, provided that you have a type class this method implicitly depends on. Most frequently, this method is used to create collections from the database.

Other methods for this API can also be used for other types of the results. However, for the purpose of this tutorial, these three will suffice.

Returning to our list example, we are calling the `to` method on it to produce a list of all of the customers. As a result, we are getting a `ConnectionIO` type, which we have already discussed. We then run it against our transactor, like we did previously.

Now, let's take a look at the `get` method of the `Customer` object:

```
def get(id: Int): IO[Customer] =
  (selectCustomerSql ++ sql"where id = $id")
    .query[Customer].unique.transact(tr)
```

The first thing to notice here is that we are performing fragment concatenation. So, the query to select the customers from the database remains the same. However, we are using the concatenation method defined on `Fragment` to concatenate it with another fragment and produce a compound fragment. The concatenation method is defined on the fragment as follows:

```
def ++(fb: Fragment): Fragment
    Concatenate this fragment with another, yielding a larger fragment.
```

Notice that the trailing white space on the left-hand `Fragment` comes in handy here. Remember that we have discussed that the `selectCustomerSql` fragment is constructed with a strength interpolator that injects a trailing whitespace into the resulting fragment. This is useful precisely for these concatenation situations where we need to concatenate two fragments sequentially. Notice that we do not need to prepend a white space to the second fragment with the filter condition because the first fragment is already built with concatenation in mind.

After that, we run the `query` method similarly to the way we did in the example of listing all customers. However, here, we are only expecting one customer. Hence, we will call the `unique` method on the query object. Finally, we will call the `transact` method to convert the `ConnectionIO` to `IO`.

Next, let's take a look at the `findByName` method:

```
def findByName(name: String): IO[Option[Customer]] =
  (selectCustomerSql ++ sql"""where name = $name""")
    .query[Customer].option.transact(tr)
```

This method performs a lookup of customers by name. Notice that it is defined very similarly to getting a customer by ID. However, we are not calling the `unique` method on the query object, but the `option` method. This is because we built the method with the possibility of an empty query result in mind. Whenever we request a user by ID, we are assuming that the user with the given ID exists in the database, at least for the purposes of this example. However, when we are looking up a user in the database, we assume that the user with a given name might not exist.

Hence, our `findByName` method returns an `Option[Customer]`.

Two final methods that we are going to discuss are the `update` and `delete` methods:

```
def update(c: Customer): IO[Int] =
  sql"""
    update customer set
      name = ${c.name}
    where id = ${c.id}
  """
  .update.run.transact(tr)

def delete(id: Int): IO[Int] =
  sql"""delete from customer where id = $id"""
    .update.run.transact(tr)
```

These methods bring nothing new in terms of the Doobie API and are constructed using the API, which we have already learned about.

Now, let 's see how this example works against a live database. To test this example, we will use the following application:

```
val customersTest: IO[Unit] = for {
  id1 <- customer.create(Customer(name = "John Smith"))
  id2 <- customer.create(Customer(name = "Ann Watson"))

  _ = println(s"Looking up customers by name")
  c1 <- customer.findByName("John Smith")
  _ = println(c1)
  c2 <- customer.findByName("Foo")
  _ = println(c2)

  _ = println("\nAll customers")
  cs <- customer.list
  _ = println(cs.mkString("\n"))

  _ = println(s"\nCustomer with id $id1")
  c3 <- customer.get(id1)
  _ = println(c3)

  _ = println(s"\nUpdate customer with id $id1")
  r <- customer.update(c3.copy(name = "Bob"))
  _ = println(s"Rows affected: $r")
  c4 <- customer.get(id1)
  _ = println(s"Updated customer: $c4")

  _ = println(s"\nClean-up: remove all customers")
  _ <- List(id1, id2).traverse(customer.delete)
```

```
   cx <- customer.list
   _ = println(s"Customers table after clean-up: $cx")
} yield ()

customersTest.unsafeRunSync()
```

The preceding application tests all of the methods that we have discussed so far. First, we create a few customers to work with. Then, we test lookup by name. After that, we test the listing of all customers in the database. After that, we test getting a customer by ID. Finally, we test the update and delete operations on the customers. The result of running the preceding application is as follows:

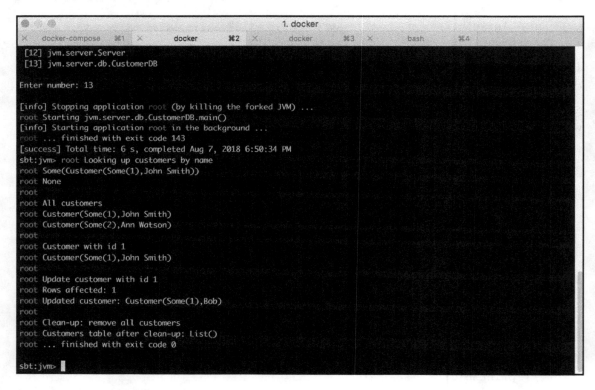

Besides the methods for the customers, we will also need methods that define how to work with the goods. So, we will need a method to create a good, and we can define it as follows:

```
def create(c: Good): IO[Int] =
  sql"""
    insert into good (
      name
    , price
```

```
  , stock)
  values (
    ${c.name}
  , ${c.price}
  , ${c.stock})
"""
  .update.withUniqueGeneratedKeys[Int]("id").transact(tr)
```

We will need methods to query the goods table, too:

```
val selectGoodSql = fr"select * from good"

def findByName(name: String): IO[Option[Good]] =
  (selectGoodSql ++ sql"""where name = $name""")
    .query[Good].option.transact(tr)

def list: IO[List[Good]] =
  selectGoodSql.query[Good].to[List].transact(tr)

def get(id: Int): IO[Good] =
  (selectGoodSql ++ sql"where id = $id")
    .query[Good].unique.transact(tr)
```

Finally, we will need `update` and `delete` methods to modify the database:

```
def update(c: Good): IO[Int] =
  sql"""
    update good set
      name = ${c.name }
    , price = ${c.price}
    , stock = ${c.stock}
    where id = ${c.id}
  """
    .update.run.transact(tr)

def delete(id: Int): IO[Int] =
  sql"""delete from good where id = $id"""
    .update.run.transact(tr)
```

We also need a database access object for the orders so that we can modify and list them. We will need the following method defined on the order object:

```
object order extends OrderDbHelpers {
  def create(o: Order): IO[Int] =
    sql"""
      insert into "order" (customer, good)
      values (${o.customer}, ${o.good})
    """
```

```
      .update.withUniqueGeneratedKeys[Int]("id").transact(tr)

  def list: IO[List[Order]] =
    selectOrderSql.query[Order].to[List].transact(tr)

  def get(id: Int): IO[Order] =
    (selectOrderSql ++ sql"where id = $id")
      .query[Order].unique.transact(tr)
}

trait OrderDbHelpers {
  val selectOrderSql = fr"""select * from "order""""
}
```

Since these methods do not introduce any new functionality and only demonstrate the use of what we have learned of Doobie so far, we will not go into detail regarding these methods.

Next, we will see how server-side programming can be performed with purely functional style, and how it can leverage the database objects we have defined so far.

Server-side programming

For the purposes of server-side programming, we will be using libraries called HTTP4S and Circe. HTTP4S is a library with which you can bootstrap an HTTP server, accept requests, and define how to respond to them. Circe is a library with which you can convert JSON strings to domain objects.

HTTP4S leverages IO under the hood so that it can be nicely integrated into our existing database infrastructure that outputs IO, as well as so that we can be sure that our server runs asynchronously. Circe uses a technique of compile-time programming via macros (which we have already discussed briefly) to define how to convert JSON strings into Scala case classes or traits.

We are going to bootstrap our server as follows:

```
BlazeBuilder[IO]
  .bindHttp(8888, "0.0.0.0")
  .mountService(all, "/")
  .serve.compile.drain.unsafeRunSync()
```

Under the hood, HTTP4S relies on the other library for server-side programming, that is, the Blaze library. As we have already mentioned, the infrastructure for server-side programming involves a wide range of various libraries, so the gist to capture here is the big picture of how server-side programming is done.

We are calling several configuration methods on the BlazeBuilder object. The bindHttp method specifies which host and port we are going to listen to. In this case, the host is set to localhost or 0.0.0.0, and the port is set to 8888.

Next, we define the handlers that the server will use. This is done by the mountService method. In this case, we bind a single handler, all, to the root path of this server. The all handler is a handler we are about to define.

When we are done configuring the server, we will call the serve method on it. The method returns a Stream which is a member of another library that is a part of the Cats infrastructure. The library is called FS2 (for Functional Streams) and is a dedicated library for working with Streams in a functional way. The Stream is lazily evaluated, and in order to run it under IO, we are going to run the compile and drain methods on this Stream. The gist of this method is that it is going to run a lazy, side-effecting Stream, under the effects type of IO. The IO is returned from the drain method. Next, we run the IO using the unsafeRunSync method.

So, as you can see, quite a lot of libraries are involved in bootstrapping an HTTP server in functional programming. However, the central idea is the same across all of these libraries. They all leverage the same effect type, IO, and they all subscribe to the idea of lazily evaluated, referentially transparent computations as values. This means that no computation is run by default; they all are stored as descriptions of computations. Since every library has its own domain, some libraries might have their own language to describe their computations. However, these domain-specific languages are ultimately translated into the single, low-level IO language.

If you are interested in understanding what is going on here in more detail, the best way to do so is to examine the Scala API documentation for the libraries that we have mentioned. Examining the methods that you are calling, the types that they are returning, and understanding the meaning of the methods and the types in question can get you a long way in understanding what is going on inside this library.

Next, we will take a look at how the handlers for the web server are defined.

The all handler is defined as follows:

```
def all = (
    createCustomer
```

```
    <+> placeOrder
    <+> listOrders
    <+> listGoods)
```

This is a combination of several other handlers. The technique to be noted here is composability. So, we are capable of composing the other handlers with the help of the composition operator.

The composition in question is an `or` composition, which means that incoming requests will be checked against every handler specified by the composition operator in turn. The first handler that is capable of handling the request will be used. The individual handlers that compose the whole `all` handler are as follows:

```
def createCustomer = HttpService[IO] {
  case req @ POST -> Root / "customer" =>
    for {
      reqBody <- req.as[Customer]
      id <- db.customer.create(reqBody)
      resp <- Ok(success(id.toString))
    } yield resp
}
```

We will create our new customer handler with the help of the `HttpService` object. The method we are calling is defined as follows:

```
def apply[F[_]](pf: PartialFunction[Request[F], F[Response[F]]])(implicit F:
    Applicative[F]): HttpService[F]
```

Lifts a partial function to an **HttpService**. Responds with **OptionT.none** for any request where **pf** is not defined.

It takes a partial function that maps a request to a response under an effect type `F`. A request contains what you would expect a request to have. Here is a definition and some of the API methods that it exposes:

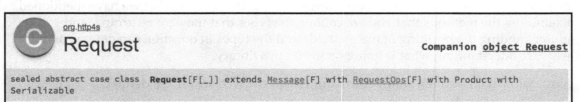

```
org.http4s
```
Request

Companion **object Request**

```
sealed abstract case class Request[F[_]] extends Message[F] with RequestOps[F] with Product with
Serializable
```

It exposes the following API:

```
Type Members

            type Self = Request[F]


Value Members

    final def addCookie(name: String, content: String, expires: Option[HttpDate] = None)(implicit F:
              Functor[F]): Self
              Add a Cookie header with the provided values

    final def addCookie(cookie: Cookie)(implicit F: Functor[F]): Self
              Add a Cookie header for the provided Cookie

    final def as[T](implicit F: FlatMap[F], decoder: EntityDecoder[F, T]): F[T]
              Decode the Message to the specified type

          def attemptAs[T](implicit F: FlatMap[F], decoder: EntityDecoder[F, T]): DecodeResult[F, T]
              Decode the Message to the specified type

          val attributes: AttributeMap


      lazy val authType: Option[AuthScheme]


          val body: EntityBody[F]
```

The partial function passed into the request returns a response under an effect type. Currently, the only supported effect type is IO. The fact that it returns the response under an effect type means that the server is built with asynchrony in mind.

A handler constructed this way will match any incoming request against the partial function.

The `HttpService` constructed by the call is defined as follows:

```
def apply[F[_]](pf: PartialFunction[Request[F], F[Response[F]]])(implicit F:
    Applicative[F]): HttpService[F]
    Lifts a partial function to an HttpService.
```

It is an alias for the `Kleisli` type. `Kleisli` is a part of the `cats` core library and is defined as follows:

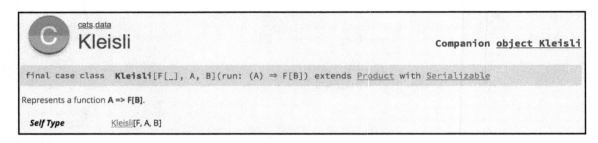

So, essentially, it is nothing more than a function you would pass to, say, the `flatMap` method. It is a function of the following kind:

```
A ⇒ F[B]
```

The partial function we are using to construct the handler does a few things here. First of all, notice that there's a DSL to conveniently extract the HTTP method and a path from the request. These extractors come from the `HTTP4S` API and can be used to match on requests conveniently.

Next, we are starting a Monadic flow over IO:

```
reqBody <- req.as[Customer]
```

The `as` call is supposed to extract the `Customer` object from the incoming request body. The assumption is made that the body is a valid JSON string, and the `Circe` library will be used under the hood to convert the incoming request body to the requested data type. You do not need to perform any other specifications of how exactly a JSON must be converted to a case class, as `Circe` defines how to do that under the hood.

The next thing that we do is we create a customer in the database. We are using the database access object that we defined previously in this section to do this. As a result, we get the ID of a newly created customer.

Finally, we construct the response to our query:

```
resp <- Ok(success(id.toString))
```

We are using the call to the `Ok` method to define the `Ok` response code `200`. `Ok` is defined as follows:

```
val Ok: Status
```

`Status` is an abstract class that does not have an `apply` method, which is necessary for the object to be callable. So, we should not be able to call it. The reason we are able to call it in our program is because the method is injected into the `Ok` object via the following Rich Wrapper:

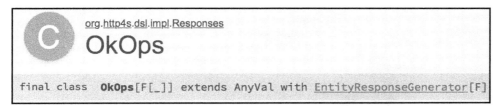

org.http4s.dsl.impl.Responses
OkOps

```
final class OkOps[F[_]] extends AnyVal with EntityResponseGenerator[F]
```

It exposes the following API:

Instance Constructors

        `new OkOps(status: Ok.type)`

Value Members

        `def apply[A](body: A, headers: Header*)(implicit F: Monad[F], w: EntityEncoder[F, A]): F[Response[F]]`

        `def apply(headers: Header*)(implicit F: Applicative[F]): F[Response[F]]`

        `def getClass(): Class[_ <: AnyVal]`

        `val status: Ok.type`

This wrapper is parametrized by an effect type under which the response is computed and returned. Currently, `HTTP4S` only supports the IO effect type, but this is not a problem since all of the other libraries of Typelevel infrastructure also speak the language of IO.

Notice that we specify a `payload` for the response. It is specified with the `success` method, which is defined as follows:

```
def success[T](payload: T): Map[String, T] =
  Map("success" -> payload)
```

So, the payload is set to an ordinary Scala, `Map[String, Int]` (Int is inferred because the argument to `success` is an integer). Since we are using `Circe`, this Scala collection will be automatically encoded into JSON and returned to the requesting client. Again, this is provided out of the box at no additional cost.

Next, the `placeOrder` handler is defined as follows:

```
def placeOrder = HttpService[IO] {
  case req @ POST -> Root / "order" =>
    for {
      cookieHeader <-
        headers.Cookie.from(req.headers).map(IO.pure).getOrElse(
          IO.raiseError(noAuthCookieError))
      jsonBody <- req.as[Map[String, Int]]
      cookie <- cookieHeader.values.toList
        .find(_.name == "shop_customer_id").map(IO.pure).getOrElse(
          IO.raiseError(noAuthCookieError))
      uId = cookie.content

      oId <- db.order.create(Order(good = jsonBody("good"), customer =
uId.toInt))
      order <- db.order.get(oId)
      resp <- Ok(success(order))
    } yield resp
}
```

It largely uses the functionality that we have already discussed. However, a few remarks should be made:

```
cookieHeader <-
  headers.Cookie.from(req.headers).map(IO.pure).getOrElse(
    IO.raiseError(noAuthCookieError))
```

First of all, HTTP4S provides the capability to extract various parameters from requests, such as cookies. In the preceding code, we extract the cookie header from all of the request headers. If the operation was not successful, we would raise an error via an IO method. Essentially, rising an error from IO gets the entire Monadic flow short-circuited. This is similar to throwing an exception from imperative code, except that the IO effect type will take care of error handling:

```
jsonBody <- req.as[Map[String, Int]]
```

In the preceding line, notice how we are able to extract the JSON body of the incoming request as a Scala map. So, not only the primitive types and case classes are supported by Circe, but also the Scala collection types. Circe automatically derives encoders and decoders for JSON on compile time:

```
resp <- Ok(success(order))
```

Notice that the preceding response sets the entire case class as its payload. We are returning a case class that's nested inside a Scala map. Circe is able to encode this data structure into JSON seamlessly.

Finally, two list handlers are defined as follows:

```
def listOrders = HttpService[IO] {
  case req @ GET -> Root / "order" =>
    db.order.list.flatMap(Ok(_))
}

def listGoods = HttpService[IO] {
  case req @ GET -> Root / "good" =>
    db.good.list.flatMap(Ok(_))
}
```

Since our database returns the result in IO and since we are using Circe to encode the model objects into JSON automatically, we can flatMap the response from the database to wrap it into the response status code. We are able to specify this entire handler as a thin wrapper on top of a database access method in just one line.

Querying the server

In the example repository, there is a shell script that you can use to query the server once you start it. You can start the server with the following command from the SBT console:

```
reStart
```

Notice that this command must be run under the Docker image. So, it will not work if you just run an SBT console on your machine from the example repository; you will need first to run the Docker image, then run the command from the SBT console that is started on that Docker image.

After that, you can use the client shell script to query the database server. For example, we can create the new customer as follows:

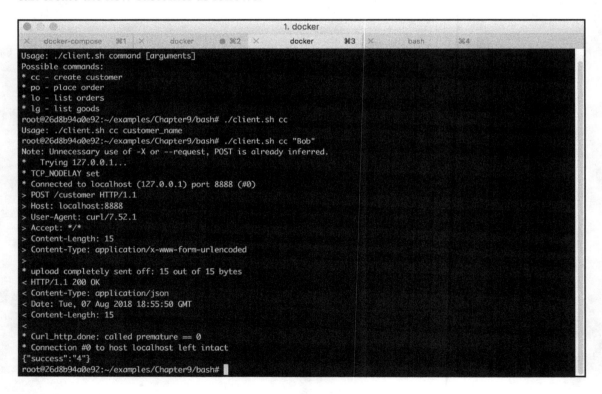

Notice how the response is a nicely formatted JSON with an ID of the created customer.

Next, we can list all of the goods that are present in the database so that we can place an order:

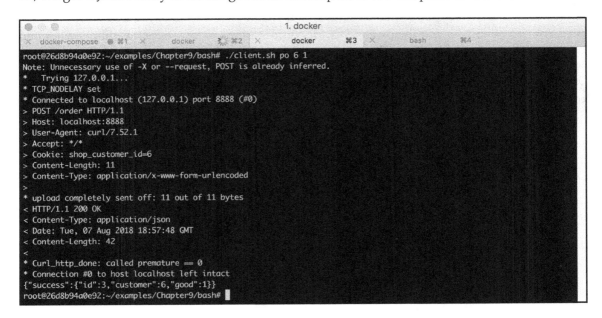

So, we got a JSON array of all the goods as the response. We can place an order as follows:

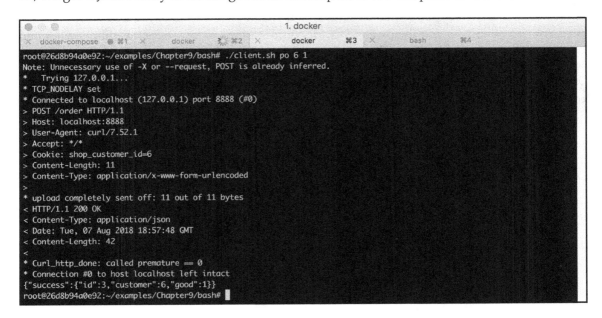

And finally, we can list all of the orders to confirm that we have the order in the database:

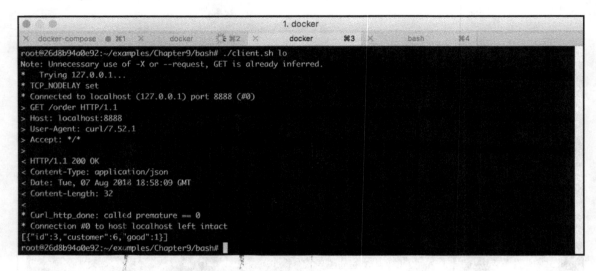

Summary

In this chapter, we have covered the broad infrastructure that the Typelevel umbrella of libraries provides for purely functional programming. First, we learned the foundation for asynchronous programming with Cats, that is, the Cats effect library. We discussed the IO concurrency primitive and the philosophy of computations as values. After that, we learned the foundations for the server-side programming, which involves a range of libraries. The libraries in question were responsible for HTTP request handling and database access, while utilizing a JSON conversion library under the hood. We have had a birds-eye overview of what programming with these may look like.

By now, we have covered enough of material for us to start writing industrial software in a purely functional way. In the next chapter, we will see more advanced patterns of functional programming. These patterns will help our architectures solve broader range of problems and make them more flexible.

Questions

1. Explain the difference between blocking and non-blocking programming.
2. Why is asynchronous programming mandatory for high-load systems?
3. How does computation as a value approach benefit concurrent programming?
4. What is an IO effect type?
5. What capabilities for asynchronous programming does IO expose?

10
Patterns of Advanced Functional Programming

We are probably already familiar with the concept of patterns from object-oriented programming. Patterns are common solutions to common problems. Whenever you have a problem that repeats from project to project, solutions also tend to repeat. Similar problems are solved similarly. And hence, such solutions become patterns that are widely accepted.

Functional programming also has its own patterns. Since it has certain problems and challenges unique to it, it will also have unique solutions. In this chapter, we will discuss solutions to common functional programming problems.

In this chapter, we will cover the following topics:

- Monad Transformers
- Tagless Final
- Type-level programming

Monad Transformers

Monad Transformers is an important pattern of purely functional programming that allows us to combine effect types. Let's now discuss it in detail.

The specialization of effect types

We've discussed how effect types are ubiquitous in purely functional programming and are used in order to abstract away side effects. You may have also noticed that these types are highly specialized, which means we have almost one-to-one mapping between side effects and effect types. For example, the ability of an application to return null is represented by an `Option` side effect type. `Option` is good for such null situations. However, it does not perform well when tasked with modeling errors and exceptions. This is because it does not preserve the information of the nature of the failure.

A data type that is good for modeling erroneous computation that can fail is `Either`. However, if you try to model a computation that returns null with `Either`, you will find that this data type is redundant for these purposes. This is because whenever you have a computation that does not return a value, you will still need to return something from it. In the erroneous scenario, we could have done the following:

```
def foo(x: Int): Option[Int] =
  if (x < 0) None
  else Some(math.sqrt(x))
```

However, what do you return in the same scenario with `Either`? If the correct result is to be modeled by `Right`, we should model an empty result with `Left`:

```
def foo(x: Int): Either[???, Int] =
  if (x < 0) Left(???)
  else Right(math.sqrt(x))
```

However, `Left` is also supposed to contain a value. What do we return in `Left`? Our best bet would be to return a string that explicitly says that the computation did not produce any result:

```
def foo(x: Int): Either[String, Int] =
  if (x < 0) Left("Can't take square root of a negative value")
  else Right(math.sqrt(x))
```

As you can see, this usage of `Either` is rather contrived in this example. This means we have a situation where side effects are fine-grained, and every side effect has its own representing effect type. This is a natural situation for Scala, as for any strongly-typed language. The finer your type system matches the side effects, the more side effects you can model out of the box.

This also means that when we have more than one side effect, we need to think about how are we going to present and combine them.

An application with multiple side effects

Modern applications aim for asynchrony. This means that whenever you need to compute anything, and it may take a long time, you do not compute it in a synchronous manner. That is, you do not wait for the computation to produce a result. Instead, you program in a non-blocking style. This means that you schedule computations to run at some point in the future and wait for the result.

Asynchrony

Consider an example of a web server tasked with handling incoming HTTP requests in a setting of a web application that manages an online forum. Consider that the requests in question are to be responded to with the data about all of the forum posts present in the database. This means that in order to reply to any given HTTP request, we first need to obtain the required data from the database. The solution may look as follows:

```
def handle(request: Request): Response = {
  val posts: List[Post] = allPosts()
  respond(posts)
}
```

In the preceding example, the types and methods are declared as follows:

```
type Request
type Response
type Post

def allPosts(): List[Post]

def respond[A](a: A): Response
```

However, this is not the only task that our application needs to do. Consider also that our forum is private, which means we need to authenticate a user prior to giving them access to the forum.

Nowadays, a popular way to authenticate is to use a cloud solution for authentication. This means that people do not implement the authentication mechanism themselves on the server side, but outsource it to some provider. Such a mechanism is known as **Authentication as a Service (AaaS)**. A number of companies provide out-of-the-box services that you can use in your application to authenticate. There are many benefits to the approach since you do not need to waste your time implementing authentication logic, and it can include not only password authentication, but also social authentications and fancy security mechanisms such as two-factor authentication.

However, if we are using a cloud-based solution for our authentication, this means that we most likely need to contact the cloud every time a user tries to log in. Modern authentication methods, such as JWT, imply a stateless authentication. It is possible to produce a JSON tag that the user can pass to a server, and the server can verify its authenticity using a cryptography mechanism. So you do not need to keep a state to authenticate a person. However, even in this scenario, you are most likely going to need to contact your cloud-based authentication platform to obtain keys that you are using as well as to verify that the user is indeed present in their databases.

How is all of the this relevant to our functional programming example? The thing to notice here is that we need to contact the web. The operation of contacting the cloud is a long-running one. For the time being, let's assume this operation is done in a synchronous manner, as follows:

```
def handle(request: Request): Response = {
  val userToken: Token = request.token
  val authenticated: Boolean = authenticate(userToken)

  if (authenticated) {
    val posts: List[Post] = allPosts()
    respond(posts)
  }
  else respond("You are not authorized to perform this action")
}
```

The following declarations were added to our environment:

```
type Token
type Request <: { def token: Token }

def authenticate(token: Token): Boolean
```

In the preceding code snippet, we ask the cloud-based authentication service whether the user is authorized to perform the action, and if they are, we reply with the forum post.

Imagine the preceding server under a high load. Immediately, questions arise about the number of threads that can be used in handling the HTTP request. Also, a question arises about how fast a web server can handle any given request. Imagine we have four threads on the task. Imagine also that it takes roughly one second to handle a given request as there is latency involved in contacting the database and the cloud-based authentication service. How much of a load can a server tolerate?

If the load is more than four requests per second, the server will start running out of threads. Imagine the server handles four requests simultaneously. This means that all of its four threads that are allocated for handling HTTP requests will be busy for one second. Consequently, the server will not be able to handle further requests until it handles those four requests. This means that if, for example, five requests arrive at the same time, the first four of them will be handled in one second, and the fifth one will take two seconds to handle. This is because it will not be started until the first four requests are handled.

The threads that handle this request do not really do anything the majority of the time. During the first call to the cloud authentication solution, the majority of the handling time is waiting to receive a reply from the server. And when it subsequently calls a database, that majority of the time it waits for the database to reply. If the thread spends the majority of its time waiting for the replies, this means that the processor does not do anything useful, that it has some free power and free capacity to work on some other tasks, such as maybe handling the other incoming requests.

This reasoning is precisely why the synchronous way of handling is not desirable in applications that are designed for high loads. An alternative is an asynchronous approach. In the asynchronous approach, whenever you have a long-running computation, you dispatch it to a thread pool using an asynchronous primitive, for example, a Future. And then, you specify what to do once the task is completed. The trick in an asynchronous application is to build it from asynchronous primitives that do not block. So, for example, the act of requesting information from the database should not involve blocking or waiting for a response, even on a thread within a future. The point is that the thread that makes a request is free to do other tasks once the request is made and it has nothing else to do.

The point is to utilize a non-blocking API to perform HTTP requests and requests to the database so that your threads, which are quite heavyweight primitives in the Java world, do not block and do not wait for responses and are not wasted, rather, they should do something useful.

An application handler in an asynchronous style would look as follows:

```
def allPosts(): Future[List[Post]]

def authenticate(token: Token): Future[Boolean]

def handle(request: Request): Future[Response] =
  for {
    authenticated <- authenticate(request.token)
    response <-
```

```
        if (authenticated) allPosts.map(respond)
        else Future { respond("You are not authorized to perform this
        action") }
    } yield response
```

It still takes about one second for a single request to get handled, because the delay that you experience once requesting external resources still exists. However, now the server will perform much better under high loads. This is because the threads themselves do not wait this entire one second on a single request. Instead, for them, the only time that counts is the time when they actually do the job, and not the time they wait on the external resource to reply to them.

So, for example, if the real processing time of a given request, meaning the time the thread is actually doing the work and not waiting for a reply, constitutes 10 milliseconds, then a single thread is capable of accepting and handling 100 requests per second.

The preceding discussion describes why you might need the side effect of asynchrony and programming with callbacks in practice. And asynchrony is a side effect that you might want to hide behind some primitives, such as a future.

However, asynchrony is not the only side effect that you might want to abstract away in the case of writing an HTTP handler. Another side effect that you might want to abstract is the side effect of an error. Now, let's discuss this side effect in detail.

The side effect of errors

In the preceding example, we saw that thing do not always go smoothly. Things can go wrong on multiple levels. So when we connect to the cloud authentication service, the connection itself may go wrong. For example, the server reply times out. Or, your application credentials are wrong and you do not end up accessing the feature of the cloud authentication service that you would like to access.

When contacting the database, things can also go wrong. For example, you may fail to establish a connection with the database. Or, for some reason, the data is not present in the database or is not in the correct format.

Finally, the business logic of the application allows for an error. This one happens when the person making the request to the server is not authorized to view the data they request. In such a situation, we will need to reply with an error message instead of the data they requested:

```
if (authenticated) allPosts.map(respond)
else Future { respond("You are not authorized to perform this action") }
```

All of the cases discussed here are a clear evidence that we have a side effect of an error here as a potential. Normally, we would abstract away this side effect into an effect type. Then, we'd use the `flatMap` function in order to combine these computations. However, we already have one effect type, `Future`, that abstracts away the asynchronous nature of request-handling. How do we introduce another side effect here?

First of all, a note should be made that `Future` itself provides a capability for error reporting. However, this is a detail specific to the Future's implementation. It is perfectly possible to imagine asynchronous primitives that provide you with the abstraction of asynchrony but do not catch the errors that happen inside them. So here, we will be viewing the situation as if the Future does not provide the capability of error-handling.

A naive way to handle that scenario would be to make the computation return a `Future` of an `Either` of a result. So, for example, the query to the database and the cloud service would look as follows:

```
def allPosts(): Future[Either[String, List[Post]]]

def authenticate(token: Token): Future[Either[String, Boolean]]
```

In the preceding code, we stack the side effects one on top of another. Will that work in practice? In principle, it is possible to imagine a computation that returns an `Either` under a `Future`. Let's have a look at how we will be using it in combination with other complications. Previously, we used the `flatMap` function to combine the computations sequentially. How would such a combination look in the case of nested side effects?

```
for {
  authenticated <- authenticate(request.token)
  response <-
    if (authenticated) allPosts.map(respond)
    else Future { Left("You are not authorized to perform this action") }
} yield response
```

The preceding code does not compile. The error is as follows:

```
                                   1. java
sbt:jvm> compile
[info] Compiling 1 Scala source to /Users/anatolii/Projects/1mastering-funprog/Chapter10/jvm/target/scala-2.12/classes .
..
[error] /Users/anatolii/Projects/1mastering-funprog/Chapter10/jvm/src/main/scala/jvm/HttpServer.scala:72:13: type mismat
ch;
[error]   found    : Either[String,Boolean]
[error]   required: Boolean
[error]         if (authenticated) allPosts.map(respond)
[error]            ^
[warn] /Users/anatolii/Projects/1mastering-funprog/Chapter10/jvm/src/main/scala/jvm/HttpServer.scala:8:13: Unused import
[warn] import cats._, cats.implicits._, cats.data._
[warn]             ^
[warn] one warning found
[error] one error found
[error] (compile:compileIncremental) Compilation failed
[error] Total time: 4 s, completed Aug 29, 2018 6:06:25 PM
sbt:jvm>
```

As you can see, the compiler says that we are using `Either` in position where `Boolean` is expected. So `authenticated` variable in the snippet above is `Either` instead of `Boolean`. However, why would we be working on `Either` under the Monadic flow? Is that not a purpose of Monadic flow to abstract away the effect types so that we are able to deal with the computed values directly without having to worry about the effect types?

Actually, we can rewrite the preceding example in terms of `flatMap` for better readability:

```
authenticate(request.token).flatMap { authenticated =>
  if (authenticated) allPosts.map(respond)
  else Future { Left("You are not authorized to perform this action") }
}
```

Let's now check the signatures and types of all the values involved. First, let's check the type that we are calling `flatMap` on, `Future[Either[/*...*/]]`. After, we are working with the result as if it were the user object retrieved from the cloud authentication service. However, let's take another look at the signature of `flatMap` as defined by `Future`:

```
def flatMap[S](f: (T) => Future[S])(implicit executor: ExecutionContext):
    Future[S]
```

Creates a new future by applying a function to the successful result of this future, and returns the result of the function as the new future. If this future is completed with an exception then the new future will also contain this exception.

Example:

```
val f = Future { 5 }
val g = Future { 3 }
val h = for {
  x: Int <- f // returns Future(5)
  y: Int <- g // returns Future(3)
} yield x + y
```

is translated to:

```
f flatMap { (x: Int) => g map { (y: Int) => x + y } }
```

S	the type of the returned **Future**
f	the function which will be applied to the successful result of this **Future**
returns	a **Future** which will be completed with the result of the application of the function

So the function already has a familiar signature: `A => Future[B]`. What is `A`? It is the type parameter of `Future`. What is the type parameter of our particular `Future`? This type parameter is `Either[String, User]`.

That means that `flatMap` does not give us the user object, but `Either`. Using this information, we can alter the example:

```
def handle(request: Request): Future[Either[String, Response]] =
  authenticate(request.token).flatMap {
    case Right(authenticated) if authenticated =>
      allPosts.map { eitherPosts =>
        eitherPosts.map(respond)
      }

    case Right(authenticated) if !authenticated =>
      Future { Left("You are not authorized to perform this action") }

    case Left(error) => Future(Left(error))
  }
```

Here, we manually extract the result value from Either. Immediately, we can say that something is very wrong and needs to be corrected. The feeling of something wrong arises because previously we have discussed that the very point of having Monadic flows and the flatMap function is to abstract away effect types. Yet here, we need to work with them explicitly.

Monad Transformers

The problem here is that the flatMap function is defined on the Future. It knows nothing about the type parameter of Future. This can be anything you can imagine. Implementation does not place any constraints on the type parameter. It also means that it knows nothing about this type signature and its properties. Hence, neither the Monad nor the Future default implementation of flatMap for Future is aware of the possibility that the type parameter to Future will be another effect type. So, when you stack our effect types in the manner discussed earlier, only the topmost effect type gets abstracted when we are using the flatMap function.

This behavior is unnatural. We didn't get what we expected. What did we expect to get? We expected that not only would the side effect be unwrapped, but its inner side effect would also be unwrapped.

When we have nested effect types, and when we expect them to be treated as one effect, we need Monad Transformers.

Monad Transformers is actually a pattern that can be used to define stackable versions of already-existing effect types. For example, let's have a look at how such a Monad Transformer is defined for the Either type in the cats library:

cats.data
EitherT

Companion **object EitherT**

```
final case class  EitherT[F[_], A, B](value: F[Either[A, B]]) extends Product with
Serializable
```

Transformer for **Either**, allowing the effect of an arbitrary type constructor **F** to be combined with the fail-fast effect of **Either**.

EitherT[F, A, B] wraps a value of type **F[Either[A, B]]**. An **F[C]** can be lifted in to **EitherT[F, A, C]** via **EitherT.right**, and lifted in to a **EitherT[F, C, B]** via **EitherT.left**.

Let's have a look at the signature of this Monad Transformer to understand what it is. First of all, notice the type parameters of this case class. Instead of the usual two type parameters of an ordinary `Either`, we have three type parameters. The first parameter is an `F[_]` effect type, and the last two parameters are ordinary left and right types. That effect type is precisely what gives this Monad Transformer its stackability. So, we can stack it with other effect types by pumping these effect types into the type variable. Notice also the argument to the constructor of `EitherT`. The argument in question has the `F[Either[A, B]]` type.

Let's imagine that the variable effect type in the preceding example is `Future`. Then, the value of `EitherT` will be `Future[Either[A, B]]`. This is precisely the signature that we had in our preceding examples when we were trying to stack these two effects types.

So the pattern essentially builds up on top of the naive stacking of effect types. However, here we have a case class defined specifically for stacking. How does it work, and how does it allow us to combine effect types?

First of all, let's have a look at how the `flatMap` function is defined by this data type:

```
def flatMap[AA >: A, D](f: (B) ⇒ EitherT[F, AA, D])(implicit F: Monad[F]):
    EitherT[F, AA, D]
```

As we can see in the preceding screenshot, the method takes the continuation function as an argument, which is something we already know. However, pay attention to the first argument of the continuation function. It is `B` here. `B` is the type of the `Right` value of `Either`. `Either` is wrapped under the `F` type. So, if we are going to use `EitherT` instead of a naive combination of `Future` and `Either`, we are going to end up with a `flatMap` function that does exactly what we are looking for.

However, also notice that this function implicitly depends on a Monad for the side effect type. Which means that in order to extract the result from `EitherT`, we need to know how to extract the result from the effect type you are combining it with:

```
def flatMap[AA >: A, D](f: B => EitherT[F, AA, D])(implicit F: Monad[F]):
EitherT[F, AA, D] =
  EitherT(F.flatMap(value) {
    case l @ Left(_) => F.pure(l.rightCast)
    case Right(b) => f(b).value
  })
```

So, arming ourselves with `EitherT`, let's rewrite the previous example:

```
def handle(request: Request): EitherT[Future, String, Response] =
  for {
    authenticated <- authenticate(request.token)
      .ensure("You are not authorized to perform this action")(identity)
    posts <- allPosts()
    response = respond(posts)
  } yield response
```

As you can see, we now have all of our computations defined in terms of the combined effects types. Also, we are able to leave our Monadic flow unchanged, meaning that we do not need to worry about extracting the results of our side effecting computations manually.

If you have a look at the `EitherT` documentation, you will see that it also provides you with a bunch of other convenience methods that you can use in the setting of nested effect types.

Generalizing the pattern

Obviously, the pattern we discussed previously is not specific to `EitherT`. It is something we are frequently going to encounter when dealing with effect types. It is not about `Future` and `Either`, but about combining two independent types.

Since this task repeats from effect type to effect type, it was generalized into a pattern. The pattern goes as follows. First, you pick up an effect type that you would like to be combinable with other arbitrary effect types. Then, you define the alternative combinable version of this type. This way, for `Either`, we have defined a combinable version of it, `EitherT`.

After that, you define all of the necessary type classes of the given effect type, optionally depending on whatever you need to make it work, including the type classes for the effect type you are going to combine this effect with.

If you have a look at the data package of the cats library, you will find that it has a number of other effects ending with the letter `T`. These are implementations of Monad Transformers for the respective effect types.

The significance of having Monad Transformers in your toolbox is that now you are able to construct effect types from existing effect types like you would from Lego blocks. This greatly increases your flexibility; now you do not need to define dedicated effect types that would express the side effects you would like to capture. If these side effects are expressible as a combination of several other side effects, you can use Transformers to create a combined effect type and use it in your applications.

We were observing the combination of two effect types. But, you are not limited to the combination of only two effects. In fact, the pattern is sufficient to combine any number of effect types into one. For example, this is how such a combination might look:

```
type Config
type Ef[A] = ReaderT[EitherT[Future, String, ?], Config, A]
```

Since `ReaderT` expects an effect type, `F[_]`, as its first argument, we manually make a **hole** in `EitherT` by the means of the question mark—`EitherT[Future, String, ?]`. The syntax is not standard to Scala and comes from the Kind Projector plugin that is imported in the project's `build.sbt`:

```
addCompilerPlugin("org.spire-math" %% "kind-projector" % "0.9.4")
```

The `?` in the type signature creates an unbound type variable in a type signature, which can be used to give the type the shape of `F[_]`.

`ReaderT[EitherT[Future, String, ?], Config, A]` is a Transformer way to express the following type:

```
Config => Future[Either[String, A]]
```

So, when talking about the Monad Transformers pattern, first and foremost we are talking about flexibility. However, this is not the only pattern that can provide you with extra flexibility when writing your programs in a purely functional manner. Next, we will have a look at the Tagless Final.

Tagless Final

Tagless Final is a popular pattern of advanced functional programming that can be used to abstract away capabilities and side effects you do not know ahead of time and cannot predict. As usual, the best way to see how it works and why it is useful is to look at some examples.

Programming to capabilities

Imagine you are writing an application that is to be executed against more than one environment. Such scenarios are common in the real world. A good example is mobile applications. You can have multiple mobile platforms. However, you would like to publish your applications to all of them. The platforms that exist are quite different from each another. And usually, it is pretty tedious to reimplement your application for every platform separately. So, you would like to write our application once, and somehow make it run against all of the platforms that currently exist.

Another example is programming server-side software that should work against a wide variety of configurations. For example, the same server-side software is executed against different databases. Relational databases are different, and procedures that are applicable to one database may not be applicable to another database.

In all of the preceding scenarios, you wanted your application's business logic not to be affected by the peculiarities of the system you are running your code on. In object-oriented programming, a standard way to tackle such an issue is to apply a Facade pattern. You declare an interface that lists all of the capabilities that you need from the underlying system your application is supposed to be run against. After that, for every specific system, you are going to provide an implementation of the interface.

The key points to notice from this discussion are the capabilities. Your application depends on some capabilities. It is built in terms of the methods exposed by the interface that specifies the capabilities in question. This idea also reiterates in the Tagless Final pattern.

To make it easier to understand the pattern, let's come up with a simple example of an application depending on some capabilities. The first one would be to read a resource from the data storage of a system. A resource is a wide notion that may include files on one filesystem, access to data over the network on other environments, or access to data that is stored in a database and other environments. Another capability will be the notification capability, which means the application is able to notify the end user of whatever job it is doing with the data retrieved from the storage.

Given these two capabilities, it is possible to write a wide range of processing applications. Once we have abstracted away the effects of reading and notifying, we can build a processing application in terms of these effects.

How would we define such capabilities in a functional manner? What would make the most sense? Previously, we discussed the idea of a type class. We have also noted that a type class is very similar to a toolbox, which means it provides you with a set of tools that you can use for a certain purpose. That analogy is ideal for our case of storing capabilities. Capabilities are also, in a sense, tools, and tools can be united into toolboxes. So, it is conceivable to define a type class with the capabilities we need as follows:

```
trait Capabilities[F[_]] {
  def resource[A](name: String): F[A]
  def notify(target: String, text: String): F[Unit]
}
```

Notice that we define the type class for an f effect type. Since we are working in the functional paradigm, and the capabilities are likely to produce side effects, we are going to describe these side effects by some effect type that we may not know ahead of time.

Next, we can define an application in terms of these capabilities provided by the type class. Imagine the resources that we are going to retrieve with the help of our capabilities are reports of the sales of some online shopping:

```
Name,Price
Bread,2
Butter,4
Cabbage,3
Water,2
```

Consider that this document is updated every day, and the objective of our application is to calculate the amount of money the business has made over the day and to notify the owner about the income. We can implement it as follows:

```
def income[F[_]](implicit M: Monad[F], C: Capabilities[F]): F[Unit] =
  for {
    contents <- C.resource("sales.csv")
    total = contents
      .split("\n").toList.tail // Collection of lines, drop the CSV header
      .map { _.split(",").toList match // List[Double] - prices of each
       of the entries
        { case name :: price :: Nil => price.toDouble }
      }
      .sum
    _ <- C.notify("admin@shop.com", s"Total income made today: $total")
  } yield ()
```

Notice how the preceding method is defined in terms of the F effect type and its subclasses. Notice how we do not know ahead of time which effect type we are going to use here. However, we know exactly which capabilities this effect type must have—the capabilities that we defined earlier, but we also need a Monad. This is because we need to sequentially combine capabilities defined in our custom type class. Then, we define our application in terms of our capabilities.

An important thing to notice here is how our capabilities become defined in the same language as the other type classes. This means that, potentially, we have the entire power of the cats library or any other libraries for functional programming.

This is what makes the Tagless Final pattern different from the Facade pattern. In Facade, you have the interfaces that hide the complex functionality that is platform-specific and that you do not care about. However, this is it. Whenever we call such a capability, we get the result you are requesting and nothing else.

In the Tagless Final pattern, whenever you are calling a capability method, you are getting a result under an effect type. An effect type is a data structure that has certain properties. You may not have control over exactly what result the capability returns because it is system-specific. However, you have control over the data structure in which this result is returned. The data structure in question is specified by the type parameter. Different data structures have different capabilities. In other functions, when we specified that we implicitly needed a Monad, we stated something about the structure we are going to work under. We can state that our effect type is to be sequentially composable. In the same way, by specifying implicit dependencies on other cats type classes, we can state other requirements of our data structure.

This control over the data structure we are working under gives us control over how we can compose our computation. So, in the Facade pattern, only the platform-specific capabilities themselves get abstracted away, and that's it. However, in the Tagless Final pattern, not only do the computations get abstracted away, but the way we compose our program gets abstracted away under the f effect type.

Now, once we have the abstract program composed, a reasonable question to ask would be how do we actually run it against different environments?

Implementations

In order to run this application against a given environment, we need to specify the effect type we are going to be working under. Besides the target effect type, we need to find the implementation for all of the implicit dependencies that our function requires. The beauty of the Tagless Final pattern is that we can run the function against any environment, as long as we can provide the implementation of our implicit dependencies for this environment and for the effect type of our choice.

The first step is to specify the effect type. A good choice would be Future, since it is a concurrency primitive, and capable of representing a wide range of computations. So, with the effect type set to Future, we will have our method called as follows:

```
import scala.concurrent.{ Future, Await }
import scala.concurrent.ExecutionContext.Implicits.global
import scala.concurrent.duration.Duration

import cats._, cats.implicits._

/*...*/
Await.result(income[Future], Duration.Inf) // Block so that the application
does not exit prematurely
```

However, the preceding code will not compile since we do not yet have an implementation of the `Capabilities` type class for Future.

Now when we are talking about the capabilities we need, we need to ask ourselves against which environment we are working in. Remember that the capabilities abstract the operations that are different from environment to environment. First, let's imagine we are working against an ordinary desktop environment and a command-line application scenario. In this case, our retrieve resource capability would be simply reading a file with a given name from a standard directory. Our notification capability will print the output to the command line:

```
implicit val capabilities: Capabilities[Future] = new Capabilities[Future]
{
  import java.io.File
  import org.apache.commons.io.FileUtils

  def resource(name: String): Future[String] =
    Future { FileUtils.readFileToString(new File(name)) }

  def notify(target: String, text: String): Future[Unit] =
    Future { println(s"Notifying $target: $text") }
}
```

We are using an Apache Commons IO library to read a file, conveniently. We are doing everything under the concurrency primitive future because this is the requirement of our application. Notice how all the technical details of notifying and reading the file are concentrated in that type class only, to the point where we can import the `File` and `FileUtils` classes only in the scope of this type class and not the scope of the entire file.

Once we run the preceding application against the given file, we are going to receive the following output:

```
Notifying admin@shop.com: Total income made today: 11.0
```

What if we now need to run the application against an environment that uses a database to store the data? What if that notification is done via email and not via the command line? No problem, we still can use the same application. However, we will need to provide a custom implementation of the capabilities for this environment:

```
implicit val anotherEnvironmentCapabilities: Capabilities[Future] = new
Capabilities[Future] {
  def resource(name: String): Future[String] = ???
  def notify(target: String, text: String): Future[Unit] = ???
}
```

In the preceding code, we have implemented a type class in terms of stubs, because implementing the database query logic and an email notification logic can be pretty tedious. However, our application now compiles. So, if you substitute the implementation of the database query and email dispatch in the preceding type class, you will also be able to run the application successfully. Since this implementation is outside the scope of this book and does not bring any value to the discussion of the Tagless Final pattern, we will not provide the implementation here.

In a similar manner, we are able to provide the implementation for almost any platform that you can imagine.

You can also do the preceding really well with the Facade pattern. So how is Tagless Final more powerful than the Facade pattern? Why would you use it instead of the object-oriented pattern? The crucial detail in discussing the power of the Tagless Final pattern is to notice that our application depends not only on the capabilities type class but also on the Monad type class. So how does that bring more power than a Facade pattern? Let's have a look at it.

Execution semantics abstraction

The capabilities type class is on equal ground with the `Monad` type class. The `Monad` type class defines how you would compose the computation sequentially. There is a saying that Monad is the semicolon of functional programming. Why would people say that? What is the role of a semicolon in object-oriented programming? In ordinary imperative programming, a semicolon is a symbol that separates one statement from another. The meaning of a semicolon is that one statement should be executed after another statement. In a sense, you can treat a semicolon as an operator of the sequential combination of two computation.

The `flatMap` function does exactly that for the functional programming world. `flatMap` defines how to sequentially composed two computations. So, this makes it a semicolon of functional programming. Also, earlier in the book, we looked at the Monadic flow pattern. We know that Monadic flow relies on `flatMap` under the hood to represent the functional code that is composed sequentially. In this way, it is very similar to the imperative semicolons.

How is that important for our discussion of the advantage of the Tagless Final pattern? The point is that an application that depends on Facade does not usually depend on any anything similar to a Monad.

This means that you may substitute a different Facade in your application for different environments. However, you will never be able to change the semantics of the sequential execution of your statements.

Let's see how it works on an example. Let's say that we need to perform logging while executing the preceding application. What do we do to make it possible? We can provide a custom implementation of Monad with its `flatMap` function, the sequential composition operator, been overloaded to log everything we need:

```
implicit val logMonad: Monad[Future] = new Monad[Future] {
  def flatMap[A, B](fa: Future[A])(f: (A) ⇒ Future[B]): Future[B] =
    fa.flatMap { x =>
      println(s"Trace of the Future's result: $x")
      f(x) }
```

You can run the application by pointing the income method explicitly to which type classes to use:

```
Await.result(income[Future](logMonad, capabilities), Duration.Inf) // Block
so that the application does not exit prematurely
```

And the output will be as follows:

```
                                    1. java
[warn] Multiple main classes detected.  Run 'show discoveredMainClasses' to see the list

Multiple main classes detected, select one to run:

 [1] jvm.HListSum
 [2] jvm.ListSum
 [3] jvm.TaglessFinalExample

Enter number: 3

[info] Application root not yet started
[info] Starting application root in the background ...
root Starting jvm.TaglessFinalExample.main()
[success] Total time: 2 s, completed Jul 26, 2018 4:25:37 PM
sbt:jvm> root Trace of the Future's result: Name,Price
root Bread,2
root Butter,4
root Cabbage,3
root Water,2
root
root Trace of the Future's result: (Name,Price
root Bread,2
root Butter,4
root Cabbage,3
root Water,2
root ,11.0)
root Notifying admin@shop.com: Total income made today: 11.0
root Trace of the Future's result: ()
root ... finished with exit code 0
```

Here, we are able to overload the very semantics of sequential composition.

Can a similar effect be achieved in the imperative world? Let's have a look at how the preceding example could be implemented with the Facade pattern:

```
trait Capabilities {
  def resource(name: String): String
  def notify(target: String, text: String): Unit
}

def income(c: Capabilities): Unit = {
  val contents = c.resource("sales.csv")
  val total = contents
    .split("\n").toList.tail // Collection of lines, drop the CSV header
    .map { _.split(",").toList match // List[Double] - prices of each of
the entries
      { case name :: price :: Nil => price.toDouble }
    }
    .sum
  c.notify("admin@shop.com", s"Total income made today: $total")
}
```

In the preceding code, we have an interface, and the method `income` depends on the type class that performs the computation.

We are not able to override sequential composition, because the only point of control is the interface. We do not have control over how the computations are executed and combined with one another.

But why is that possible in the functional world and not in the imperative world? What makes the functional approach so special that we are able to do this kind of abstraction of combinational semantics?

Computation as a value

When discussing side effects and abstraction, we argued that functional programming aims for purity. And whenever we have some computation that has a side effect, we are reifying this computation into some value. Here, the value is `Future`. All our computations are reified into Future. And we are able to combine `Future` using the operators defined for it.

In the imperative world, we are not able to perform the similar combination of computations, since the computations are not reified to values. We are not able to play around with computations in the imperative world because computations are not a thing there. There is no way for us to refer to a computation. At least no obvious way. Of course, in Java, we can stuff the computation under the Runnable interface. However, it will be quite cumbersome. In the functional world, Monads are ubiquitous in sequential composition. Everything is composed using `flatMap`. In Java, wrapping everything in Runnable would introduce too much architectural overhead, so it is not worth it.

However, one might argue that Futures are not pure. Whenever we instantiate Future, we give an instruction for a computation to start. Is there an even stronger version of the Tagless Final pattern that provides us with some more expressive power?

Free Monad

The Free Monad pattern is a stronger version of the Tagless Final pattern. Actually, the free object is a structure from abstract algebra. Hence the name comes from this domain.

The application of the pattern is rather limited, and most likely we will not encounter any real necessity for the pattern while only starting purely functional programming. So we will not go in depth about the Free Monad here. However, we will describe in general how it works.

Basically, the idea behind the Free Monad is that all of our computations become a value. The idea is that whenever we define our application, it does not really execute itself, but constructs an abstract syntax tree that describes the application that we can run later. And it is our responsibility to execute it afterward.

The pattern is quite heavyweight, so the preceding example offers only the gist of it. Another thing to notice is that whenever we need to apply the Free Monad pattern, we can still leverage the Tagless Final pattern. Here, we saw how defining a custom implementation for the Monad can be helpful to inject custom functionality, such as logging. The same idea can be used to construct a tree out of our application. Ordinarily, the meaning of the sequential composition is to run one statement after another. It is easy to imagine an implementation of the sequential composition where the statements are not executed one after another but are reified into tree nodes and get injected into a tree that represents your application. Remember that `flatMap` has full control over how it continues the computation. So it is perfectly normal to imagine a `flatMap` function that does not run statements but uses them to construct a tree.

Why might we want to use the Free Monad pattern? The idea here is to be able to run the computation against more than one interpreter. A concrete example comes from the `doobie` library for working with SQL. In Doobie, a SQL statement can be written as follows:

```
sql"""select * from customers where id = $id""")
```

Here, we are using string interpolation, a feature of Scala that allows us to generate objects from strings on compile-time.

After executing this statement, we will perform several calls on the object specifying what we want to do with the SQL statement, such as whether we want to query or update the database. For example, if we want to query the database, we can do the following:

```
sql"""select * from customers where id = $id""")
  .query[User].unique.transact(tr)
```

One common task when working with SQL from programming languages is to provide as much safety as possible while calling the database. For example, we might want to answer the question of whether our query is formed correctly. We might want to have an entire test suite where we have all of our queries that we are using, and we test them to check whether they are formed correctly and whether their return types are the ones that we expect.

Internally, Doobie represents its SQL queries with free objects, which means that they are just data structures that specify the computation to be performed against a database. Since it is just a description of the computation and not the computation itself, we can either run it or do anything else with it. One of the things that we might want to do is to check whether it is correct against certain rules. This is done in Doobie. Here, we can either run our queries against an interpreter that will query the database, or that will check their correctness.

So basically, in such situation when we have a computation that we might want to run against different interpreters, or we might want to pass around and modify by other computational, we might want to use a Free Monad.

A word of caution should be said as the pattern is heavyweight, it should not be used without a good reason, or else the overhead in terms of architecture will be pretty high.

Speaking of the safety of your application, you can achieve a high grade of safety and stability if you perform as many computations as possible at compile-time. The very basics of programming to type classes is having a strong compiler with a strong type system that is capable of injecting proper type classes for you. Can such a strong compiler be harnessed to perform more than just injecting capabilities and type classes into your computations? Let's step into the world of type-level programming in the next section.

Type-level programming

The job of the compiler is to translate your program from one set of instructions into another. In high-level languages, you translate higher-level instructions that are easy to read and write for people to lower-level instructions that are easy for machines to execute.

Since the compiler needs to perform a conversion of one set of symbols into another set of symbols, it builds some internal model of the program that you are writing. In a sense, we can say that the compiler understands the program, for some definition of **understands**.

If the compiler builds an internal model or understands your program in some other way, we can also harness the power of compiler to make the compiler check for the correctness of the program. We can make the compiler impose and enforce certain styles or guarantees that your program must obey. We have already seen an example of `annotation.tailrec`. The job of the annotation was to instruct the compiler to check the annotated function to have certain guarantees about it. Concretely, the compiler checked the function to be tail-recursive.

To ensure correctness of your program, we may well use a strongly typed language, and encode the guarantees and the semantics of your program in types. The types are known to the compilers, and hence, it can perform certain checks on these types. For example, it can make sure that you supplied an argument of the correct type to a function because it knows the input type of the function. So, in a strongly-typed language, no longer can you make the mistake of passing an argument of the wrong type to a function.

The advantage of having strong compilers that check the program for mistakes is that you are able to catch more errors at compile-time. In general, errors that are caught at compile-time are much easier to debug and fix. If an error happens at runtime, it means that it is not discovered right away. You may release your application to the end user, and for particularly tricky bugs, months and even years can pass before they are discovered. Once they are discovered, you need to investigate the erroneous behavior yourself throughout the codebase and try to reproduce it so that you can fix it.

Compile-time errors are manifested right away. When you compile the code, you see exactly how and where you went wrong. So there is an obvious advantage to making sure the compiler can catch as many errors as possible.

Can we push our compiler even further? Let's have a look at an example of the type-level programming in Scala. It is called type-level because we aim to encode as many guarantees about our program as possible in the types. This way, these guarantees are checked at compile-time.

A naive implementation of the heterogeneous list

Consider that we have the following list:

```
val list: List[Any] = List(0, 2.0, "3", Fraction(4, 2))
```

So, in the preceding list, we have elements of different types, and hence we are forced to declare this list as List[Any]. Fraction is defined for the purpose of our example as follows:

```
case class Fraction(numerator: Int, denominator: Int)
```

Notice that in the preceding list, each element can be represented as a floating-point number. They have different types, but it is possible to define certain common behavior on all of these types. Since the elements are very similar to each other, we might want to perform a common operation on them. For example, we may want to find the sum of all the numbers in the list:

```
val sum = list.map {
  case x: Int => x.toDouble
  case x: Double => x
  case x: String => x.toDouble
  case Fraction(n, d) => n / d.toDouble
}.sum
```

Notice that we are not able to sum all elements right away because the type of the list is
List [Any]. We can only add up a list composed of numbers. Hence, we map our list so
that it becomes List [Double]. After that, we call the same method on this list, which is a
standard method defined for all numeric collections defined by the Scala collections
framework.

In the screenshot below, we can see the output of the program:

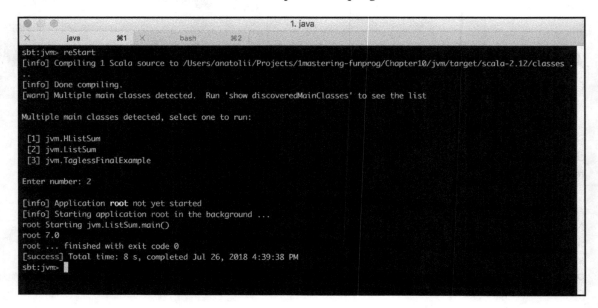

However, notice the body of the map method. The body of the map method is actually a
partial function. A partial function is a function that is not guaranteed to be able to handle
an entire domain on which it is defined. Let's look at the signature of the map function, as
follows:

```
final def map[B](f: (A) ⇒ B): List[B]
        [use case]
        Builds a new collection by applying a function to all elements of this list.

        B           the element type of the returned collection.
        f           the function to apply to each element.
        returns     a new list resulting from applying the given function f to each element of this list
                    and collecting the results.
```

In the preceding screenshot, you can see that it expects a function from the type of the elements of the list to some other type, B. The type of our elements is any. However, the function that we have passed to our function is a partial function, meaning that it is only capable of handling a subset of all possible object in Scala.

That problem with partial functions is that they are computed at runtime. This means, if you forget to specify a certain clause in the partial function, you will not find out about that until the runtime when the application will throw a match error signifying that the partial function was not able to handle its input. Let's simulate this situation:

```scala
val sum = list.map {
  case x: Int => x.toDouble
  case x: Double => x
  case x: String => x.toDouble
  // case Fraction(n, d) => n / d.toDouble
}.sum
```

We have commented out one of the `case` clauses of our partial function that we used to map the list. What happens if we run this application? See the following:

```
                                    1. java
  ×      java        ⌘1   ×      bash      ⌘2

Multiple main classes detected, select one to run:

[1] jvm.HListSum
[2] jvm.ListSum
[3] jvm.TaglessFinalExample

Enter number: 2

[info] Application root not yet started
[info] Starting application root in the background ...
root Starting jvm.ListSum.main()
[success] Total time: 6 s, completed Jul 26, 2018 4:40:43 PM
sbt:jvm> root[ERROR] Exception in thread "main" scala.MatchError: Fraction(4,2) (of class jvm.Fraction)
root[ERROR]    at jvm.ListSum$.$anonfun$sum$1(HListSum.scala:10)
root[ERROR]    at jvm.ListSum$.$anonfun$sum$1$adapted(HListSum.scala:7)
root[ERROR]    at scala.collection.immutable.List.map(List.scala:287)
root[ERROR]    at jvm.ListSum$.delayedEndpoint$jvm$ListSum$1(HListSum.scala:7)
root[ERROR]    at jvm.ListSum$delayedInit$body.apply(HListSum.scala:5)
root[ERROR]    at scala.Function0.apply$mcV$sp(Function0.scala:34)
root[ERROR]    at scala.Function0.apply$mcV$sp$(Function0.scala:34)
root[ERROR]    at scala.runtime.AbstractFunction0.apply$mcV$sp(AbstractFunction0.scala:12)
root[ERROR]    at scala.App.$anonfun$main$1$adapted(App.scala:76)
root[ERROR]    at scala.collection.immutable.List.foreach(List.scala:389)
root[ERROR]    at scala.App.main(App.scala:76)
root[ERROR]    at scala.App.main$(App.scala:74)
root[ERROR]    at jvm.ListSum$.main(HListSum.scala:5)
root[ERROR]    at jvm.ListSum.main(HListSum.scala)
root ... finished with exit code 1
```

As you can see, an exception was thrown. The program was compiled successfully, however, when we tried to run it, we had an exception. This means something went wrong at runtime. Is there a way to make the compiler track these kinds of errors, and handle them at compile-time?

Type-level solution to the heterogeneous list problem

The strategy for solving this problem is to encode the guarantees that we want to have in types. We will leverage the highly-developed mechanism of implicit resolution to enforce that guarantee on a certain type. The general idea is to have a guarantee presented by an implicit value. And if we need a certain guarantee about our program, we make our program implicitly depend on the value that represents this guarantee.

The catch is that the application will not compile if the compiler does not find any of the implicits the program depends on. So, by making the program depend on the implicits that represent our guarantees, and making sure these values are present in scope only if the guarantee is satisfied, we can make sure is that the compiler will not compile a program that does not satisfy this guarantees.

However, first of all, we need types. The preceding solution of a `List[Any]` is not good for our application because the compiler does not have the information about the precise types of the elements of the list. Instead, we can define a data structure called a heterogeneous list. The code for this new list is as follows:

```
package jvm
/*...*/
sealed trait HList {
  def :::[H](h: H): H ::: this.type = jvm.:::(h, this)
}
case class :::[+H, +T <: HList](head: H, tail: T) extends HList {
  override def toString() = s"$head ::: $tail"
}
trait HNil extends HList
case object HNil extends HNil
```

Above, `jvm` is a package under which the JVM examples of this book are implemented.

A heterogeneous list is a recursive data structure. If you have a look at the `:::` value, this `case` class is composed of a head and a tail. The head can be anything you like, and the tail must be another instance of the heterogeneous list. The terminal case of the recursive data type is `HNil`.

Here is how we can define such a list in your application:

```
val hlist: String ::: Int ::: Fraction ::: HNil =
  "1" ::: 2 ::: Fraction(3, 4) ::: HNil
```

Notice how this list is aware of the types of each of its arguments. Also, notice how in Scala, we can leverage the infix notation that allows us to use names of types as operators. Take a look at the following type:

```
String ::: Int ::: Fraction ::: HNil
```

It is equivalent to the following standard notation:

```
:::[String, :::[Int, :::[Fraction, HNil]]]
```

This is syntactic sugar to facilitate so-called algebraic data types. Algebraic data types are data types that are composed of other data types in a type-safe manner.

Next, how would we define an application that will compute a sum on a heterogeneous list? Previously, in a partial function example, we saw that another problem was compile-time safety. And here, we would like to include certain guarantees into our code. We want the compiler to check these guarantees. What guarantees would you like to impose? First of all, we need to make sure that our list can be mapped to a list where everything is a double. Previously, we did it using a partial function that is only run on the runtime. Here, we have agreed to use implicit to specify the guarantees about our application. Hence, we can have our summation method as follows:

```
def sumSimple[L <: HList](hlist: L)(implicit m: MapToDouble[L]): Double
```

`MapToDouble` is a type class that we have just come up with. The job of the type class is to convert a heterogeneous list so that all of its elements are doubles. Notice that we pass a type parameter to this type class. It is the `L` type, which extends the heterogeneous list. `L` extends the heterogeneous list and is an algebraic data type, which means it is a composite data type that is composed of the types of all of the elements of this list. This means that at compile-time, the type class will be aware of the types of all the elements present in this heterogeneous list, which means it is possible to define the type class so that we will not be able to resolve it if the members of the list are not convertible to double.

Are those all the guarantees we need? In principle, once we have a guarantee and a way to convert our heterogeneous list to a list of doubles, it may not be difficult to traverse the data structure recursively and sum up all of its values. So, the summation method using the `MapToDouble` type class only can be implemented as follows:

```
def sumSimple[L <: HList](hlist: L)(implicit m: MapToDouble[L]): Double = {
  val mapped: m.Result = m.map(hlist)
```

```
def loop(l: HList): Double = l match {
  case :::(h: Double, t) => h + loop(t)
  case HNil => 0
}
loop(mapped)
}
```

Notice that we again are using a partial function to abstract the values from the recursive data structure of the heterogeneous list. We terminate our or question once we reach `HNil`. However, we have argued previously that partial functions are bad because they can fail at runtime. Therefore, it can be instructive to see how we can avoid usage of a partial function here.

So, let's introduce a new type class responsible for computing a sum on a heterogeneous list. We can do so as follows:

```
def sum[L <: HList, LR <: HList](hlist: L)(implicit m: MapToDouble.Aux[L,
LR], s: Sum[LR]): Double =
  s.sum(m.map(hlist))
```

So, we make our mapping capability and summation capability outsourced to the type classes we have just discussed. However, what is `Aux` at the end of the `MapToDouble` type class all about? Also, what is that new `LR` type parameter added to the type of the sum function?

Basically, `LR` is the type of this list mapped to by `MapToDouble`. So, for our list of the following type:

```
String ::: Int ::: Fraction ::: HNil
```

This type will be as follows:

```
Double ::: Double ::: Double ::: HNil
```

In the preceding code, you can see the auxiliary pattern. The entire point of it is that we do not know the `LR` type variable and rely on the Scala compiler to compute it. Compiler computes the `LR` type is by means of implicitly resolving the `MapToDouble` type class. The big picture is that the Scala compiler is able to leverage the implicit mechanism to compute entire types and store the result in a type argument variable, and then, we can reuse it in the implicit resolution of other type classes. So, we are using this type computed by the auxiliary mechanism to resolve the `Sum` type class.

Why do we need to compute the HList type if we know ahead of time that all of its elements are doubles? We may know the type of the elements, but we still need the compiler's help to know how many doubles to stack into the resulting HList. Remember that HList stores the type of every element, so if we say that all of the elements are doubles, we still need to know the length of the list to construct it. Here, the compiler is able to help us with this task.

So how exactly does the auxiliary pattern work and how exactly is the compiler capable of computing new types? To answer this question, let's proceed to the definition of our type classes. Let's start with the MapToDouble type class:

```
trait MapToDouble[L <: HList] {
  type Result <: HList
  def map(l: L): Result
}
```

Notice that the type class has two members. The first is the Result type, which represents the result type of mapping a given heterogeneous list so that all of its members are doubles. Then, we have the method that performs map in itself. Notice also that MapToDouble has only one type parameter, L.

The Result type is an abstract type, which means it is up to implementations of the type class to define it. We'll see in a moment how to leverage this ability to compute the result type.

The catch is that, technically, the result type is not reflected in the type of the type class. Which means, whenever we need this type class, for some L type, we can resolve it as follows:

```
type L = String ::: Int ::: Fraction ::: HNil
val mapper: MapToDouble[L] = implicitly[MapToDouble[L]]
```

In the preceding code, the implicit method is defined as follows:

```
def implicitly[T](implicit e: T): T

Annotations          @inline()
```

So basically, the method is a utility to resolve an implicit value of a certain type.

Notice that when we request the implicit dependency on this type class, we do not specify the result type, which means we are not required to know this type when we resolve their implicit dependency. Now, imagine that you had your type class defined as follows:

```
trait MapToDoubleNoAux[L <: HList, Result <: HList] {
  def map(l: L): Result
}
```

Now, with the preceding type class defined, we are no longer able to resolve it without knowing the result it is going to compute. Indeed, we have no other way to refer to this type class but as follows:

```
type In = String ::: Int ::: Fraction ::: HNil
type Out = Double ::: Double ::: Double ::: HNil
val mapper: MapToDoubleNoAux[In, Out] = implicitly[MapToDoubleNoAux[In,
Out]]
```

Since the type class has two type arguments, we must to provide it with both of them. We might know the first type argument, however, because it is present in our program, in the type of our `HList`. The type of our heterogeneous list is constructed for us by the compiler when we construct the list itself. However, the result of the conversion of this list to a list of doubles is not currently known to the compiler. And we must provide it to resolve the implicit dependency. Hence, we are forced to compute it ourselves.

Is there a way to make the compiler compute that, similarly to how it computes the type of the list when you construct it? For this, we have the Aux pattern.

The auxiliary pattern looks as follows:

```
object MapToDouble {
  type Aux[L <: HList, LR <: HList] = MapToDouble[L] { type Result = LR }
  /*...*/
}
```

So, it is nothing more than a type definition inside the companion object of our type class. Notice that here we are using structural types to define our auxiliary type. The preceding program says that the Aux type of is `MapToDouble`, whose body will contain a type member of `Result` set to a certain type variable.

The catch is that we still are able to capture both of the type variables that are significant to us, the input and output types, in a single `Aux` type. However, when we are trying to resolve the type class implicitly, we are no longer obliged to know both of the types.

And so, we can implicitly depend on the `Aux` type, and the compiler resolves this type without the knowledge of the second type parameter:

```
def sum[L <: HList, LR <: HList](hlist: L)(implicit m: MapToDouble.Aux[L,
LR], s: Sum[LR]): Double
```

Instead, the resolution will go as follows in this case:

1. The compiler will infer the first type parameter, `L`. It will infer it by looking at the input argument. So, you do not need to provide it explicitly.
2. It will start the implicit resolution. First, we need `MapToDouble.Aux`. This type expands to the `MapToDouble[L] { type Result = LR }` type.
3. The compiler will interpret this as a command to resolve the `MapToDouble` type, whose first type argument must be `L`. The second type parameter of the `Aux` type is unknown, but it is not a problem, because, as we have discussed previously, the compiler does not need it to resolve the type class. However, this second type parameter has a name and is bound to a certain type, which is a member of the type class we are about to resolve. The compiler will, therefore, infer this second type parameter from the `Result` type of `MapToDouble`.
4. After this type class is resolved, we now have the `LR` type parameter. We can now use it as an input to the next implicit resolution—that of `Sum[LR]`.

The reason the preceding logic works, and that the compiler does not need the second type parameter, `LR`, of `MapToDouble.Aux` is as follows. The type of the type `MapToDouble` does not include the second type parameter `LR`, and `MapToDouble.Aux` is an alias for `MapToDouble`. The type `L`, which is a type parameter to `MapToDouble`, is all that the compiler needs to resolve the type class. If you think about it, when resolving something implicitly, or specifying a type of some variable, you do not need to explicitly specify the members of this variable. Since the second type parameter is a member of an object to be resolved, we do not need to know it when resolving our type.

The Aux pattern is used to capture the types that are structural members of type classes into type arguments that can be referred to from the implicit group of a method signature.

So basically, it is all about having the types that we do not know on call-time as structural members of the type classes, not the type parameters of these type classes. This way, the types that we will not know ourselves and will need to be computed will not be members of the signature the type signature of the type class. And hence, we can resolve these type classes without knowing their member types. So, we can compute these types on implicit-resolution time, leveraging algebraic data types principle. We will see how exactly we can compute these types using the mechanism of implicit resolution in the following code snippet.

This is how the function that we have just defined can be applied to a heterogeneous list:

```
val s = sum(hlist)
println(s"Sum of $hlist is $s")
```

The output of running the program is as follows:

Sum of 1 ::: 2 ::: Fraction(3,4) ::: HNil is 3.75

Next, let's have a look at how the implicit mechanism resolves all of the dependencies we need.

Reclusive implicit resolution

Let's get a big picture understanding of what the members of the `MapToDouble` companion object look like:

```
object MapToDouble {
  type Aux[L <: HList, LR <: HList] = MapToDouble[L] { type Result = LR }
  def apply[L <: HList](implicit m: MapToDouble[L]) = m

  implicit def hcons[H, T <: HList, TR <: HList](implicit
    td: ToDouble[H]
  , md: MapToDouble.Aux[T, TR]
  ): Aux[H ::: T, Double ::: TR]

  implicit def hnil[H <: HNil]: MapToDouble.Aux[H, HNil]
}
```

So as you can see, we have an Aux type, and `apply` function definitions, which are common for the type class pattern. Also, we have two implicit members, which define implementations for the `MapToDouble` type class for `hlist`. Since there are two possible instances of `hlist`, we have two possible implementations of MapToDouble, both for `:::` and `HNil`.

Notice the implicit dependencies that these two implicit values have. First of all, `hnil` does not depend on anything. Let's have a look at its body:

```
implicit def hnil[H <: HNil]: MapToDouble.Aux[H, HNil] = new MapToDouble[H]
{

  type Result = HNil
  def map(h: H) = HNil
}
```

The result of mapping an empty heterogeneous list is just another empty heterogeneous list. This is because we do not have anything to map.

hcons, however, has implicit dependencies. As you can see in the preceding example, it implicitly depends on two other type classes: ToDouble and MapToDouble. As you can see, ToDouble is parametrized by the H type. The H type is the head type of our heterogeneous list. Any heterogeneous list is defined in terms of its head type and its tail type only.

The meaning of all these implicit dependencies is that we are able to convert any heterogeneous list that is not empty to a list of doubles if we are able to convert its head to double, and if we are able to map its tail to a list of doubles. The definition of the ToDouble type class is as follows:

```
trait ToDouble[T] {
  def toDouble(t: T): Double
}
```

One critical thing to notice about these implicit dependencies is that they are recursive. hcons itself is of the MapToDouble.Aux type. But in order to generate this MapToDouble, we need to also have MapToDouble for the tail of the heterogeneous list in question.

Since the Scala compiler is capable of resolving implicit dependencies recursively, we are able to make an implicit dependency of one type depend recursively on the implicit dependency of the same type. The only thing to watch out for here, as with any other recursion, is for it to be able to terminate. This means, on every step of recursion, we must get closer, in some defined sense, to the terminal case of this recursion. That terminal case of recursion in our case is HNil. And with every step, we resolve the MapToDouble type class for a heterogeneous list that is one element shorter than the previous list because we take only the tail without the head. This guarantees that recursion will terminate.

Now, let's have a look at the implementation of hcons:

```
implicit def hcons[H, T <: HList, TR <: HList](implicit
  td: ToDouble[H]
, md: MapToDouble.Aux[T, TR]
): Aux[H ::: T, Double ::: TR] = new MapToDouble[H ::: T] {

  type Result = Double ::: TR
  def map(l: H ::: T): Double ::: TR =
    td.toDouble(l.head) ::: md.map(l.tail)
}
```

The body of the map function is defined in terms of the `ToDouble` type class that converts the head to double, and then uses the `MapToDouble` type class in order to convert the tail to double.

In a similar fashion, we can define the `Sum` type class that we will be using in order to compute the sum of the heterogeneous list with all doubles:

```
trait Sum[L] {
  def sum(l: L): Double
}

object Sum {
  def apply[L <: HList](implicit s: Sum[L]) = s

  implicit def hcons[T <: HList](implicit st: Sum[T]): Sum[Double ::: T] =
    { (l: Double ::: T) => l.head + st.sum(l.tail) }

  implicit def hnil[H <: HNil]: Sum[H] =
    { (x: HNil) => 0 }
}
```

In the companion object, we also have two cases of recursive implicit resolution—one terminal and one non-terminal case. The terminal case is `hnil`, and the non-terminal case is `hcons`. The terminal case is simple because if we take an empty list, its sum is always 0 because there are no elements in this list. However, if we have a non-empty list, our ability to compute its sum depends on our ability to compute the sum of its tail. If we are able to compute the sum of its tail, as notified by its implicit dependency, we can compute the sum of the tail, and add the value of the head to it.

Finally, the last piece that we have not yet discussed is the implementation of the `ToDouble` type class:

```
trait ToDouble[T] {
  def toDouble(t: T): Double
}

object ToDouble {
  def apply[T](implicit t: ToDouble[T]) = t

  implicit def double: ToDouble[Double] = identity
  implicit def int : ToDouble[Int ] = _.toDouble
  implicit def string: ToDouble[String] = _.toDouble

  implicit def fraction: ToDouble[Fraction] =
    f => f.numerator / f.denominator.toDouble
}
```

As we can see, the `ToDouble` type class is implemented for every type that we are going to use in practice.

What are the benefits of using the type class approach and the type-level computations instead of simply doing a recursive pattern-matching using a recursive function? The answer is compile-time safety. Remember how at the beginning of this chapter, we argued that in case of recursive pattern-matching when we forgot to perform a pattern match on a single instance, we only found out about our mistake on runtime? Let's have a look at what happens if we fail to specify one case in the situation of type-level computations.

The equivalent of pattern-matching for the type-level computation scenario are the `ToDouble` type class implementations. If you have a look at them, they specify how exactly to convert every type. Let's have a look at what happens if you comment out one of the implementations that we need:

```
implicit def double: ToDouble[Double] = identity
implicit def int : ToDouble[Int ] = _.toDouble
implicit def string: ToDouble[String] = _.toDouble

// implicit def fraction: ToDouble[Fraction] =
//   f => f.numerator / f.denominator.toDouble
```

Now let's have a look at what happens when we run the program:

```
sbt:jvm> reStart
[info] Compiling 1 Scala source to /Users/anatolii/Projects/1mastering-funprog/Chapter10/jvm/target/scala-2.12/classes .
..
[error] /Users/anatolii/Projects/1mastering-funprog/Chapter10/jvm/src/main/scala/jvm/HListSum.scala:32:14: could not fin
d implicit value for parameter m: jvm.MapToDouble.Aux[String ::: Int ::: jvm.Fraction ::: jvm.HNil,LR]
[error]    val s = sum(hlist)
[error]            ^
[error] one error found
[error] (compile:compileIncremental) Compilation failed
[error] Total time: 1 s, completed Jul 26, 2018 5:11:10 PM
sbt:jvm> 
```

The error is a compile-time error this time, so the application did not even compile. However, notice also that the error message is rather cryptic and hard to read. Next, we will have a look at how you can debug this kind of compile-time message. Type-level computations give rise to an entirely new style of programming in advanced languages such as Scala, so it is imperative that you know how to work with the compile-time errors in this setting.

Debugging type-level computations

Currently, type-level computations represent the leading edge of modern programming technology. The technology is rather experimental, and hence, it still does not have much support in terms of comprehensive error messages and tools for debugging.

So, the preceding error message can be debugged step by step by leveraging algebraic data types. This means that you trace every step of recursion, and make sure that every implicit during every step is resolved correctly. At some point, you come to the place where the resolution produces errors, and then you can see which case produces an error.

These checks can be done with `implicitly` keyword in Scala. The process of debugging with the `implicitly` function may look as follows:

```
implicitly[MapToDouble[String ::: Int ::: Fraction ::: HNil]]
implicitly[MapToDouble[Int ::: Fraction ::: HNil]]
implicitly[MapToDouble[Fraction ::: HNil]]
implicitly[ToDouble[Fraction]]
```

The output of the preceding program's compilation will be as follows:

```
                                    1. java
  ×      java      ⌘1  ×      bash      ⌘2
sbt:jvm> reStart
[info] Compiling 1 Scala source to /Users/anatolii/Projects/1mastering-funprog/Chapter10/jvm/target/scala-2.12/classes .
..
[error] /Users/anatolii/Projects/1mastering-funprog/Chapter10/jvm/src/main/scala/jvm/HListSum.scala:32:13: could not fin
d implicit value for parameter e: jvm.MapToDouble[String ::: Int ::: jvm.Fraction ::: jvm.HNil]
[error]    implicitly[MapToDouble[String ::: Int ::: Fraction ::: HNil]]
[error]              ^
[error] /Users/anatolii/Projects/1mastering-funprog/Chapter10/jvm/src/main/scala/jvm/HListSum.scala:33:13: could not fin
d implicit value for parameter e: jvm.MapToDouble[Int ::: jvm.Fraction ::: jvm.HNil]
[error]    implicitly[MapToDouble[Int ::: Fraction ::: HNil]]
[error]              ^
[error] /Users/anatolii/Projects/1mastering-funprog/Chapter10/jvm/src/main/scala/jvm/HListSum.scala:34:13: could not fin
d implicit value for parameter e: jvm.MapToDouble[jvm.Fraction ::: jvm.HNil]
[error]    implicitly[MapToDouble[Fraction ::: HNil]]
[error]              ^
[error] /Users/anatolii/Projects/1mastering-funprog/Chapter10/jvm/src/main/scala/jvm/HListSum.scala:35:13: could not fin
d implicit value for parameter e: jvm.ToDouble[jvm.Fraction]
[error]    implicitly[ToDouble[Fraction]]
[error]              ^
[error] four errors found
[error] (compile:compileIncremental) Compilation failed
[error] Total time: 0 s, completed Jul 26, 2018 5:13:54 PM
sbt:jvm> 
```

So, the error is caused because the compiler is not able to find the implicit `ToDouble` type class for Fraction. Notice how with each statement, we gradually shrink the search space by reducing the size of our `HList` algebraic type. At each step, we are looking at whether the error will manifest itself. Finally, we arrive at `implicitly[ToDouble[Fraction]]`, and realize there is no such implicit type-class implementation in scope. Notice also that all the preceding errors happen at compile-time.

The current state of affairs for the type-level computations may be not as good as you might want in Scala. However, you should keep in mind that the technology is still experimental. Scala itself is a language that is a playground for experimenting with new technologies. So, the main catch is the power of this new technology to bring the runtime errors in the scope of compile-time by leveraging the power of the type system and implicit resolution to specify certain guarantees about your program in terms of types. In Future, it is reasonable to expect that such kinds of technologies will get better tooling as they become more widely adopted.

Libraries for type-level programming

As in the case of cats being a library for purely functional programming in Scala, there exist libraries that facilitate type-level programming in Scala. One such library is `Shapeless`. In fact, `Shapeless` is a part of the same ecosystem of libraries as `cats`. It provides a set of classes and types, including the heterogeneous list type, that facilitate some advanced purely functional programming on the type level.

This approach deserves its own book, so we will not be going much deeper into it in this chapter. If you would like to learn more about this approach, please consult the official documentation and learning resources on `Shapeless`.

Summary

In this chapter, we learned about the patterns of advanced functional programming.

First, we looked at Monad Transformers. These are used to construct compound effect types. Given two independent effect types that describe their own side effects, you can stack them one on top of another to get a combined type from them.

After that, we explored the Tagless Final pattern. The main benefit is inversion of control when you can have a single implementation of your business logic run against different effects systems to gain different semantics.

Finally, we learned about a pattern of type-level computations in functional programming. The main benefit of these is that they allow you to impose guarantees on your program encoded in terms of types, and have these guarantees checked at compile-time. This checking can be achieved with the mechanism of type-level computational, such as Scala implicit-conversion resolution, or any similar mechanisms that allows for type-level programming.

The techniques for purely functional programming covered so far are powerful and promising, but are not yet widely accepted in the industry. The current de facto standard for concurrent programming is the actor model. In the next chapters, we will look at it. We will start with introduction of the model in the next chapter.

Questions

1. Explain the benefits of Monad Transformers.
2. Explain the benefits of the Tagless Final pattern.
3. Explain the benefits of type-level computations.

Introduction to the Actor Model 11

In the previous chapter, we the discussed patterns and techniques of advanced functional programming in modern programming languages. However, you may have noticed that we were always dealing with cases of sequential programming. The closest that we have ever gotten to real parallelism was when we discussed the Applicative type class.

In this chapter, we will go deeper into the topic of modern functional solutions for parallelism. The following are the topics that we will be covering in this chapter:

- Overview of parallelism solutions
- Traditional model synchronization on monitors
- The actor model as a replacement for the traditional model

Overview of parallelism solutions

If you remember, the Applicative type class gives us an abstraction to define parallel computations. It was set against the `Monad` class, which is an abstraction to define sequential computational.

In the *Type Classes* section in `Chapter 8`, *Basic Type Classes and Their Usage*, we reasoned that Applicatives are needed to provide you with a primitive to define independent computational. Parallelism can also be modeled by the Applicative. However, it is precisely the idea of independence for motivating force behind this type class.

Parallelism and concurrency require a different approach. They give rise to problems that are not normally encountered in sequential programming, and these problems have their own techniques so that they can be solved in object-oriented programming. However, these techniques are even more error-prone and hard to reason about than regular object-oriented and imperative programming. Hence, a bunch of other techniques were devised in order to simplify the process of developing concurrent software.

So far, we still cannot say that we have an ideal approach to parallel and concurrent programming. Whenever concurrency is involved, programming gets much more difficult than in a single-threaded case, even in the case of the use of the most modern techniques and approaches. Modern systems tend to be distributed, and there is a high demand on the scalability of such systems. This means that in the modern world, it is often the case that a single application must run on several machines that can be located in different parts of the world. Also, there is a requirement on the scalability of such systems. Scalability means that whenever you add extra processing power, such as extra machines to the cluster, the existing program must run seamlessly on these new machines without you needing to write extra programming code. Basically, scalability means that software must run on any number of machines as well as it does on a single machine.

Obviously, in such scenarios, chaos is inevitable. So far, we do not have a single solution to the issues that arise in the context of distributed fault-tolerant and highly available systems. Attempts were made to create approaches and mathematical theories that address this issue in the 20th century. Here, we are talking primarily about a class of mathematical theories called process calculi. Process calculi is a set of mathematical theories that are precisely aimed to describe processes that happen concurrently with the help of mathematical logic and mathematical laws. Some notable examples of process calculi include **Algebra of Communicating Processes** (**ACP**), which has an implementation in Scala called SubScript (see `subscript-lang.org`), pi-calculus, **Calculus of Communicating Systems** (**CCS**). Attempts were made to implement these theories in practice. However, today, we cannot say that any given theory addresses the entire range of problems faced by modern programmers in-depth and with convenience.

Also, in recent years, a range of engineering approaches have been developed specifically for the development of concurrent and parallel applications. One such approach is reactive programming. This approach is mostly based on engineering your application in terms of streams, data sources, and sinks. This kind of approach can be very useful in the context of an application that is heavy on data flow, which means that there is a large volume of data that is constantly moving from one part of an application to another.

A practical application of such reactive programming is applications that are heavy on events. For example, many mobile applications rely on event propagation and reacting to events. This means that a good strategy to describe this kind of application would be to reason about data streams and data sources, as well as reactions to data as first-class citizens of the application. Normally, these kinds of application would be described in terms of callbacks and reactions to events. However, reasoning in terms of streams gets you a toolset of proper abstractions. In the previous chapter, we saw that when we frequently encounter errors and side effects, then making them first-class citizens of your programs and reasoning about them explicitly can be very beneficial to troubleshoot your application and to reduce the chance of an error.

It's the same thing here—when we have an application that is heavy on data and events, then reasoning in terms of streams can be pretty beneficial. There is an entire range of implementations of this approach for a wide range of programming languages.

However, programming in terms of event streams and reactive programming is not always what you want. It's true that certain applications that are heavy on events and data processing may be reasonable to describe in terms of data streams. However, this is not always the case.

As we have discussed previously, a wide range of theories and approaches have been developed to address the difficulties of parallel programming. Some of them can be regarded as more functional. For example, some libraries for functional programming for Scala, such as `Cats` or `ScalaZ`, provide certain primitives to allow for concurrent and parallel programming. Some of these approaches have a more object-oriented flavor. For example, some of the process calculi mentioned previously tend to have a deal of object-oriented spirit in them, which means that they introduce certain kinds of primitives that are very much comparable to objects in object-oriented programming. Some theories and approaches reside on the edge between functional programming and object-oriented programming and cannot be clearly classified as members of any of these approaches. For example, this can be the reactive approach to programming. Although it is heavy on functions and uses Lambda calculus to compose these functions, the trade-off is often type safety.

The presence of the amount of theories and approaches for concurrent programming means that this topic is highly speculative. It is often the case that techniques and theories that work well for one application will not show themselves as being well for another. Therefore, it is necessary to remark this book's stance on the topic. In this book, we take a pragmatic approach to functional programming, which means that the aim of this book is to give you a toolset to solve practical problems in a functional manner. So far, one of the most pragmatic and best approaches toward parallel programming is the actors model. While it is possibly not the most elegant modal from a functional programming perspective, since it still lacks a satisfactory type safety, it is something that is highly scalable and works well in practice. In this chapter of this book, we will be studying the actor approach to the functional programming of parallel applications, and we will see how to use modern actor-based technology to write real-world parallel and scalable applications with the help of the actor model.

However, before we jump into discussing the actor model and its practical applications, it is necessary to understand all of the challenges that are faced by parallel programming, and how they are solved in the traditional model of object-oriented programming with the traditional approach. So, first of all, let's take a look at the traditional approach to parallel programming, that is, multi-threading with synchronization and monitors.

Traditional model synchronization on monitors

Concurrency scenarios occur when you have two or more operations that are executed in parallel one with another. This parallelism can be either true parallelism or simulated parallelism. True parallelism is when your application is executed in parallel on two different CPU cores, like so:

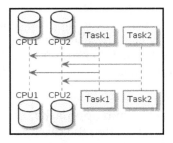

Simulated parallelism is when all of your parallel tasks are executed on the same processor core, however the processor switches from one task to another from time to time. Every task is composed of so-called atomic actions—smallest tasks that cannot be interrupted until they complete. The processor can take a certain amount of atomic actions from one task, and then execute a certain number of atomic tasks from another task:

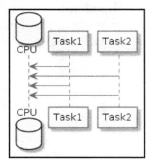

When you are writing a parallel application, you will often come across a situation where your tasks need to communicate one with another. One such situation when this may happen is when your concurrent tasks need to access some kind of resource that can be external or internal to the application, which is not thread-safe. In this situation, they will need to coordinate their access to this resource. Here, we have stumbled upon a very important concept to parallel programming, that is thread safety. Thread-safe resources can be accessed from any number of threads in parallel without worrying about whether something can go wrong. However, resources that are not thread-safe must be accessed from one side at a time. A typical example of a thread-safe resource is an immutable data structure. A typical example of a non-thread-safe resource is a shared mutable state.

What can possibly go wrong if you access a resource that is not thread-safe from more than one thread? Consider the example of writing to a file. Consider that you are writing an application for an online shop that is intended to generate a list of goods in some format. Consider that you need to read from a file listing goods in CSV and then transform them in some way:

```
Name,Price
TV Set,100
iPhone 8,300
Samsung Galaxy S5,300
MacBook Pro,2500
MacBook Air,1500
```

Consider that you need to output the same goods in JSON using the `Circe` library that we have already learned about:

```
{"Name":"TV Set","Price":100}
{"Name":"iPhone 8","Price":300}
{"Name":"Samsung Galaxy S5","Price":300}
{"Name":"MacBook Pro","Price":2500}
{"Name":"MacBook Air","Price":1500}
```

Also consider that you want to perform this operation in parallel. What you need to do here is take every row of the CSV file and convert it into some JSON output. Then, we need to write this output into the output file. Here, we have a bunch of operations that are not dependent one on another. Every transformation of every row is independent on any other transformation of any other row. So, what we might want to do is take these tasks in parallel from two threads. Therefore, one thread will process the first half of the list, and the other thread will process the second half of the list.

The output to a file can be modeled as a certain transaction, like so:

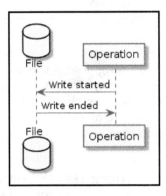

In the preceding diagram, you can see that we have the operation of opening the file for writing, then executing certain atomic actions that write the data into the file, and then closing the file. For simplicity, the process of writing a string called `Hello` into a file may not look like the following:

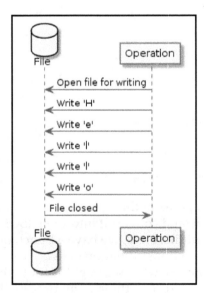

In the preceding diagram, we can see that the entire transaction is not atomic. It is composed of atomic operations, and is writing individual characters in our case. A note should be made here that the preceding example is only an example. Different implementations of writing logic might implement the transaction process differently so that the preceding atomic operations might not hold true for all environments. However, the preceding example illustrates this point very well, since most implementations still write to a file in a non-thread-safe manner using atomic actions. The entire writing transaction is not atomic.

Let's consider what happens if we try and write into the same file from two different threads:

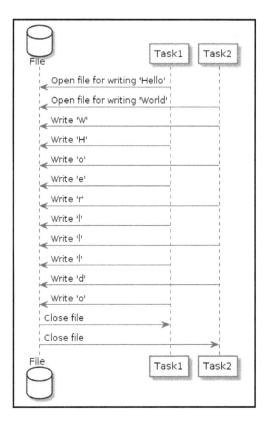

So, as you can see, we do not have any guarantee regarding the order in which the atomic tasks of every transaction get executed. So, as the preceding scenario comes through, you will end up with the following output to a file:

WHoerllldo

That is what we mean when we say that an operation or a resource is not thread-safe. This means that it is only permitted to work with the source from a single thread. Working from two threads with the same resource can be done as follows:

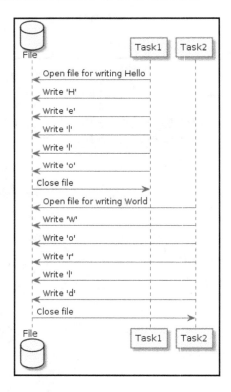

So, obviously, the preceding two threads must be aware of one another and of the order in which they should be executed. More precisely, we should somehow impose a guarantee that only one thread at a time will have access to the shared resource. In other words, we need to synchronize the threads somehow.

Synchronization

The simplest approach that can be used to synchronize the threads is called synchronization. It is implemented on the language level and is a standard construct in most programming languages.

The idea is as follows. Certain chunks of your programming code can be made guarded, which means they cannot be executed by the thread unless a certain condition is true. The condition in question is ownership of a so-called monitor. Therefore, a thread can own certain monitors. In a JVM setting, a monitor can be any object. So, on the JVM level, we can declare that a thread owns a monitor. Threads can take ownership and release the ownership of monitors at their own discretion. Another rule is that a monitor can only be held by one thread at a time. When a thread wants to take a monitor that is already held by another thread, then this thread must wait until this monitor is released and becomes available to it once more.

The preceding framework can be used in order to synchronize threads with one with another. You can do so as follows. Whenever we have a resource that is not thread-safe and needs to be accessed from more than one thread, we guard the code by accessing it with the `synchronized` keyword, that is, in the case of Java or Scala. This can be done as follows:

```
val target = new File("sample.txt")
 target.synchronized {
    FileUtils.writeStringToFile(target, "Hello World", "utf8")
}
```

The preceding code is executed in the context of some thread. Every instruction is executed in the thread in sequence. When the thread reaches the `synchronized` keyword, it attempts to take the object in question as a monitor. If this object is owned by some other thread, this thread goes into sleep mode. This means it does nothing until notified that the monitor is released and available for it to acquire. Once the monitor is available, it is acquired by this thread. This thread now has a guarantee that no other threat will take the same monitor until it is held by itself. Then, this thread executes the code in a `synchronized` block.

After the code is executed, the monitor is released by the current thread. The semantics of the execution will be as follows:

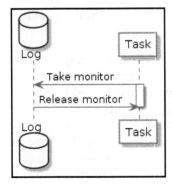

The preceding approach might look good in theory. However, there are a bunch of serious problems that can be encountered in such a scenario. These problems are pretty hard to debug, and they cannot be spotted by modern compilers. The existence of such problems demands a better framework for reasoning and defining concurrent and parallel applications. Next, let's take a look at what these problems are.

Problems with the traditional model – race conditions and deadlocks

The problems start to appear when more than one resource gets involved. Consider, for example, a slightly modified version of the preceding program. In the previous example, we had to write the result of the computation into a file. Consider that, at the same time as doing the computations themselves, we need to keep track of what they're doing in a log file. This kind of practice can be useful in a real-world scenario for debugging purposes.

So, the plan is as follows. First, the entire input file is read into the program memory. In our current scenario, threads are heterogeneous, which means that they have different tasks to accomplish. Homogeneous threads are generally easier to work with because they behave similarly and are controlled from one place. However, this is not always the case in the real world. So, let's consider threads with the following tasks. The first thread will be tasked with the conversion from CSV to JSON, as in the previous example. Also, it must report about how the conversion goes into the log file. The other thread will perform a different task. Let it compute some statistics over the file in question, for example, an average price of all the goods that the online shop is trading.

Let's see how such a program might be implemented in a traditional synchronization scenario. Before diving into this example, let's define some convenience methods and values that we will use in the example. You will need the following imports:

```
import scala.collection.JavaConverters._

import java.io.File
import java.nio.charset.Charset

import org.apache.commons.io.FileUtils
```

For file operations, we will use the Apache Commons IO library. The dependency on it must be declared in `build.sbt`:

```
libraryDependencies += "commons-io" % "commons-io" % "2.6"
```

The convenience methods are as follows:

```
// Files we will be working with
val input = new File("goods.csv" )
val log = new File("log.txt" )
val output = new File("goods.json")

// Encoding for the file I/O operations
val encoding = "utf8"

// Convenience method to construct threads
def makeThread(f: => Unit): Thread =
 new Thread(new Runnable {
   override def run(): Unit = f
 })

// Convenience method to write log
def doLog(l: String): Unit = {
  FileUtils.write(
    log
  , l + "\n"
  , encoding
  , true // Append to the file rather than rewrite it
  )
  println(s"Log: $l") // Trace console output
}

// Convenience method to read the input file
def readInput(): List[(String, Int)] =
  FileUtils.readLines(input, encoding).asScala.toList.tail
```

```
    .map(_.split(',').toList match {
      case name :: price :: Nil => (name, price.toInt)
    })
```

With the stage set, let's proceed to the example. First of all, let's take a look at the first thread tasked with the conversion from CSV to JSON. The first thing you might want to do in this thread is open the file we're going to work on and read it to a list:

```
val csv2json: Thread = makeThread {
  val inputList: List[(String, Int)] =
    input.synchronized {
      val result = readInput()
/*...*/
```

Since files are not thread-safe resources, the first thing that we need to do is take a monitor on the file. Immediately after reading this file, we might want to report to the log that the operation was performed successfully. So, we might want to take a monitor on the log file and report the operation as follows:

```
log.synchronized {
  doLog(s"Read ${result.length} lines from input")
}
```

Notice that the monitor of the log file is released immediately after we are done with that reporting. So, `inputList`code looks as follows:

```
val inputList: List[(String, Int)] =
  input.synchronized {
    val result = readInput()
    log.synchronized {
      doLog(s"Read ${result.length} lines from input")
    }
    result
  }
```

Once we are done with reading the file, we perform the operation of conversion on every row of the input file, and then we write the result into the output file:

```
val json: List[String] =
  inputList.map { case (name, price) =>
    s"""{"Name": "$name", "Price": $price}""" }

FileUtils.writeLines(output, json.asJava)
```

So, the entire code for the first thread looks as follows:

```
val csv2json: Thread = makeThread {
  val inputList: List[(String, Int)] =
    input.synchronized {
      val result = readInput()
      log.synchronized {
        doLog(s"Read ${result.length} lines from input")
      }
      result
    }

  val json: List[String] =
    inputList.map { case (name, price) =>
      s"""{"Name": "$name", "Price": $price}""" }

  FileUtils.writeLines(output, json.asJava)
}
```

Now, let's take a look at the other thread. It is tasked by the objective of computing certain statistics to our input file. More precisely, what we can do is compute some sort of aggregate function on all of the prices of the goods. For example, we might consider computing the average, the maximum value, and the minimum value of the set. However, we might also want to configure this thread with the exact metrics we want to compute:

```
def statistics(avg: Boolean = true, max: Boolean = false, min: Boolean =
false): Thread
```

As you can see, we were able to specify which exact metrics we need to compute. A reasonable step would be to report this information to a log file before doing anything else:

```
log.synchronized {
  doLog(s"Computing the following stats: avg=$avg, max=$max, min=$min")
}
```

The first thing that we do here is take a monitor on the log file and report the metrics. The next thing we need to do is actually read the file:

```
val inputList: List[(String, Int)] = log.synchronized {
  doLog(s"Computing the following stats: avg=$avg, max=$max, min=$min")
  val res = input.synchronized { readInput() }
  doLog(s"Read the input file to compute statistics on it")
  res
}
```

Since we also need to report the fact that the file was read successfully to the log, we decide to release the log monitor, but only after the file is successfully read. Notice how the snippet that reports the metrics gets incorporated into the `inputList` code, so that both the statistics and the `Read the input file` reporting can be done under the same `synchronized` code block.

After reading the input file, we are able to compute the required metrics on this input file based on the parameters specified by the user as follows:

```scala
val prices: List[Int] = inputList.map(_._2)
def reportMetrics(name: String, value: => Double): Unit = {
  val result = value
  log.synchronized { doLog(s"$name: $result") }
}

if (avg) reportMetrics("Average Price", prices.sum /
  prices.length.toDouble)
if (max) reportMetrics("Maximal Price", prices.max)
if (min) reportMetrics("Minimal Price", prices.min)
```

Therefore, the entire code for the `statistics` thread will look like the following:

```scala
def statistics(avg: Boolean = true, max: Boolean = false, min: Boolean =
false): Thread = makeThread {
  val inputList: List[(String, Int)] = log.synchronized {
    doLog(s"Computing the following stats: avg=$avg, max=$max, min=$min")
    val res = input.synchronized { readInput() }
    doLog(s"Read the input file to compute statistics on it")
    res
  }

  val prices: List[Int] = inputList.map(_._2)
  def reportMetrics(name: String, value: => Double): Unit = {
    val result = value
    log.synchronized { doLog(s"$name: $result") }
  }

  if (avg) reportMetrics("Average Price", prices.sum /
prices.length.toDouble)
  if (max) reportMetrics("Maximal Price", prices.max)
  if (min) reportMetrics("Minimal Price", prices.min)
}
```

What happens if you run this thread in parallel with the first thread?

```
csv2json.start()
statistics(true, true, true).start()
```

You may notice that, sometimes, the program hangs and becomes non-responsive. This situation is called a **deadlock**.

Basically, the problem here is that the two threads are racing for the resources. It is a race condition of who takes which monitor first. The first thread takes the monitor on the input file, and then it takes the monitor on the log. Then, it releases the monitor on the lock, and then it releases the monitor on the input file:

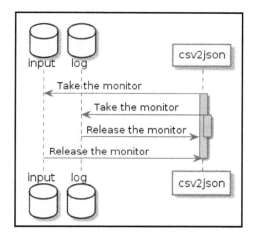

In the preceding diagram, the orange bar represents the code that is executed under the input monitor. The blue bar is the code under the log monitor. In this particular case, the blue code also owns the input monitor, since it has not been released from the time of its execution yet.

The second thread, in contrast, does these operations in a different order. First, it takes a lock on the log file. Then, it takes the lock on the input file, and then it releases the lock on the input file, before releasing the lock on the log file:

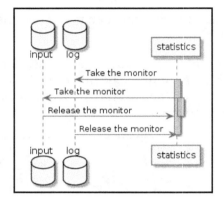

The two threads depend on the same set of resources, and the order in which they acquire them is not defined. This means that they will be competing for these resources, and when you run the program several times, the order of resources in acquisition will be different from run to run.

Let's take a look at a case where an application works well:

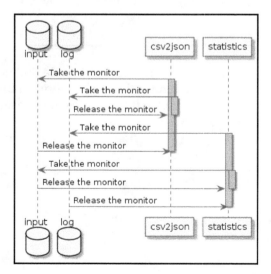

In the preceding diagram, the first thread takes the monitor on input and then it takes a monitor on the log, but after that, the second thread attempts to take the lock on the log, but it is late to do that. Therefore, it is forced to wait until the other thread finishes. The first thread has acquired all of the locks it is dependent on, and so it finishes successfully. After it finishes, it releases all of monitors it owns, and the second thread is capable of taking them.

Now, let's take a look at how and why exactly the application gets a deadlock:

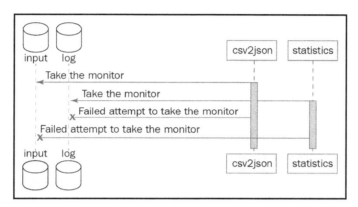

So, in the example above, the first thread takes the monitor on the input file. Together with it, the second thread takes the monitor on the log file. After that, in order to proceed, the first thread needs a monitor on the log file, but it cannot take it because the second thread has already taken it, and so it is forced to wait.

The second thread needs the monitor on the input file in order to proceed. However, it cannot take it because it is owned by the first thread, and so it is also forced to wait. This means we have ended up in a situation where neither of the threads can proceed until the other thread finishes, and so neither of the threads ever finishes. This kind of situation is called a deadlock.

A quick fix may be to make the threads and take the monitor in the same order. For example, if the first thread takes the monitor on the input file and then a monitor on the log file, we might want to enforce the same order on the second thread as well. So, the second thread will look as follows:

```
def statisticsSafe(avg: Boolean = true, max: Boolean = false, min: Boolean
= false): Thread = makeThread {
  val inputList: List[(String, Int)] = input.synchronized {
    log.synchronized {
      doLog(s"Computing the following stats: avg=$avg, max=$max, min=$min")
      val res = readInput()
```

```
      doLog(s"Read the input file to compute statistics on it")
      res
  }
}

  val prices: List[Int] = inputList.map(_._2)
  def reportMetrics(name: String, value: => Double): Unit = {
    val result = value
    log.synchronized { doLog(s"$name: $result") }
  }

  if (avg) reportMetrics("Average Price", prices.sum /
prices.length.toDouble)
  if (max) reportMetrics("Maximal Price", prices.max)
  if (min) reportMetrics("Minimal Price", prices.min)
}
```

The preceding chunk of code in bold is what was changed compared to the statistics thread definition. Now, whoever takes the monitor on the input file first is guaranteed to finish the execution. This is because, in the preceding application, it is impossible to take the monitor on the log file unless you already own the monitor on the input file. So, whoever takes the monitor on the input file is guaranteed to be able to take the same monitor on the log file.

The fix might work in the short term. However, you might have already noticed that it is suboptimal. In the previous example, we had a pretty simple situation. We only had two threads and two resources they depend on. That kind of simple setting is not likely to happen in the real world. Real-world applications are likely to have dozens of threads in them and depend on dozens of resources. Also, debugging the preceding complexity was tricky. If only two threats were capable of producing such complexity and required a lot of our brain power to do the analysis and find the problem, imagine how this complexity can grow in magnitude in a real-world setting.

This is precisely why the standard synchronization approach to parallel programming is not practical in the long run. It's fine as a low-level model of programming so that people build some high-level primitives on top of it. However, we cannot use it in practice efficiently. These kinds of problems with threads and concurrent applications provided a motivation to create newer, more robust approaches to reasoning about concurrent programming. We already discussed some of them briefly at the beginning of this chapter. Now, let's talk about the actor model in more detail.

The actor model as a replacement for the traditional model

One of the most popular approaches to dealing with the complexity discussed previously is the actor approach to concurrent programming. If you look at the preceding examples in detail, you will notice one thing about them, that is, global reasoning. Whenever we have several threads that need to communicate in one with another, we are forced to reason about them together. So, we cannot take one thread and reason about it independently from other threads.

As we saw previously, the solution to the deadlock problem was to change the order in which the monitors were taken in the second thread so that the order matched the one in the first thread. Basically, when we are working in the scope of the second thread, we are forced to take into account the operations done in the first thread.

Global reasoning produces mental load on the programmer's mind. One of the central points of this book is that purely functional programming aims to reduce the mental load on the programmer's mind by reducing the scope of reasoning about the programs.

How can we tackle the problem of the global scope and shared mutable state as the means of communication between threads in the context of concurrent programming? The response of the actors model would be to provide a set of abstractions to ensure that whenever you are programming a parallel application, you are able to forget that you are working in a concurrent environment. The central point behind the actors model, the central idea of why it is created, and why it exists, is to make your program within a concurrent environment as if you were dealing with a single threaded application, which means you no longer need to think about taking monitors or accessing resources in a thread-safe manner.

The actor model does this by providing you with a set of abstractions and a set of conventions that you must follow as part of the model. A central abstraction of the actor model is, not surprisingly, an actor. An actor can be roughly thought of as a thread. It is not necessarily mapped one-to-one on threads; in fact, it is a more lightweight primitive, and you might have thousands upon thousands of actors. The way their concurrency is managed is in abstracted away. However, the right way to think about actors is that they are the concurrency primitives of the actor model.

An actor can own certain resources, and if it does, it is guaranteed that no other actor owns or has access to these sources. For example, if an actor has a reference to a file, it is guaranteed that no other actor has the same reference to the same file, so it is not able to write or read from the file. If it does need to access a resource owned by another actor, it needs to ask the owner actor to perform the required operation on behalf of this actor. Since all of the operations over a non-thread-safe or resource are done by one and only one actor, and actors are sequential and single threaded entities, there is no danger that some non-thread-safe behavior will emerge in this context.

How exactly does one actor ask another actor to perform an action? This is done by messaging. Every actor has a so-called **mailbox**. A mailbox is a place where all of the incoming communications to this actor are stored. A single unit of communication in the actor model is a message. A message can be anything as long as it complies with the constraints of the actor model, which we will be discussing later. A mailbox is a queue. Therefore, the messages from many actors that run and send messages in parallel may arrive to the single actor, and they will get sorted into a single sequential queue. An actor is guaranteed to process only one message at a time. So, the way it works is that the actor waits on its mailbox for mail. Then, it takes one letter at a time and processes it sequentially.

One way regarding how exactly to process the incoming mail is defined in the body of an actor in terms of reactions to different kinds of incoming mail. So, for every type of mail the actor is capable of handling, it defines a certain function that is supposed to be executed whenever this letter arrives to the actor.

Deadlock example revisited

So far, we have looked at the actors model at a glance. We have not learned any practical implementations of the actor model just yet. However, it can be instructive to take a look at how our previous example can be implemented so that we are rid of the complexity that we have faced with it.

First of all, we have discussed that actors are primitives of concurrency of the actors model. In the preceding example, the primitives of concurrency were two threads that performed some operations. So, it is reasonable to map the operations that we need to perform from the two threads onto two actors of the actor model. So now, instead of two threads, we have two actors. One actor is supposed to generate JSON from CSV, and the other actor is supposed to compute some statistics on the CSV file.

In the preceding example, we had two files that we were supposed to work with and two threads that needed to get access to both of the files. The actors model requires that only one actor must own a given resource. So, if the first actor needs a resource, the second actor cannot have it. In our situation, the first and second actors need to work with the input file and the log file. How should we tackle this situation? How should we make it compliant with the actor model?

The solution is that none of the two actors should own this resource. Instead, we should create a third actor that is responsible for running operations that involve these resources. Then, whenever we need to do something with a result, we send a message to that actor asking to perform the required operation.

Since our actor, let's call it process manager, controls access to the input file and the log file, we must expect the request from other actors to perform operations relevant to this resource. In other words, we also need to define the reactions to all the possible messages that it might receive. Hence, we need to think about what kind of operations request we might get from other actors. We can consider the following requests:

- First, we get the input file. This message is a request to read the input file and send it back to the requesting actor as an immutable collection. Sharing an immutable resource between two actors is perfectly fine since immutable resources are thread-safe.
- Secondly, we may be expecting a request to write into the log file. Upon receiving this request, the resource manager actor will perform a write operation into the log file with the message that was sent to it.

Once we have the resource manager actor, we can express the example like so:

Now, the first two actors that do the actual job are defined in terms of messages and communication with the resource manager. The first actor asks the process manager to send it an input file. Upon receiving a response from the resource manager, it starts its operations, and whenever it performs a significant action that requires logging, it sends the log message to the resource manager. No monitors are taken in this situation since all of the resources are owned by a single actor. All of the other actors are not calling them directly—they are just asking the resource actor to perform the operations on their behalf.

The second actor has a similar situation to itself. First of all, it sends a log message to the resource manager with the statistics it is going to compute. Secondly, it requests the input file from the resource manager. Finally, upon receiving the input file as a separate message, it performs the computation and also contacts our resource manager whenever it needs logging.

None of the actors need to take monitors or synchronize one with another in order to ensure that the non-thread-safe resources are safe to work with. They are all owned by a single actor, and this single actor works with them sequentially from its own single thread. The messages that the other actors send to it may arrive in parallel, but they will be aggregated in a single mailbox, and they will not be processed right away. The resource actor processes messages at its own pace, at its own time, whenever it has the resources and the processing time allocated to the underlying system. It is guaranteed that this actor will process the messages one at a time, and no two messages will be processed in parallel. Hence, we have a greatly increased level of thread safety.

Also, noticed that in the preceding diagram, we have a scenario that would cause a deadlock in the standard synchronization model. The first actor needs to access the file, and then it needs to access the log, and the second actor needs to access the log and then the file. Previously in this chapter, we discussed how this kind of situation yields the possibility of a deadlock. Here, the deadlock is no longer possible, since the resources are controlled by a single actor.

Summary

In this chapter, we had a brief overview of the motivation and the idea behind the actor model. We saw how the architecture of applications can be expressed in terms of what the actor model might look like. In the next chapter, we will dive deeper into the model and see how to use it in practice. We will learn some practical implementations and frameworks of the models that we can use in our projects right away.

Questions

1. How does the synchronization model work in synchronizing parallel computations?
2. How does a deadlock occur? Describe a scenario in which a deadlock can occur.
3. What are the main abstractions and constraints of the actor model?
4. How does the actor model help prevent the problems that usually arise under the synchronization model?

The Actor Model in Practice

12

In the previous chapter, we started to look at the actors model as one of their concurrency models available in Scala. In Chapter 9, *Libraries for Pure Functional Programming*, we saw how challenges of asynchronous and multithreaded programming can be solved using IO and the infrastructure it provides. However, this kind of technology is still not widely adopted. In practice, when working with multithreading, concurrency, and asynchrony in Scala, you will need to deal with more robust libraries in real-world situations.

In this chapter, we will look at the following topics:

- Akka overview
- Defining, creating, and messaging actors
- Working with actor systems

Akka overview

Akka is an implementation of the actor model, which we discussed in the previous chapter for its industrial purposes. If the Cats effect focuses on experimentation and trials with new technologies, then Akka focuses on providing the industry with the tools that can solve large-scale problems. Of course, we can expect cats to mature to that level as well, however, if you are going to work with concurrency and asynchrony in Scala in a real-world situation, it is likely you will encounter Akka.

The purpose of this book is to make you comfortable with modern technologies in functional programming that are in demand in real-world situations. Since concurrent and asynchronous programming is ubiquitous, we are going to discuss the tools that are most widely used to tackle its challenges. We will start by looking at the principles on which Akka is built.

Principles of Akka

The central abstraction of Akka is an actor. An actor is an entity that can receive and send messages to other actors.

Actors are lightweight concurrency primitives. Similarly to how you can have millions of Fibres in cats, you can have millions of actors in Akka. This is because they utilize asynchrony and provide abstractions on top of standard Java virtual machine threads. By utilizing the resources of the JVM, you can have millions of actors in parallel on a single machine.

Akka is built with scaling in mind. The library does not stop at providing you with the abstractions for actors themselves. Similarly to how cats has an infrastructure of libraries for various specific cases of functional programming, Akka has a host of libraries for special cases of asynchronous programming. You will encounter an HTTP server as part of this library, which is an infrastructure to allow you to communicate between actors that reside on different machines.

The purpose of the actors model is to provide you with a concurrency framework that will reduce your mental overhead and allow for robust and scalable software.

To overcome the challenges that concurrent programming poses, Akka imposes a range of pretty harsh restrictions on a programmer. One can expect to benefit from the model only if they follow these restrictions. It is important to remember that the rules the actor model imposes are not encoded and enforced by the compiler. So it is up to you to follow them. Breaking them at will is easy. It is important to remember that if you do so, it is very likely that you are going to end up with even more of a headache than you had without the actor model.

Encapsulation

One problem with concurrent programming is the shared mutable state. Akka eliminates this problem by providing a restriction that it is impossible to access your actors as ordinary objects. This means your business logic does not have a single variable that would store an actor. Hence, it is impossible to access the values defined on the actors by ordinary object-oriented means.

The actors are exposed to the outer world via proxy types—`ActorRefs`. The Akka library defines this type, and only safe operations are permitted on an actor.

If you want to do something with an actor, you should do so via this proxy. Also, you do not instantiate an actor as an ordinary Java or Scala object. You do not call a constructor on it. Instead, you will instruct `ActorSystem` to instantiate it. With these constraints, it becomes impossible to accept the data of an actor by any means other than messaging it.

Messaging

Every actor has a mailbox, where any other messages can be sent. Akka guarantees that the messages are handled by the actor one at a time, and no concurrent handling happens. In fact, the actor model provides a guarantee that no more than one thread accesses the internal state of an actor at a time. However, keep in mind that it is up to the programmer to follow the actor model precisely. It is easy to break the model by spawning extra threads (e.g. with a `Future`) in an actor, thus breaking the single-threaded access guarantee.

This restriction is essential to enforce in the presence of other convenient concurrency libraries, such as Future. Akka works hand-in-hand with Scala Future. It is important to remember that futures start and work from other threads. So, the moment you start a Future in Akka, you lose the guarantee of single-threaded access to the state of an actor. If you follow this road, you will need to specify the synchronization and utilize the monitor mechanism provided to you by the JVM. This is an anti-pattern, it kills the very purpose of Akka, and is a big no-no in actor programming.

Remember that the model is going to help you only if you follow its rules, and there is nothing to enforce you to do so.

No leaking of mutable state

Another thing that you must look out for when programming with Akka is leaking mutable state of the actors. Remember the previous principle that no more than a single thread must access the inner state of an actor? Well, if you send a reference to a mutable object that is owned by one actor to another one, this object may be accessed from two threads at a time in parallel. If you leak mutable state to other actors, you may end up with a worse headache than when starting a Future from an actor. In the case of starting a Future, at least you have control over that Future and the thread it started from; you can define some monitors and protocols to access the actor's state. Of course, you should not do it, but in theory, it is possible.

However, if you leak a reference to a mutable state from one actor to another, you will have no control whatsoever over how that actor will use it.

Again, this rule is not enforced by Akka. In Akka, you can pass any object as a message to another actor. This includes mutable references. So, you should be aware of the possibility and actively avoid it.

Fault-tolerance and supervision

Akka is built with resilience and fault-tolerance in mind. This means that if an actor fails as a result of an exception, there is a well-defined way it will automatically restart and restore its state. Akka organizes actors in hierarchies, and parent actors are responsible for the performance of their children. So, if a child fails, its parent is supposed to be responsible for restarting it. The idea is that the external world should not be affected by the problems of an actor's subordinates. If the problem happens, it is the supervisor's responsibility to solve it rather than escalating it further. And when the child actor restarts, it should be able to restore itself to the state it was at when it failed.

Messaging guarantees

Akka is built to be deployed in clusters, over the network. This means that you have fewer delivery guarantees about the messages than when you are working on a single JVM application. If you are sending a message from an actor that resides in one computer to an actor on another side of the world, you cannot guarantee that this message will get delivered.

So, the actor model as implemented by Akka requires you to build your applications with no guarantees whatsoever about delivering the messages. Your application must be robust to the situations of the impossibility of message-delivery.

However, Akka provides you with a guarantee about the order in which messages from one actor to another get delivered. This means that if from the same actor, you send a message before another, you can be sure that message also arrives before the second one.

The best thing to do after learning the preceding theory is to have a look at how it works in practice. Next, we will be discussing an example that relies on the numerous functionalities that Akka exposes. We will be learning these functionalities as we encounter them.

Asynchrony

Remember when we discussed IO, we stressed the importance of asynchrony and non-blocking computations? Threads of the underlying operating system are scarce, and on a system with high load, you need to utilize them well. Blocking is not a wise utilization of the threads.

We have discussed that you should not invoke other threads from the current actor. The motivation for this is to prevent access to the mutable state of the current actor from more than one thread. We have discussed that whenever we need to process something, we schedule the processing as a message to the current actor.

Therefore, to enforce single-threaded processing, you might be tempted to block on a future from a message-handling logic, as follows:

```
Await.ready(future, 3 seconds)
```

However, this blocks the underlying thread. Blocking turns an actor that does so into a heavyweight concurrency primitive. If you use it in a setting of a high-load application, it will eat system-concurrency resources fast. The rationale here is the same as when we were discussing IO. Bottom line: do not block your concurrency primitives because the threads are scarce. If you need to wait for the result of some asynchronous computation to continue the current computation, make sure that that the computation will send this actor a message when it finishes, register a handler on the current actor saying what to do once the task finishes, and release the current thread.

Defining, creating, and messaging actors

The actors are defined as classes that inherit from the `Actor` class from the Akka library:

```
class HelloWorld extends Actor {
```

Actor exposes the following abstract API:

Type Members

        type **Receive** = PartialFunction[Any, Unit]

Abstract Value Members

        abstract def **receive**: Actor.Receive
                Scala API: This defines the initial actor behavior, it must return a partial function with the actor logic.

The only method that is abstract in `Actor` is the `receive` method. Akka calls this method when an actor needs to handle an incoming message. It returns a partial function from `Any` to `Unit`. This means that it is capable of handling a message from a domain of all objects, and it is supposed to produce some side effects while handling this message, which is indicated by the `Unit` return type. That function is a partial function, which means that it can handle only a part of the input `Any` domain that your actor is interested in.

When your define an actor, you override this method to define what the actor must do:

```
val log = Logging(context.system, this)

def receive = {
  case Ping ⇒ log.info("Hello World")
}
```

The message is defined as follows:

```
case object Ping
```

So, when an actor receives the ping message, it will output the `hello world` string to the log. We can construct the log with the help of the following function:

```
def apply[T](system: ActorSystem, logSource: T)(implicit arg0: LogSource[T]):
LoggingAdapter
```

Obtain LoggingAdapter for the given actor system and source object. This will use the system's event stream and include the system's address in the log source string.

Do not use this if you want to supply a log category string (like "com.example.app.whatever") unaltered, supply system.eventStream in this case or use

```
Logging(system, this.getClass)
```

The source is used to identify the source of this logging channel and must have a corresponding implicit LogSource[T] instance in scope; by default these are provided for Class[], Actor, ActorRef and String types. See the companion object of akka.event.LogSource for details.

You can add your own rules quite easily, see akka.event.LogSource.

This function is defined over the following object:

akka.event

Logging

`object` **Logging**

Main entry point for Akka logging: log levels and message types (aka channels) defined for the main transport medium, the main event bus. The recommended use is to obtain an implementation of the Logging trait with suitable and efficient methods for generating log events:

```
val log = Logging(<bus>, <source object>)
...
log.info("hello world!")
```

One of the abstractions Akka relies upon is the event system. Events can be used to track the changes in the state of an actor and restore it to the previous state in case of failure. Since logging is also an event stream in a sense, Akka provides you with an elaborate logging infrastructure that also integrates with its general event system. When constructing a logger, you will need to provide the `ActorSystem` you are defining it for, as well as the reference to the current actor. You will then be able to display the log messages properly while specifying the current actor.

Notice that here, to construct the logger, we are accessing some other API defined on the actor. We are calling the context method and its member-system method. So, next, let's have a look at the API the actor exposes.

All of the concrete members of the `Actor` class can be divided into several groups.

Callbacks

The following methods belong to the callbacks group:

```
def postRestart(reason: Throwable): Unit
    User overridable callback: By default it calls preStart().

def postStop(): Unit
    User overridable callback.

def preRestart(reason: Throwable, message: Option[Any]): Unit
    Scala API: User overridable callback: By default it disposes of all children and then calls postStop().

def preStart(): Unit
    User overridable callback.
```

The Akka framework in different situations calls these callbacks. For example, `postStop` is called after the actor stops. `preStart` is called before the actor starts. `preRestart` is called before, and `afterRestart` is called after, the actor has restarted. The restart callbacks take a `reason` as an argument. The `reason` is an exception due to which this actor had to restart itself. It is also part of Akka's fault-tolerance strategy. When building your actors, you should keep the possibility of such restarting in mind.

Finally, the `unhandled` method is called whenever a message arrives at an actor that it is not capable of handling it:

```
def unhandled(message: Any): Unit
```
User overridable callback.

Is called when a message isn't handled by the current behavior of the actor by default it fails with either an akka.actor.DeathPactException (in case of an unhandled akka.actor.Terminated message) or publishes an akka.actor.UnhandledMessage to the actor's system's akka.event.EventStream

Remember that we have discussed that the `receive` method returns a partial function. This means it is defined only on a part of its domain type. So, whenever a message arrives at an actor that it is not able to handle, the unhandled callback is called instead.

Supervision

Also, part of the fault-tolerance strategy that Actor provides is the `supervisorStrategy` method:

```
def supervisorStrategy: SupervisorStrategy
```
User overridable definition the strategy to use for supervising child actors.

You can override this method to provide the actor with different ways to supervise its children. Supervision is the concept of watching the children's life cycle and taking actions on significant events, such as when an actor fails with an exception. In Akka, parent actors are supposed to supervise child actors. The supervision strategy is defined as follows:

akka.actor
SupervisorStrategy

Companion **object SupervisorStrategy**

abstract class **SupervisorStrategy** extends AnyRef

An Akka SupervisorStrategy is the policy to apply for crashing children.

IMPORTANT:

You should not normally need to create new subclasses, instead use the existing akka.actor.OneForOneStrategy or akka.actor.AllForOneStrategy, but if you do, please read the docs of the methods below carefully, as incorrect implementations may lead to "blocked" actor systems (i.e. permanently suspended actors).

Source   FaultHandling.scala

Linear Supertypes

Known Subclasses

AllForOneStrategy, OneForOneStrategy

As you can see, there are two subclasses defined for this class, and the documentation suggests you shouldn't implement additional subclasses because an incorrect implementation can lead to erroneous behavior:

akka.actor
AllForOneStrategy

case class **AllForOneStrategy**(maxNrOfRetries: Int = -1, withinTimeRange: Duration = Duration.Inf, loggingEnabled: Boolean = true)(decider: Decider) extends SupervisorStrategy with Product with Serializable

Applies the fault handling **Directive** (Resume, Restart, Stop) specified in the **Decider** to all children when one fails, as opposed to akka.actor.OneForOneStrategy that applies it only to the child actor that failed.

`AllForOneStrategy` will apply a given action to all of the children if one fails:

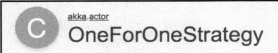

```
case class OneForOneStrategy(maxNrOfRetries: Int = -1, withinTimeRange: Duration = Duration.Inf,
loggingEnabled: Boolean = true)(decider: Decider) extends SupervisorStrategy with Product with
Serializable
```

Applies the fault handling **Directive** (Resume, Restart, Stop) specified in the **Decider** to the child actor that failed, as opposed to akka.actor.AllForOneStrategy that applies it to all children.

`OneForOneStrategy` will apply an action only to the child that failed.

Notice also that both strategies are parameterized by various parameters that define how it should handle situations with failed children. One of these parameters is `Decider`:

```
type Decider = PartialFunction[Throwable, Directive]
```

The `Decider` type is a partial function from a `Throwable` to a `Directive`. It takes a `Throwable` (which can be an `Exception` or an `Error`) that has occurred in the actor, and the job of `Decider` is to provide information to the actor system on how to handle this exception.

`Directive` defines what to do on a given exception with an actor:

There are four subclasses to the `Directive` trait. The `Escalate` directive escalates the exception to the parent of the supervising actor. So, when the child fails, the parent will also fail and will rely on its own parent to handle the exception.

akka.actor.SupervisorStrategy
Escalate

`object` **Escalate** extends Directive with Product with Serializable

Escalates the failure to the supervisor of the supervisor, by rethrowing the cause of the failure, i.e. the supervisor fails with the same exception as the child.

The `Restart` directive will discard the actor that failed and will create a new actor in its place:

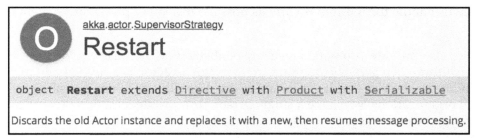

akka.actor.SupervisorStrategy
Restart

`object` **Restart** extends Directive with Product with Serializable

Discards the old Actor instance and replaces it with a new, then resumes message processing.

The `Resume` directive will instruct the actor that had an exception to continue processing the messages:

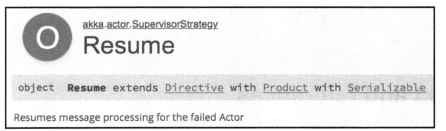

akka.actor.SupervisorStrategy
Resume

`object` **Resume** extends Directive with Product with Serializable

Resumes message processing for the failed Actor

The exception will be ignored, and no action will be taken to handle it. The child actor will continue as it did previously.

Finally, the `Stop` directive will stop the current actor without starting another one in its place.

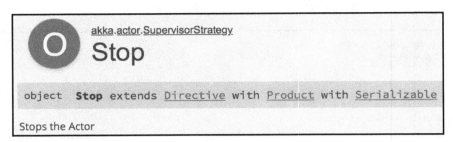

The preceding infrastructure provides you with the capability to construct hierarchies where parents are responsible for the sound operation of the children. This approach provides a separation of concerns and enables a degree of local reasoning. This means that actor systems handle the failures as early as possible instead of propagating them up the hierarchy.

Hierarchies also provide you with a measure of abstraction, because you no longer care about the children of a given actor, you can treat a given actor as a single point of responsibility for the task that it was asked to do. A single point of responsibility is similar to how, in organizations, you have a single person responsible for a department, and whenever you need the department to do something, you talk to the responsible person. You expect them to run the department properly. Akka is built the same way. Whenever you have a concern, you have an actor responsible for this concern. It may or may not have child actors that help them work on this concern, however, as an outside observer, you do not need to be aware of these factors. You do not need to care about the errors that happen to these subordinates. This is, of course, only if the errors in question can be localized to a given department. If the error is more significant than what the department can handle, it propagates up the chain.

Context and references

Apart from the callbacks that give you control over how an actor reacts to various life cycle events, an actor has an API for managing the context of its execution:

```
implicit final val self: ActorRef
```

> The 'self' field holds the ActorRef for this actor.
>
> Can be used to send messages to itself:
>
> ```
> self ! message
> ```

```
final def sender(): ActorRef
```

> The reference sender Actor of the last received message. Is defined if the message was sent from another Actor, else **deadLetters** in akka.actor.ActorSystem.
>
> WARNING: Only valid within the Actor itself, so do not close over it and publish it to other threads!

Actors have references to the `ActorRef` of themselves and the sender actor. These references are supposed to be accessed from the `receive` method. Through them, you can interact with the sender actor, as well as with this actor as with `ActorRefs`. This means that you can send messages to these actors, and do other things you would usually do as an external observer.

Aside from references, an actor has a `context` reference that provides information and control over the context of the actor's execution:

```
implicit val context: ActorContext
```

> Scala API: Stores the context for this actor, including self, and sender. It is implicit to support operations such as **forward**.
>
> WARNING: Only valid within the Actor itself, so do not close over it and publish it to other threads!
>
> akka.actor.ActorContext is the Scala API. **getContext** returns a akka.actor.AbstractActor.ActorContext, which is the Java API of the actor context.

`ActorContext` provides various APIs that may be useful when handling messages.

Managing the actor hierarchy

The central concept for managing actor hierarchies is the `ActorContext` type. It is defined as follows:

akka.actor

ActorContext

trait **ActorContext** extends <u>ActorRefFactory</u>

The actor context - the view of the actor cell from the actor. Exposes contextual information for the actor and the current message.

`ActorContext` allows you to perform various operations on the actor's hierarchy. For example, you can create new actors with the `actorOf` method which is defined as follows:

```
abstract def actorOf(props: Props, name: String): ActorRef
        Create new actor as child of this context with the given name, which must not be null, empty or start with "$".

abstract def actorOf(props: Props): ActorRef
        Create new actor as child of this context and give it an automatically generated name (currently similar to
        base64-encoded integer count, reversed and with "$" prepended, may change in the future).
```

So, with `ActorContext`, you can create child actors of this actor. We will cover the exact procedure of creating a new actor with the `Props` object a bit later when we will be discussing actor systems.

The current actor is capable of accessing the child actors it created with the `child` and `children` methods:

```
abstract def child(name: String): Option[ActorRef]
```

> Get the child with the given name if it exists.
>
> *Warning*: This method is not thread-safe and must not be accessed from threads other than the ordinary actor message processing thread, such as java.util.concurrent.CompletionStage and scala.concurrent.Future callbacks.

```
abstract def children: Iterable[ActorRef]
```

> Returns all supervised children; this method returns a view (i.e. a lazy collection) onto the internal collection of children. Targeted lookups should be using **child** instead for performance reasons:
>
> ```
> val badLookup = context.children find (_.path.name == "kid")
> // should better be expressed as:
> val goodLookup = context.child("kid")
> ```
>
> *Warning*: This method is not thread-safe and must not be accessed from threads other than the ordinary actor message processing thread, such as java.util.concurrent.CompletionStage and scala.concurrent.Future callbacks.

Similarly, you can access the parent actor of this actor:

```
abstract def parent: ActorRef
```

> Returns the supervising parent ActorRef.
>
> This method is thread-safe and can be called from other threads than the ordinary actor message processing thread, such as java.util.concurrent.CompletionStage and scala.concurrent.Future callbacks.

`ActorSystem` is a collection of actors:

```
implicit abstract def system: ActorSystem
```

> The system that the actor belongs to. Importing this member will place an implicit ActorSystem in scope.
>
> This method is thread-safe and can be called from other threads than the ordinary actor message processing thread, such as java.util.concurrent.CompletionStage and scala.concurrent.Future callbacks.

We will cover actor systems later in the *Creating actors* section, but for now, you should understand that `ActorSystem` is accessible from `ActorContext`.

Managing the life cycle

Akka context provides you with various methods for the life cycle management of an actor:

```
abstract def stop(actor: ActorRef): Unit
```
> Stop the actor pointed to by the given akka.actor.ActorRef; this is an asynchronous operation, i.e. involves a message send. If this method is applied to the **self** reference from inside an Actor then that Actor is guaranteed to not process any further messages after this call; please note that the processing of the current message will continue, this method does not immediately terminate this actor.
>
> ***Definition Classes***   ActorRefFactory

You can stop this or another actor from using `ActorContext`. A widespread pattern with actor-based programming is the following:

```
context stop self
```

The preceding idiom is often used to terminate actors that have accomplished their job and have nothing more to do.

Actors can change their behavior. The behavior of an actor is defined by its `receive` method:

```
abstract def become(behavior: Receive, discardOld: Boolean): Unit
```
> Changes the Actor's behavior to become the new 'Receive' (PartialFunction[Any, Unit]) handler. This method acts upon the behavior stack as follows:
>
> o if **discardOld = true** it will replace the top element (i.e. the current behavior)
> o if **discardOld = false** it will keep the current behavior and push the given one atop
>
> The default of replacing the current behavior on the stack has been chosen to avoid memory leaks in case client code is written without consulting this documentation first (i.e. always pushing new behaviors and never issuing an **unbecome()**)
>
> *Warning*: This method is not thread-safe and must not be accessed from threads other than the ordinary actor message processing thread, such as java.util.concurrent.CompletionStage and scala.concurrent.Future callbacks.

However, as part of handling messages, you may want to change the way messages are handled by an actor. For this purpose, you can use the `become` method.

An actor remembers past behaviors you have overridden and keeps them in a stack. This means that you can call an `unbecome` method to pop the current behavior from the stack and use the previous behavior:

```
abstract def unbecome(): Unit
```

    Reverts the Actor behavior to the previous one on the behavior stack.

    Warning: This method is not thread-safe and must not be accessed from threads other than the ordinary actor message processing thread, such as java.util.concurrent.CompletionStage and scala.concurrent.Future callbacks.

Supervision

An actor can watch another actor for its life cycle events:

```
abstract def watch(subject: ActorRef): ActorRef
```

    Registers this actor as a Monitor for the provided ActorRef. This actor will receive a Terminated(subject) message when watched actor is terminated.

    watch is idempotent if it is not mixed with **watchWith**.

    It will fail with an IllegalStateException if the same subject was watched before using **watchWith**. To clear the termination message, unwatch first.

    Warning: This method is not thread-safe and must not be accessed from threads other than the ordinary actor message processing thread, such as java.util.concurrent.CompletionStage and scala.concurrent.Future callbacks.

    returns   the provided ActorRef

Whenever you need this actor to be aware of when another actor terminates, you can instruct it to watch that other actor with actor context. When that actor terminates, the supervising actor will receive a `Terminated` message. You can register a handler of a `Terminated` message the same way you handle any other message from the received message.

Creating actors

All of the actors belong to some `ActorSystem`, which is a hierarchy of actors:

akka.actor **ActorSystem**	Companion **object ActorSystem**

abstract class **ActorSystem** extends ActorRefFactory

An actor system is a hierarchical group of actors which share common configuration, e.g. dispatchers, deployments, remote capabilities and addresses. It is also the entry point for creating or looking up actors.

The most important methods when creating new actors are as follows:

```
abstract def actorOf(props: Props, name: String): ActorRef
```
> Create new actor as child of this context with the given name, which must not be null, empty or start with "$".

```
abstract def actorOf(props: Props): ActorRef
```
> Create new actor as child of this context and give it an automatically generated name (currently similar to base64-encoded integer count, reversed and with "$" prepended, may change in the future).

Every actor is created using an `actorOf` method called over an actor system or an actor context. You can create the actor system itself using its companion-object API:

```
def apply(name: String, config: Option[Config] = None, classLoader: Option[ClassLoader] =
    None, defaultExecutionContext: Option[ExecutionContext] = None): ActorSystem
```
> Creates a new ActorSystem with the specified name, the specified ClassLoader if given, otherwise obtains the current ClassLoader by first inspecting the current threads' getContextClassLoader, then tries to walk the stack to find the callers class loader, then falls back to the ClassLoader associated with the ActorSystem class.

When calling this method, you can specify the name of this system. You can also specify the configuration that defines certain aspects of the behavior of the actor system. The configuration is a file that is placed under the path specified under the CLASSPATH environmental variable. CLASSPATH is a standard way to let a JVM program know where to look for the classes it uses. For example, in an SBT project, you can place the configuration under the following path under the project root directory: `src/main/resources/application.conf`. In this configuration file, we can, for example, disable logging of so-called dead letters—messages intended for nonexistent actors:

```
akka.log-dead-letters=0
```

The configuration is quite flexible and grants you a degree of control of how your actor system is executed. For more information, please consult the Akka documentation on configuration.

You are also able to specify which execution context this `ActorSystem` is going to use to run its actors. Just as when we discussed IO, for a concurrency library, we need a way to specify what threading strategy the library should use. Finally, you can provide a class loader to `ActorSystem`, which will be used for things such as resolving configurations. All these parameters are optional. If you do not specify one of them, Akka will use reasonable defaults.

Now, let's have a look at how we run our Hello World example:

```
val system = ActorSystem()
val helloWorld = system.actorOf(Props[HelloWorld], "hello-world")
helloWorld ! Ping
```

First, we create `ActorSystem`. We create a `HelloWorld` actor. We do not call its constructor. We do so by using a `Props` object. We specify the class that we are going to create in the `Props` type parameters. We also specify the name of the actor to be created. `Props` is a case class defined as follows:

akka.actor

Props

Companion **object Props**

```
final case class Props(deploy: Deploy, clazz: Class[_], args: Seq[Any]) extends Product with
Serializable
```

Props is a configuration object using in creating an Actor; it is immutable, so it is thread-safe and fully shareable.

Its companion also defines a bunch of convenience methods to create `Props`:

```
def apply(clazz: Class[_], args: Any*): Props
    Scala API: create a Props given a class and its constructor arguments.

def apply[T <: Actor](creator: ⇒ T)(implicit arg0: ClassTag[T]): Props
    Scala API: Returns a Props that has default values except for "creator" which will be a function that creates an
    instance using the supplied thunk.

def apply[T <: Actor]()(implicit arg0: ClassTag[T]): Props
    Scala API: Returns a Props that has default values except for "creator" which will be a function that creates an
    instance of the supplied type using the default constructor.
```

After we create an actor with the help of `Props`, we can send a message to this actor. We do so with the `!` operator that `ActorRef` defines.

Actor parameters

Ordinary classes can have constructors that take arguments that can be used to parametrize the resulting instance. In the same way, an alternative version of the `Props` factory method can be used to create an actor with constructor parameters.

Imagine we have an actor whose constructor takes arguments:

```
class HelloName(name: String) extends Actor {
  val log = Logging(context.system, this)

  def receive = {
    case "say-hello" ⇒ log.info(s"Hello, $name")
  }
}
```

The preceding actor specifies the name of a person it is going to greet when it does its output. Also, notice how it accepts a string as a message. This is to show that you can send any object as a message to an actor.

When you have an actor that takes constructor parameters, a standard practice is to declare a `Props` factory method as a companion of an actor:

```
object HelloName {
  def props(name: String): Props =
    Props(classOf[HelloName], name)
}
```

This method abstracts away the `Props` needed to create this actor. Now, you can construct this actor and use it as follows:

```
val system = ActorSystem("hello-custom")
val helloPerson = system.actorOf(HelloName.props("Awesome Person"), "hello-
name")
val helloAlien = system.actorOf(HelloName.props("Alien Invaders"), "hello-
aliens")
helloPerson ! "say-hello"
helloAlien ! "say-hello"
helloAlien ! "random-msg"
```

The output is as follows:

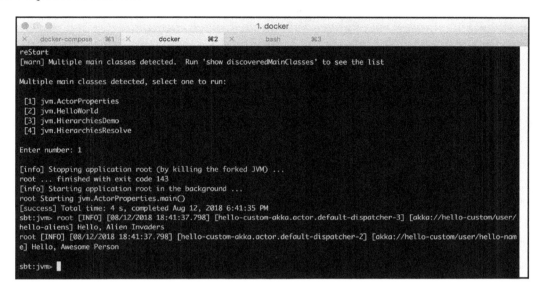

Working with actor systems

The strength of the actor model is that actors are lightweight, which means you can use millions of them on a single JVM running on an ordinary computer. Most of the time, you are not going to use a single actor but many actors. This requires a model to handle multiple actors.

In Akka, actors are organized in hierarchical trees—meaning that every actor has a parent and can have multiple children. Next, we will have a look at a slightly more complicated example that will showcase how actors work in hierarchies.

Task specification

Imagine we need to have multiple actors that all output a greeting to a given name to the log. Imagine also that we need to abstract away the fact that there are multiple actors in the system from the end user. We are going to do so by creating a single supervising actor that is going to be in charge of the execution of all its child actors. The child actors will be the actors that output the greeting message to the log, and the parent actor will be a manager that represents them.

The protocol is going to be as follows. First, create a `GreetingsManager` actor. Then, you are going to send a `SpawnGreeters` message to spawn a number of greeter actors parameterized by the number of greeters required. These spawned greeters must override the ones we already had. That overriding is done by stopping the previous actors and creating new ones.

Next, the user sends a `SayHello` message to the manager actor, which will instruct all of its children to perform output to the log. However, in a situation where the manager does not have any child actors spawned, we are going to output an error that asks the user to spawn the actors first.

Implementation

Let's start by defining the `Greeter` actor, as it is the simpler one:

```
class Greeter extends Actor {
  val log = Logging(context.system, this)

  def receive = {
    case SayHello(name) => log.info(s"Greetings to $name")
    case Die =>
      context stop self
      sender ! Dead
  }
}
```

The actor is going to accept a say hello message that is parameterized by the name the actor is supposed to greet. On receiving this message, it is going to perform a log output.

The `Greeter` actor has the means for the other actors to stop it. We have already discussed that one of the requirements of the task is that the manager actor should be able to terminate its existing actress to spawn a new actor. This can be accomplished by sending a message to this `Greeter` actor.

That message will use the `context stop self` pattern and will report to the sender actor that it is dead with the `Dead` message. Note that `context stop self` terminates the `self` actor only once it is done processing its current message. So the `sender ! Dead` code will be executed once the actor is still alive. The actor will terminate after it finishes processing the `Die` message.

We are using case classes as messages to communicate between actors because they are convenient for pattern-matching. The entire protocol looks as follows:

```
case class SpawnGreeters(n: Int)
case class SayHello(name: String)
case class Execute(f: () => Unit)
case object JobDone
case class GreetersResolution(result: Try[ActorRef])
case class GreetersTerminated(result: List[Any])
case object GreetersCreationAuthorised
case object Die
case object Dead
```

We will introduce every message as we encounter it.

Also, notice that Akka has a built-in message that can be used to stop actors. Whenever you send `PoisonPill` to an actor, its default behavior is to terminate itself:

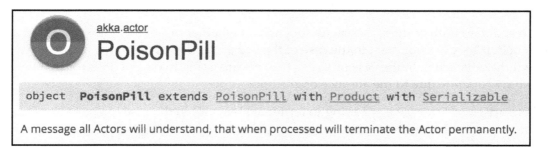

The reason we are not using `PoisonPill` here is that it does not play well with the pattern that we are going to use down the line.

Next, let's start working on the `GreetingsManager` actor:

```
class GreetingsManager extends Actor {
  val log = Logging(context.system, this)

  def baseReceive: Receive = {
    case SpawnGreeters(n) =>
      log.info("Spawning {} greeters", n)
      resolveGreeters()
      context become spawningGreeters(sender, n)
    case msg@SayHello(_) =>
      resolveGreeters()
      context become sayingHello(sender, msg)
  }
```

```
    def receive = baseReceive
 /*To be continued...*/
  }
```

The `receive` method is set to `baseReceive`. The reason we are not defining the API the actor exposes directly under `receive` is that we are going to leverage the `context become` functionality to change the behavior of the actor. `context become` can be used to override the functionality of the receive method. Every new behavior is going to be implemented as a separate method inside of this actor, for easy switching.

The `baseReceive` method enables the actor to handle two API messages: `SpawnGreeters` and `SayHello`. They will manage the underlying greeters and instruct them to perform output.

Notice that both of these methods follows a pattern. First, they optionally perform a log output, after that, they call the `resolveGreeters` method, and finally, they use the `context become` pattern to change the behavior of the current actor.

The reaction to both of these messages depends on whether or not the `Greeter` actors are spawned. If they are not, then in the case of the `SpawnGreeters` message, we are going to spawn them as usual. In the case of `SayHello`, we are going to output an error that we are not able to operate due to the absence of greeters.

If there are child actors, we are going to terminate them all in the case of `SpawnGreeter` to create new ones. In case of `SayHello`, we are going to instruct the child actors to output the greeting to the log.

In principle, you can track the state of all of your child actors from a mutable variable inside this actor. So, whenever you spawn a child actor, you save the references to it to a collection inside of this actor. This way, you will be able to quickly check for whether or not we have the child actors defined.

However, in this example, we are going to explore how to check for child actors using the built-in actor-hierarchy-management API.

The API is asynchronous and messaging-based. We have discussed already that it is crucial for the actors to be non-blocking. They are lightweight concurrency primitives, and threads are scarce, hence, to keep actors lightweight, we need to make sure that they utilize as little of their threading as necessary. Hence, we cannot afford to block on a children's query operation. The strategy is to request the children, register listeners to the responses as reactions to actor messages, and release the thread the actor is using to execute this strategy.

This strategy is what you see in the `baseReceive` example. The `resolveGreeters` method initiates the children resolution, and the results are going to arrive at the actor back as a message. We are going to change the `receive` implementation of this actor to handle this message.

Once the appropriate response arrives, these new behaviors will perform the requested functionality. We have separate behaviors for the `SpawnGreeters` and `SayHello` messages. Notice also that we parametrize these behaviors by the original sender of the current message and the data they provide. So, we will be able to execute the response request when we are ready, as well as notify the requester of the successful execution of this request.

Let's have a look at how the `resolveGreeters` function is implemented:

```
def greeterFromId(id: Any) = s"greeter-$id"

def resolveGreeters() =
  context.actorSelection(greeterFromId("*")).resolveOne(1 second)
    .transformWith {
      case s@Success(_) => Future.successful(s)
      case f@Failure(_) => Future.successful(f)
    }
    .map(GreetersResolution) pipeTo self
```

The `actorSelection` API is documented as follows:

---

def **actorSelection**(path: <u>ActorPath</u>): <u>ActorSelection</u>

    Construct an <u>akka.actor.ActorSelection</u> from the given path, which is parsed for wildcards (these are replaced by regular expressions internally).

def **actorSelection**(path: String): <u>ActorSelection</u>

    Construct an <u>akka.actor.ActorSelection</u> from the given path, which is parsed for wildcards (these are replaced by regular expressions internally).

In Akka, every actor has a name and a chain of parent actors it belongs to. Every actor also has a name. This allows you to identify actors by a path to them. For example, let's have a look again at the output of our hello world application:

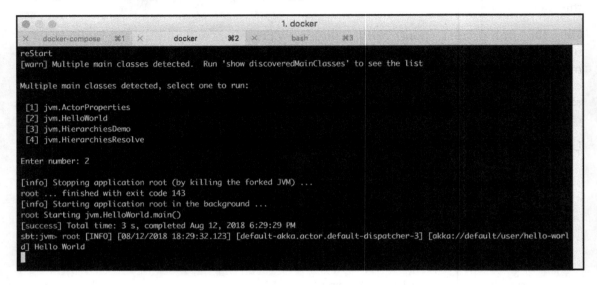

The log provides a path to the current actor in square brackets:

```
akka://default/user/hello-world
```

In Akka, it is possible to query actors by their path. It is possible to query entire slices of actors and send messages to entire collections of actors.

So, the actor selection function is a function that accepts a path to the actor that can include wildcards to query lots of actors at the same time, and it will return an actor selection under a Future.

Actor-selection provides you with some of the capabilities you would have on an ordinary `ActorRef`. However, for the `resolveGreeters` function, our objective is to check whether the greeters exist at all. This can be done by calling a `resolveOne` function and observing whether it returns a successful Future or a failed Future.

`resolveOne` takes the timeout as an argument and produces a Future that is going to result in a random actor from the collection of actors you are selecting. If the selection is empty, it is going to fail.

After that, we have an Akka pattern for Future interoperability. The pattern is called the pipe pattern, and in our example, it follows some transformations of the Future we are going to ignore for a moment:

```
/*...*/
  .map(GreetersResolution) pipeTo self
```

The `pipeTo` method is available on actor references via a Rich Wrapper:

The API it injects is as follows:

```
Instance Constructors

        new PipeableFuture(future: Future[T])(implicit executionContext: ExecutionContext)


Value Members

        val future: Future[T]


        def pipeTo(recipient: ActorRef)(implicit sender: ActorRef = Actor.noSender): Future[T]


        def pipeToSelection(recipient: ActorSelection)(implicit sender: ActorRef =
            Actor.noSender): Future[T]

        def to(recipient: ActorSelection, sender: ActorRef): PipeableFuture[T]
```

As we have discussed already, it is an anti-pattern to call a Future from an actor. Whenever you have an asynchronous computation that this actor depends upon, you need to make sure that this computation sends a message to this actor upon termination, and defines how to handle the message from the actor. Akka defines such a pattern for futures—the pipe pattern. The pattern makes sure that the message will be sent to a given actor upon future completion.

In our example, we request the `actorSelection` results and schedule a message with the results of this resolution to be sent to the current actor.

The transformations we are doing before the pattern are required to make sure that the failed future also sends a message to the current actor:

```
.transformWith {
  case s@Success(_) => Future.successful(s)
  case f@Failure(_) => Future.successful(f)
}
.map(GreetersResolution)
```

Finally, we use the map method to wrap the result of this future into a message that we want to send to the actor.

Let's have a look at how `actorSelection` works in practice with a small example. Consider the following case clause added to the base handler:

```
case "resolve" =>
  val selection = context.actorSelection(greeterFromId("*"))
  selection.resolveOne(1 second).onComplete { res =>
    log.info(s"Selection: $selection; Res: $res") }
```

Our actor manager is now capable of receiving a `resolve` string as a message, upon which it will perform an actor-selection of all the current greeters and put the results into the log.

We can run the resolution as follows:

```
implicit val timeout: Timeout = 3 seconds
val system = ActorSystem("hierarchy-demo")
val gm = system.actorOf(Props[this.GreetingsManager], "greetings-manager")

Await.ready(for {
  _ <- Future { gm ! "resolve" }
  _ <- gm ? SpawnGreeters(10)
  _ <- (1 to 10).toList.traverse(_ => Future { gm ! "resolve" })
} yield (), 5 seconds)
```

We are working under the Future Monadic flow here. This is because, on some occasions, we are going to wait on the response of an actor system before we proceed. Let's have a look at the example line by line.

First, we have a `resolve` message sent to the current actor:

```
  _ <- Future { gm ! "resolve" }
```

The ? operator is injected by the following Rich Wrapper in Akka.

```
_ <- gm ? SpawnGreeters(10)
```

Next, we have an ask pattern:

Here is the API it injects:

```
Instance Constructors

          new AskableActorRef(actorRef: ActorRef)


Value Members

          def ?(message: Any)(implicit timeout: Timeout, sender: ActorRef = Actor.noSender):
              Future[Any]

          val actorRef: ActorRef


          def ask(message: Any)(implicit timeout: Timeout, sender: ActorRef = Actor.noSender):
              Future[Any]
```

The pattern sends a message to an actor reference, just like the ordinary ! operator. However, it also expects the actor to respond to the current actor. The response message is returned under a Future. Under the hood, this ask method creates a temporary child actor that actually sends the message to the original addressee. If the addressee responds to this temporary actor, the response will be available as the Future's result.

We are using the ask pattern because we want to suspend the execution of the example until the manager reports that the actors were successfully created. The first line of this example models a case where the greeting manager had no child actors. With the second line, we create the child actors and wait until they are created. The next line will test how actor-selection works against a non-empty selection:

```
_ <- (1 to 10).toList.traverse(_ => Future { gm ! "resolve" })
```

With this line, we are sending 10 resolve messages to the greeting manager. The result of the execution of the program is as follows:

```
                                    1. docker
 ×   docker-compose   ⌘1   ×        docker        ⌘2   ×      bash      ⌘3

sbt:jvm> root [INFO] [08/12/2018 18:33:36.254] [scala-execution-context-global-14] [akka://hierarchy-demo/user/greetings
-manager] Selection: ActorSelection[Anchor(akka://hierarchy-demo/user/greetings-manager#-335253773), Path(/greeter-*)];
Res: Failure(akka.actor.ActorNotFound: Actor not found for: ActorSelection[Anchor(akka://hierarchy-demo/user/greetings-m
anager#-335253773), Path(/greeter-*)])
root [INFO] [08/12/2018 18:33:36.254] [hierarchy-demo-akka.actor.default-dispatcher-3] [akka://hierarchy-demo/user/greet
ings-manager] Spawning 10 greeters
root [INFO] [08/12/2018 18:33:36.310] [hierarchy-demo-akka.actor.default-dispatcher-3] [akka://hierarchy-demo/user/greet
ings-manager] Created 10 greeters
root [INFO] [08/12/2018 18:33:37.093] [scala-execution-context-global-8] [akka://hierarchy-demo/user/greetings-manager]
Selection: ActorSelection[Anchor(akka://hierarchy-demo/user/greetings-manager#-335253773), Path(/greeter-*)]; Res: Succe
ss(Actor[akka://hierarchy-demo/user/greetings-manager/greeter-6#1542315700])
root [INFO] [08/12/2018 18:33:37.103] [scala-execution-context-global-8] [akka://hierarchy-demo/user/greetings-manager]
Selection: ActorSelection[Anchor(akka://hierarchy-demo/user/greetings-manager#-335253773), Path(/greeter-*)]; Res: Succe
ss(Actor[akka://hierarchy-demo/user/greetings-manager/greeter-1#-449866333])
root [INFO] [08/12/2018 18:33:37.123] [scala-execution-context-global-8] [akka://hierarchy-demo/user/greetings-manager]
Selection: ActorSelection[Anchor(akka://hierarchy-demo/user/greetings-manager#-335253773), Path(/greeter-*)]; Res: Succe
ss(Actor[akka://hierarchy-demo/user/greetings-manager/greeter-1#-449866333])
root [INFO] [08/12/2018 18:33:37.126] [scala-execution-context-global-8] [akka://hierarchy-demo/user/greetings-manager]
Selection: ActorSelection[Anchor(akka://hierarchy-demo/user/greetings-manager#-335253773), Path(/greeter-*)]; Res: Succe
ss(Actor[akka://hierarchy-demo/user/greetings-manager/greeter-1#-449866333])
root [INFO] [08/12/2018 18:33:37.128] [scala-execution-context-global-8] [akka://hierarchy-demo/user/greetings-manager]
Selection: ActorSelection[Anchor(akka://hierarchy-demo/user/greetings-manager#-335253773), Path(/greeter-*)]; Res: Succe
ss(Actor[akka://hierarchy-demo/user/greetings-manager/greeter-1#-449866333])
root [INFO] [08/12/2018 18:33:37.136] [scala-execution-context-global-8] [akka://hierarchy-demo/user/greetings-manager]
Selection: ActorSelection[Anchor(akka://hierarchy-demo/user/greetings-manager#-335253773), Path(/greeter-*)]; Res: Succe
ss(Actor[akka://hierarchy-demo/user/greetings-manager/greeter-1#-449866333])
root [INFO] [08/12/2018 18:33:37.136] [scala-execution-context-global-14] [akka://hierarchy-demo/user/greetings-manager]
 Selection: ActorSelection[Anchor(akka://hierarchy-demo/user/greetings-manager#-335253773), Path(/greeter-*)]; Res: Succ
ess(Actor[akka://hierarchy-demo/user/greetings-manager/greeter-1#-449866333])
root [INFO] [08/12/2018 18:33:37.136] [scala-execution-context-global-14] [akka://hierarchy-demo/user/greetings-manager]
```

The result is nondeterministic. This means that every time we send a message to the actor, we are not sure which actor will be returned. Notice how, at first, the greeter with ID 6 is returned, and on subsequent invocations, the greeter with ID 1 is returned.

Let's now have a look at how this pattern plays with the rest of the application. Let's explore the `SayHello` message-handling example first. After calling `resolveGreeters`, we use the `context become` pattern to change the way the actor handles messages and set a new `receive` function to `sayingHello`. Let's have a look at how `sayingHello` is defined:

```scala
def sayingHello(requester: ActorRef, msg: Any): Receive = {
  case GreetersResolution(Failure(_)) =>
    log.error("There are no greeters. Please create some first with
SpawnGreeters message.")
    context become baseReceive
    requester ! JobDone
```

```
    case GreetersResolution(Success(_)) =>
      log.info(s"Dispatching message $msg to greeters")
      context.actorSelection(greeterFromId("*")) ! msg
      context become baseReceive
      requester ! JobDone
  }
```

sayingHello is going to react on the `GreeterResolution` message. This is precisely the message we are sending from the result of the `Greeter` functions we just discussed. The message has the following definition:

```
case class GreetersResolution(result: Try[ActorRef])
```

So we have two cases of the payload of that message—the success and failure. We have a failure in which there are no greeters registered:

```
case GreetersResolution(Failure(_)) =>
  log.error("There are no greeters. Please create some first with
SpawnGreeters message.")
  context become baseReceive
  requester ! JobDone
```

In this case, we log an error saying that there are no greeters. We then switch the actor's receive logic back to base and report to the original requester that the job is done, so that it is aware that the actor system has finished processing its request, in case the requester needs to wait upon such an event:

```
case GreetersResolution(Success(_)) =>
  log.info(s"Dispatching message $msg to greeters")
  context.actorSelection(greeterFromId("*")) ! msg
  context become baseReceive
  requester ! JobDone
```

In the case of a successful resolution of greeters, we select the greeters using actor-selection logic and send the message to this selection. Finally, we switch back to base-handling logic and report to the requester that the job is done.

Now, let's have a look at how the spawning greeters logic works:

```
def spawningGreeters(requester: ActorRef, numGreeters: Int): Receive = {
  case GreetersResolution(Failure(_)) =>
    self ! GreetersCreationAuthorised
  case GreetersResolution(Success(_)) =>
    log.warning(s"Greeters already exist. Killing them and creating the new
ones.")
    context.children
      .filter(c => raw"greeter-\d".r.unapplySeq(c.path.name).isDefined)
```

```
      .toList.traverse(_ ? Die)
      .map(GreetersTerminated) pipeTo self

  case GreetersTerminated(report) =>
    log.info(s"All greeters terminated, report: $report. Creating the new
ones now.")
    self ! GreetersCreationAuthorised

  case GreetersCreationAuthorised =>
    (1 to numGreeters).foreach { id =>
      context.actorOf(Props[Greeter], greeterFromId(id)) }
    log.info(s"Created $numGreeters greeters")
    requester ! JobDone
    context become baseReceive
}
```

The method takes a requester actor and the number of greeters to create. Let's have a look at the message handlers:

```
case GreetersResolution(Failure(_)) =>
  self ! GreetersCreationAuthorised
```

If there are no children registered, we send a GreetersCreationAuthorised message to ourselves specifying that it is safe to create greeters. We need this authorization because sometimes it is not safe to create new greeters—namely when the current actor has old greeters still alive. In this case, we can have naming conflicts we want to avoid:

```
case GreetersResolution(Success(_)) =>
  log.warning(s"Greeters already exist. Killing them and creating the new
ones.")
  context.children
    .filter(c => raw"greeter-\d".r.unapplySeq(c.path.name).isDefined)
    .toList.traverse(_ ? Die)
    .map(GreetersTerminated) pipeTo self
```

In case the resolution was successful, we must kill this actor's greeters first. We output a warning message to that log specifying that we are going to kill the existing greeters. After that, we obtain the children from the actor context. children provides us with an iterator of all the children of this actor. We are then going to filter the actors by name with a regular expression:

```
c => raw"greeter-\d".r.unapplySeq(c.path.name).isDefined
```

Above, `raw` is needed so that \ is not treated as an escape character, but is interpreted literally. `r` turns the string it is called on into a regular expression object – this API is a part of Scala Core library. `unapplySeq` attempts to match the regex it is called on against the string passed to it as an argument. If the match succeeds, the method returns `Some`, otherwise – `None`. See Scala Core API on `scala.util.matching.Regex` for more information.

In case we have any other children, only the greeters that follow a specific naming convention will get selected. We do not have any other children in this example. However, it is still a good idea to identify the target children.

After we have filtered the actors to kill, we send them a termination message:

```
.toList.traverse(_ ? Die)
```

We are using the ask pattern again in the body of the `traverse` method to produce a Future. The greeter actors will respond with a message reporting that they were terminated. This allows us to block the execution asynchronously and continue once all the greeters are dead. We can achieve this by using the ask pattern to track the termination of individual actors, then combine the returned Futures into one Future with the `traverse` method. This Future will succeed once all of the actors are terminated.

Finally, we wrap the Future's contents into the `GreetersTerminated` message. Next, let's look at the `GreetersTerminated` branch:

```
case GreetersTerminated(report) =>
  log.info(s"All greeters terminated, report: $report. Creating the new
ones now.")
  self ! GreetersCreationAuthorised
```

We output the report of the termination to the log and send the authorization message to `self` to begin the greeters' creation process:

```
case GreetersCreationAuthorised =>
  (1 to numGreeters).foreach { id =>
    context.actorOf(Props[Greeter], greeterFromId(id)) }
  log.info(s"Created $numGreeters greeters")
  requester ! JobDone
  context become baseReceive
```

`GreetersCreationAuthorised` is a branch that will only be executed once it is safe to create new greeters. It will create new greeters from a loop:

```
(1 to numGreeters).foreach { id =>
  context.actorOf(Props[Greeter], greeterFromId(id)) }
```

Here, the second argument to `actorOf` is defined as follows:

```
def greeterFromId(id: Any) = s"greeter-$id"
```

Next, we notify the requesting actor that the job of creating the greeters is completed. Finally, we switch the context back to `baseReceive`. Now, let's write a test program to see how the example works:

```
implicit val timeout: Timeout = 3 seconds
val system = ActorSystem("hierarchy-demo")
val gm = system.actorOf(Props[this.GreetingsManager], "greetings-manager")

def printState(childrenEmpty: Boolean, isHelloMessage: Boolean) =
  Future { println(s"\n=== Children: ${if (childrenEmpty) "empty" else
"present"}, " +
    s"Message: ${if (isHelloMessage) "SayHello" else "SpawnGreeters"}") }

Await.ready(for {
  _ <- printState(true, true)
  _ <- gm ? SayHello("me")

  _ <- printState(true, false)
  _ <- gm ? SpawnGreeters(3)

  _ <- printState(false, false)
  _ <- gm ? SpawnGreeters(3)

  _ <- printState(false, true)
  _ <- gm ? SayHello("me")
} yield (), 5 seconds)
```

We first send a hello message to an empty greeter manager. Then, we spawn the greeters with a corresponding message. Then we send the `SpawnGreeters` message once more, to see how the greeters manager will first kill its existing greeters and only then spawn the new ones. Finally, we send the `SayHello` message again.

We have two messages and two possible states of the manager's children greeters. This gives us four possible combinations. Every one of the messages in the example checks the behavior of each of these cases. Notice, how we are using the ask pattern to block the execution flow asynchronously until the actor responds that it has completed the operation. This makes sure that we do not send messages too early.

The output of the message looks as follows:

```
                                    1. docker
 ×   docker-compose  ⌘1   ×      docker      ⌘2   ×      bash      ⌘3
root === Children: empty, Message: SayHello
root [ERROR] [08/12/2018 18:36:15.393] [hierarchy-demo-akka.actor.default-dispatcher-2] [akka://hierarchy-demo/user/gree
tings-manager] There are no greeters. Please create some first with SpawnGreeters message.
root
root === Children: empty, Message: SpawnGreeters
root [INFO] [08/12/2018 18:36:15.434] [hierarchy-demo-akka.actor.default-dispatcher-2] [akka://hierarchy-demo/user/greet
ings-manager] Spawning 3 greeters
root
root === Children: present, Message: SpawnGreeters
root [INFO] [08/12/2018 18:36:15.486] [hierarchy-demo-akka.actor.default-dispatcher-2] [akka://hierarchy-demo/user/greet
ings-manager] Created 3 greeters
root [INFO] [08/12/2018 18:36:15.493] [hierarchy-demo-akka.actor.default-dispatcher-2] [akka://hierarchy-demo/user/greet
ings-manager] Spawning 3 greeters
root [WARN] [08/12/2018 18:36:15.525] [hierarchy-demo-akka.actor.default-dispatcher-5] [akka://hierarchy-demo/user/greet
ings-manager] Greeters already exist. Killing them and creating the new ones.
root [INFO] [08/12/2018 18:36:16.222] [hierarchy-demo-akka.actor.default-dispatcher-5] [akka://hierarchy-demo/user/greet
ings-manager] All greeters terminated, report: List(Dead, Dead, Dead). Creating the new ones now.
root [INFO] [08/12/2018 18:36:16.225] [hierarchy-demo-akka.actor.default-dispatcher-5] [akka://hierarchy-demo/user/greet
ings-manager] Created 3 greeters
root
root === Children: present, Message: SayHello
root [INFO] [08/12/2018 18:36:16.234] [hierarchy-demo-akka.actor.default-dispatcher-5] [akka://hierarchy-demo/user/greet
ings-manager] Dispatching message SayHello(me) to greeters
root [INFO] [08/12/2018 18:36:16.236] [hierarchy-demo-akka.actor.default-dispatcher-4] [akka://hierarchy-demo/user/greet
ings-manager/greeter-2] Greetings to me
root [INFO] [08/12/2018 18:36:16.235] [hierarchy-demo-akka.actor.default-dispatcher-3] [akka://hierarchy-demo/user/greet
ings-manager/greeter-1] Greetings to me
root [INFO] [08/12/2018 18:36:16.237] [hierarchy-demo-akka.actor.default-dispatcher-3] [akka://hierarchy-demo/user/greet
ings-manager/greeter-3] Greetings to me
```

Summary

In this chapter, we discussed the Akka framework, which is a de-facto standard for actor-oriented programming in Scala. We have learnt how to create new actors, how to define them, and how to run an actor-based application. We saw how actors are organized into actor systems, and how they work together in hierarchies. Also, we briefly discussed the patterns that Akka provides for working with actors and futures.

In the next chapter, we will see the usage of the actors model in practice by looking at an example application implemented with this model.

Questions

1. What are the principles of the Actor model in Akka's implementation?
2. How do you define an actor in Akka?
3. How do you create a new actor?
4. How do you send a message to an actor?
5. What is the ask pattern and how do you use it?
6. What is the pipe pattern and how do you use it?

13
Use Case - A Parallel Web Crawler

In the previous chapter, we discussed the actors model and a framework that you can use to program with actors. However, the actor model is a paradigm just like functional programming. In principle, if you know the actors model from one language, you can use it in another language even if it doesn't have a framework that supports the actor model. This is because an actor model is an approach to reasoning about parallel computations, not some language-specific set of tools.

This state of things, just like functional programming, has its own benefits and drawbacks. The benefit is that you are not language-dependent if you depend on concepts. Once you know a concept, you can come to any programming language at all, and be capable of using them. However, the learning curve is steep. Precisely because it is all about paradigm and approach, it is not enough to install a library and start using it after skimming its documentation, as it is frequently the case with many other libraries or general-purpose languages that are similar one to another. Since it is all about shifting the paradigm, you need to apply some learning effort in order to understand the paradigm and how to use it in practice.

In the previous chapter, we built up a theoretical foundation on the toolset the actor model provides, as well as discussed the main concepts of the actor model and how to use it in practice. However, since it is a set of ideas and not just a library, it is necessary to develop an intuition for how it works. The best way to develop an intuition for a new paradigm is to have a look at some practical examples that will demonstrate how this paradigm is applicable in practice.

For this reason, in this chapter, we will be looking at a practical example of where an actors model can be applied. We will be looking at an example of web crawling.

In this chapter, we will cover the following topics:

- Problem statement
- Sequential solution
- A parallel solution with Akka

Problem statement

In this chapter, we will be addressing the problem of building a web crawler. Web crawlers are important, for example, in the domain of indexing and searching the web.

The graph structure of the web

All the websites can be imagined as a graph of pages. Every page contains some HTML markup and content. As part of this content, most web pages contain links to other pages. Since links are supposed to take you from one page to another, we can visualize the web as a graph. We can visualize links as edges that take you from one node to another node.

Given such a model for the entire internet, it's possible to address the problem of searching for information over the web:

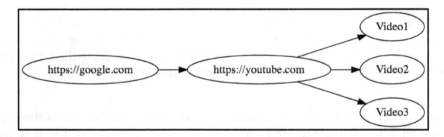

We are talking about a problem that is faced by the search engines. The objective of a search engine is to index the information stored online and devise algorithms that will find the required pages—nodes of the graph—efficiently based on certain queries by the end user. The algorithms required to index those nodes and to match the user requests to the information stored in the nodes are complex, and we will not be addressing them in this chapter. Often, these algorithms involve advanced machine learning and natural-language processing solutions to understand and evaluate the content stored in the pages. The brightest minds in machine learning and natural language processing work on search tasks for companies such as Google.

Therefore, in this chapter, we will be addressing a task that is also faced by search engines but is easier to tackle. Before indexing the information stored online, this information needs to be collected. A collection of information is a task of traversing the graph of all the pages and storing the contents in a database. The task of web crawling is precisely the task of traversing the graph starting from one node and following to other nodes through links. In the example in this chapter, we will not be storing website information in a database but will focus on the web crawling task.

Collecting information from the graph

Collecting information from a graph can be depicted as follows:

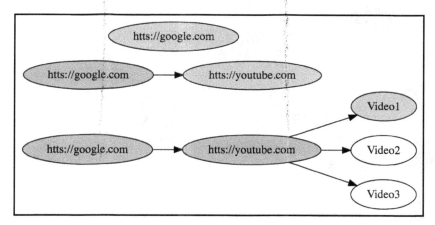

In the preceding illustration, the blue nodes are the ones currently being processed, the green ones are the ones that have already been processed, and the white ones are the ones not yet processed. This preceding task can be implemented as follows:

1. Specify which URL you would like to start from, that is, the starting node from which the traversal will start.

2. The crawler will visit the URL by issuing a GET request to it, and receive some HTML:

```
                                          1. java
Progress for depth 1: 153 of 165
Progress for depth 1: 154 of 165
Progress for depth 1: 155 of 165
Progress for depth 1: 156 of 165
Progress for depth 1: 157 of 165
Progress for depth 1: 158 of 165
Progress for depth 1: 159 of 165
Progress for depth 1: 160 of 165
Progress for depth 1: 161 of 165
Progress for depth 1: 162 of 165
Progress for depth 1: 163 of 165
Progress for depth 1: 164 of 165
http://mvnrepository.com/artifact/com.github.paulcwarren
http://mvnrepository.com/artifact/io.micrometer/micrometer-registry-influx/1.0.5
http://central.maven.org/maven2/com/nepxion/discovery-plugin-config-center/4.0.0
http://mvnrepository.com/artifact/org.webpieces/http1_1-parser/1.9.45
http://mvnrepository.com/artifact/net.nemerosa.ontrack/ontrack-extension-git/3.35.8#ivy
http://mvnrepository.com/artifact/net.nemerosa.ontrack/ontrack-json/3.35.8#sbt
http://mvnrepository.com/artifact/org.webpieces/core-channelmanager2/1.9.35/usages
http://mvnrepository.com/artifact/io.github.lukehutch/fast-classpath-scanner/2.12.2
http://mvnrepository.com/artifact/org.webpieces/core-channelmanager2
http://mvnrepository.com/artifact/com.github.paulcwarren/spring-content-solr
1664
background log: debug:  Thread run-main-0 exited.
background log: debug: Interrupting remaining threads (should be all daemons).
background log: debug: Not interrupting system thread Thread[Keep-Alive-Timer,8,system]
background log: debug: Sandboxed run complete..
background log: debug: Exited with code 0
[success] Total time: 22 s, completed Jul 16, 2018 2:02:01 PM
>
```

3. After receiving this HTML text, the crawler will extract the edges of the current node—the links to other nodes. The links are well defined in HTML markup. They are specified as follows:

```
<a herf="link_address">link_text</a>
```

So, once we have the HTML markup, we can look it up for the contents matching the preceding pattern. After that, we may want to collect all of the links presented on the page into one single collection structure, for example, a list. Once we have that, we may want to execute the same operation recursively on every node linked to the current one.

Parallel nature of the task

The preceding task was chosen as an example for this chapter because it is parallelizable by nature. Basically, whenever you have a bunch of tasks that are not dependent one on another, it may be a good idea to parallelize the tasks. In our example, the preceding task can be very well conceptualized as a set of independent operations. A single unit of operation is the task of visiting a URL, abstracting all of the other nodes that are linked by the page of this URL, and then executing the same task on these URLs recursively.

This makes our crawling example a very good case for parallel actor application. Running all these tasks sequentially for every URL may be very time consuming, and therefore it is much more efficient to apply some strategy to the tasks. Even on a single-core CPU computer processing power, even in the case when most of the tasks are processed in a simulated parallelism manner, the operation will still be dozens of times more efficient than in the sequential case. This is because a lot of waiting is involved in requesting HTML from the internet or a GET request.

In the succeeding diagram, you can see an example of a request to have a process performed from a single thread:

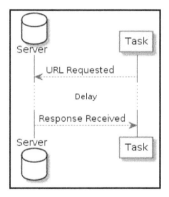

 So, as you can see, the thread issues a request, and then it waits for the response to be derived. From your own browsing experience, you can easily say that sometimes a response from a website may take seconds to arrive. So essentially, these seconds will be wasted by the thread because it will block on this task, and the processor will do nothing useful at the time.

Even when you have a single core and even when you have only an option of simulated parallelism, the processor can still be utilized much more efficiently, if when one thread waits for the request to arrive at it, another thread issues a request or processes a response that has already arrived at it.

As you can see from the diagram, requests are issued much more efficiently, and while one thread waits for a request and sleeps, the processor is busy with other threads that have a real job to do:

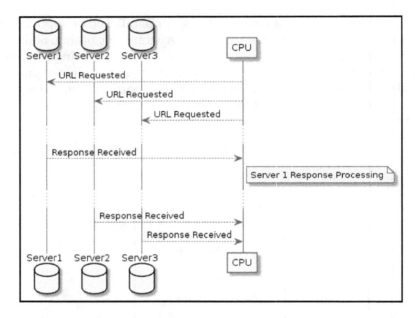

In general, such kind of blocking can be very frequently the case. For example, you may have some operations that wait on a database to give a response, or on a message to arrive from the outer world. So even in the case of simulated parallelism, these kinds of situations can be greatly sped up. Needless to say, most modern machines work in a setting of several cores that will speed up the execution greatly.

Now that we know the exact specification of the task, and we why exactly it makes sense to parallelize this task, let's get our hands dirty and see some implementation in action. However, before we dive into the details of the actor-based implementation of the task, let's first have a look at how this can be implemented sequentially, just so that we have a baseline to work against.

Sequential solution

First of all, let's have a look at how we would like to use the solution once it is built. Also, let's have a look at exactly which output we expect from the solution:

```
val target = new URL("http://mvnrepository.com/")
val res = fetchToDepth(target, 1)
 println(res.take(10).mkString("\n"))
 println(res.size)
```

In the preceding code, we perform the following things. First of all, we would like to be able to define our URL in terms of a Java-native URL object. In this example, we are using the Maven repository website as a crawling target. mvnrepository.com is a website that provides an easy search through all of the Maven packages.

After that, we have a call to fetchToDepth. This is the method that is supposed to do the actual work for us and actually crawls the website for links. As a first argument, we supply it a URL we want to process. As the second argument, we supply it the depth to which you want to search the graph.

The idea behind having the depth is to avoid infinite recursion. The web is a very interconnected place. So, when we start from one node and begin to descend recursively into the nodes it is connected to, it may take a very long time to arrive at the terminal nodes, that is, a node that does not have any further links. It is quite possible that for the majority of the websites out there, such a lookup will be infinite or will take an unreasonably long time to accomplish. Therefore, we would like to limit our lookup depth. The semantics of how it will work is that for every edge the algorithm searches, the depth will be decreased by one. Once the depths reach zero, the algorithm will not try to follow the edges any further.

The result of this from function-execution will be a collection. Precisely, a set of links that were collected from this website. After that, we take the first 10 links and output them to the standard output, one link per line. Also, we output the number of links that the system managed to extract in total. We do not print all the links because there will be too many of them.

The output we are aiming to get is as follows:

```
                                    1. java
Progress for depth 1: 153 of 165
Progress for depth 1: 154 of 165
Progress for depth 1: 155 of 165
Progress for depth 1: 156 of 165
Progress for depth 1: 157 of 165
Progress for depth 1: 158 of 165
Progress for depth 1: 159 of 165
Progress for depth 1: 160 of 165
Progress for depth 1: 161 of 165
Progress for depth 1: 162 of 165
Progress for depth 1: 163 of 165
Progress for depth 1: 164 of 165
http://mvnrepository.com/artifact/com.github.paulcwarren
http://mvnrepository.com/artifact/io.micrometer/micrometer-registry-influx/1.0.5
http://central.maven.org/maven2/com/nepxion/discovery-plugin-config-center/4.0.0
http://mvnrepository.com/artifact/org.webpieces/http1_1-parser/1.9.45
http://mvnrepository.com/artifact/net.nemerosa.ontrack/ontrack-extension-git/3.35.8#ivy
http://mvnrepository.com/artifact/net.nemerosa.ontrack/ontrack-json/3.35.8#sbt
http://mvnrepository.com/artifact/org.webpieces/core-channelmanager2/1.9.35/usages
http://mvnrepository.com/artifact/io.github.lukehutch/fast-classpath-scanner/2.12.2
http://mvnrepository.com/artifact/org.webpieces/core-channelmanager2
http://mvnrepository.com/artifact/com.github.paulcwarren/spring-content-solr
1664
background log: debug:  Thread run-main-0 exited.
background log: debug: Interrupting remaining threads (should be all daemons).
background log: debug: Not interrupting system thread Thread[Keep-Alive-Timer,8,system]
background log: debug: Sandboxed run complete..
background log: debug: Exited with code 0
[success] Total time: 22 s, completed Jul 16, 2018 2:02:01 PM
>
```

Next, let's explore the sequential implementation of the preceding objectives. Let's have a look at `fetchToDepth`:

```
def fetchToDepth(url: URL, depth: Int, visited: Set[URL] = Set()): Set[URL]
```

As you can see, the function accepts the three arguments. Two of them are the ones that we have already seen before and discussed in our example API usage. The third one is the set of URLs that the crawler has already visited. Why might we have such a set? Why does the crawler need it at all? How will it behave if we do not store the set of all visited links?

In fact, the same set must be stored for any similar graph-traversal situation. The problem here is the presence of cycles in a graph.

In the diagram below, you can see how a graph with cycles might emerge in a web crawler application:

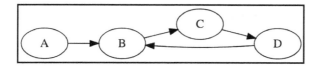

It is enough for website **A** to reference website **B**, and then website **B** references website **A** for a cycle to emerge. If the graph has a cycle, there is a risk that our traversal algorithm will enter an infinite loop if it tries to traverse it without keeping track of the nodes that it has already visited. For this reason, we need to keep track of the visited nodes. The first thing to do in the `fetchToDepth` function is to fetch the given URL:

```
val links = fetch(url).getOrElse(Set())
```

We are using the following function to do fetch the given URL:

```
def fetch(url: URL): Option[Set[URL]] = Try {
  Jsoup.connect(url.toString)
    .get
    .getElementsByAttribute("href")
    .asScala.map( h => new URL(url, h.attr("href")) ).toSet
}.toOption
```

The `fetch` function is a function that takes a URL and outputs `Option[Set[URL]]`, the data structure with the links that this page contains.

Inside this function, nothing really remarkable happens except the side effects. We are using `Try` to capture the side effect of an error. Then, we convert `Try` to `Option` because we are not interested in the error type, as explained below.

The logic of this function is straightforward. We are using a popular Java library, called `Jsoap`, in order to connect to the given URL, issue a get request, retrieve all of the elements that have an `href` attribute that contains a link, and afterwards, map the resulting elements by extracting their links.

The logic is wrapped into `Try`, which is later converted into `Option`. Why have such a system involving `Try` and `Option`? As we learned in the first part of this book, both `Try` and `Option` are effect types. The entire idea behind an effect type is to abstract away some side effects that might happen. Since our business logic is wrapped into the `Try` effect, some side effects that are abstracted by `Try` might happen in this logic.

`Try` abstracts away the possibility of an error or an exception. In fact, a lot of things can go wrong when we are performing a request to a remote server. For example, the request can time out, or we may lose internet connection, or the server can return an erroneous status code.

In the context of massive data processing, things inevitably go around for some of the data nodes. This means that when performing the crawling operation discussed previously, we can be almost certain that sometimes it will fail. What happens if you design a function that does not account for such errors? Most likely, our algorithm will encounter an exception and will fail midway through the dataset. This is why fault tolerance is a crucial property of this kind of system.

In the preceding example, fault tolerance is achieved by wrapping the possibility of an error into the `Try` effect type. Another thing to notice here is not only the `Try` type but the fact that it is converted into `Option`. `Option` indicates that a function may or may not produce a result. In the context of converting from `Try` to `Option`, `Try` is mapped to `Some` if it is a successful attempt, and it is mapped to `None` if it is a failure. In the case of a failure, some information about the error that has happened gets lost when we convert `Try` to `Option`. This fact reflects the attitude that we don't care about the type of the error that might occur.

This kind of attitude demands further explanation, as it is usually the case everywhere where we intentionally drop data. We discussed that in this kind of massive data-processing, errors are inevitable. Of course, it is nice to have your algorithm catch and handle gracefully most of the errors that it will encounter, however, it is not always possible. You cannot remove the fact that sooner or later the algorithm will encounter an error since the algorithm works not on some dummy data but on real-world websites. Whenever you are working with real-world data, errors are a fact of life, and you cannot plan to handle every possible error that occurs gracefully.

Hence, a proper way to structure a program that is certain to encounter errors is fault tolerance. This means that we build the program as if it is certain to encounter errors and we plan for recovering from any error without actually specifying the type of the error. The fact that we are converting our `Try` to `Option` here reflects the attitude toward errors. The attitude is that we don't care about which error might happen during execution, we only care that an error can happen.

Fault tolerance is one of the fundamental principles of the design of Akka. Akka is built with fault tolerance and resilience in mind, which means that actors are designed as if they are certain to encounter errors, and Akka provides you with a framework to specify how to recover from them.

Let's now return to our `fetch` line from the `fetchToDepth` method and see how exactly this attitude plays out in the logic of our example:

```
fetch(url).getOrElse(Set())
```

Let's return to our `fetchToDepth` example. After we perform the affect statement on a given URL, we also perform a `getOrElse` call on it. `getOrElse` is a method defined on a Scala `Option` that has the following signature:

```
final def getOrElse[B >: A](default: ⇒ B): B
```

    Returns the option's value if the option is nonempty, otherwise return the result of evaluating **default**.

    default   the default expression.

    Annotations   @<u>inline</u>()

So basically, this method tries to extract a value from `Option`. If the value is not present in `Option`, it outputs the default value that is supplied to the method. `getOrElse` is equivalent to the following code:

```
type A
val opt: Option[A]
val default: A

opt match {
  case Some(x) => x
  case None => default
}
```

So now we have a set of links extracted from a given link. Let's now have a look at how it is traversed in our sequential example:

```
if (depth > 0) links ++ links
 .filter(!visited(_))
 ./*...*/
```

In the preceding code, you can see a chunk of the code in the `fetchToDepth` method. First of all, we check whether the depth is greater than 0. Previously, we discussed how specifying depth constraints could save us from infinite execution.

The first statement after the `if` check is the current link accumulator, the `links` variable, being united with some larger right-hand statement. In the snippet above, only a fragment of this statement is presented, and we will discuss it step by step. The big picture is that this statement applies `fetchToDepth` recursively to all the links in the `links` set.

This means that the right side of the ++ operator takes every link from the set that we have retrieved and extracts all the links present in its page. This must be done recursively. But first, we need to clean up the set of all abstracted URL from the current link so that it doesn't contain the links that we have previously visited. This is to tackle the problem of cycles in the graph:

```
.toList
.zipWithIndex
```

Next, we have the resulting set further transformed by the call to the `toList` and `zipWithIndex` methods. Basically, these two methods are required for logging purposes. Inside data-processing operations, you would like to have some reporting in order to keep track of the operations. In our case, we would like to assign a numeric ID to every link that we are going to visit, and we are going to log the fact that we are visiting a link with a given ID into the standard output. The signature of `zipWithIndex` is as follows:

```
def zipWithIndex: List[(A, Int)]
    [use case]
    Zips this list with its indices.

    returns     A new list containing pairs consisting of all elements of this list paired with their index. Indices
                start at 0.

    Definition Classes    IterableLike → GenIterableLike

    Full Signature

    Example:
    List("a", "b", "c").zipWithIndex = List(("a", 0), ("b", 1), ("c", 2))
```

So basically, a list of elements, A, becomes a list of pairs of A and Int:

```
.foldLeft(Set[URL]()) { case (accum, (next, id)) =>
 println(s"Progress for depth $depth: $id of ${links.size}")
 accum ++ (if (!accum(next)) fetchToDepth(next, depth - 1, accum) else
Set())
 }
```

In the preceding code, you can see the logic that actually performs the processing of every given URL. We are using a `foldLeft` method. Let's have a look at its signature:

```
def foldLeft[B](z: B)(op: (B, A) ⇒ B): B

    Applies a binary operator to a start value and all elements of this sequence, going left to right.

    Note: will not terminate for infinite-sized collections.

    B           the result type of the binary operator.

    z           the start value.

    op          the binary operator.

    returns     the result of inserting op between consecutive elements of this sequence, going left to right
                with the start value z on the left:

                    op(...op(z, x_1), x_2, ..., x_n)

                where x_1, ..., x_n are the elements of this sequence. Returns z if this sequence is empty.

    Definition Classes    LinearSeqOptimized → TraversableOnce → GenTraversableOnce
```

Basically, this method folds your entire collection into a single value. For a simpler example of its use case, consider the following chunk of code:

```
(1 to 10).toList.foldLeft(0) { (total, nextElement) => total + nextElement
}
```

So basically, we start with some empty accumulator and specify what to do for each element given a value accumulated so far in scope. Every subsequent element of the list must be added to the accumulator.

Returning to our example of `fetchToDepth`, the justification for the usage of `foldLeft` is as follows. Ultimately, we have a set of links, and for every element of this set, we need to calculate the set of URLs it links to. However, we are interested in a combined set with all the links from all of the URLs we have just called. Hence, the example is similar to the example of the addition of integers. Except here, we are computing a union over a collection of sets of links.

Let's now have a look at the code block that is passed as the second argument to `foldLeft`. First, we perform a logging statement. Next, we perform a step of calculating the links that belong to the current URL. We are then adding these links into the combined accumulator.

Notice also that before actually crawling a link, we perform a check to see whether it is contained already in the accumulator. It is crawled only if it is not contained in the current accumulator. This check is used to prevent redundant work. If the link is already contained in the accumulator, this means it was already processed by the algorithm since it is a depth-first traversal of the graph. So we do not need to process it again.

Also, notice that we perform the processing using a recursive call to the `fetchToDepth` function with the depth reduced by one:

```
else links
```

Finally, if the depth is 0, we will return the set of links that we have extracted from the current page. Which means we will stop the algorithm at this point.

The entire code for the `fetchToDepth` function looks as follows:

```
def fetchToDepth(url: URL, depth: Int, visited: Set[URL] = Set()): Set[URL]
= {
    val links = fetch(url).getOrElse(Set())

    if (depth > 0) links ++ links
      .filter(!visited(_))
      .toList
      .zipWithIndex
      .foldLeft(Set[URL]()) { case (accum, (next, id)) =>
        println(s"Progress for depth $depth: $id of ${links.size}")
        accum ++ (if (!accum(next)) fetchToDepth(next, depth - 1, accum)
else Set())
      }
      .toSet
    else links
}
```

Next, let's discuss what a parallel solution to the preceding problem might look like.

A parallel solution with Akka

Before approaching the problem of parallelizing our crawler, let's discuss our strategy of how we are going to approach it.

Strategy

We are going to model our problem of creating the actors' system with a tree of actors. This is because the task itself naturally forms a tree.

We have already discussed how all the links and pages on the internet comprise a graph. However, we have also discussed, in our example, two things that are not desirable when processing and traversing this graph—cycles and repetitions of work. So, if we have visited a certain node, we are not going to visit it anymore.

This means that our graph becomes a tree on processing time. This means you cannot get to a parent node from a child node when descending from a child node. This tree may look as follows:

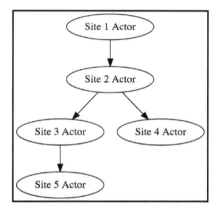

We are going to communicate with the root-level node. So basically, we will send this node a link that we are going to start crawling from, and afterward, this actor is going to crawl it. Once it extracts all the links from that link, it will for each such link spawn a child actor that will do the same operation on that link. This is a recursive strategy.

These worker actors will report the results to their parent actors. The results from the bottom-most actors are going to get propagated to the top-level actors all the way through the tree.

In this implementation, notice how we do not restrict our usage of actors. Every link gets worked on by a dedicated actor, and we don't really care about how many actors will get spawned. This is because actors are very lightweight primitives, and you should not be afraid to be generous with spawning actors.

Let's have a look at how to implement this strategy.

Implementation

First of all, let's have a look at the API we want and its usage:

```
val system = ActorSystem("PiSystem")
val root = system actorOf Worker.workerProps

(root ? Job(new URL("http://mvnrepository.com/"), 1)).onSuccess {
  case Result(res) =>
  println("Crawling finished successfully")
  println(res.take(10).mkString("\n"))
  println(res.size)

}
```

In the preceding code, you can see the main method of the parallelized actor application. As you can see, we create an actor system and a root-level worker actor. The idea is to represent all of the processing actors as a single class, `Worker`. The job of a single worker is to process a single URL and spawn additional workers to process the links extracted from it.

Next, you can see an example of querying the actor. First of all, we have the following line:

```
(root ? Job(new URL("http://mvnrepository.com/"), 1)).onSuccess {
```

Ordinarily, you send messages to actors using the `!` operator. However, here we are using `?` because we are using an ask pattern. In essence, `?` is the act of sending a message to an actor and waiting for it to respond with another message. The ordinary `!` returns `Unit`, however, the `?` ask pattern returns a `Future` of a possible response:

```
def !(message: Any)(implicit sender: ActorRef = Actor.noSender): Unit
    Sends a one-way asynchronous message.
def ?(message: Any)(implicit timeout: Timeout, sender: ActorRef = Actor.noSender):
    Future[Any]
```

So essentially, we are sending a message `Job` to the root actor, and we are expecting some response in `Future`.

Job is an ordinary case class that specifies the URL we are going to scrape, as well as the depth to which we are going to descend. The semantics of these two parameters are the same as that in the sequential example.

After that, we call the onSuccess method on Future to set the callbacks. So, once the result arrives at our location, we are going to report to the standard output.

Now, let's have a look at how the worker actor is implemented and how it works:

```
def receive = awaitingForTasks
```

In the preceding code, the receive method is implemented in terms of another method called awaitingForTasks. This is because we are going to change the implementation of receive in the future based on the information that is sent to the actor in the messages. Basically, our actor is going to have several states in which it is going to accept different sets of messages and react to them differently, but the idea is to encapsulate every state in a separate callback method, and then switch between the implementations of these callbacks.

Let's take a look at the default state of the actor, awaitingForTasks:

```
def awaitingForTasks: Receive = {
  case Job(url, depth, visited) =>
  replyTo = Some(sender)

  val links = fetch(url).getOrElse(Set()).filter(!visited(_))
  buffer = links
  /*...*/
```

awaitingForTasks specifies how an actor should react when it receives the Job message. The message is supposed to tell the actor to start crawling a certain URL for a certain depth. Also, as you can see, we store all the visited nodes in a visited collection. Visited is a set of all visited URLs, and the semantics of it and some motivation for it are the same as in the sequential example, to avoid repeating unnecessary work.

After that, we set the replyTo variable. It specifies the sender of the task, which is interested in receiving the result of our crawling.

After setting this variable, we start the process of crawling. First of all, we are using the fetch method we are already familiar with from the sequential example to obtain the set of all the links present on a given URL's page, and filter out the links that we have already visited.

After that, similar to our sequential example, we check whether the depth permits further descent, and if it does, we are going to perform the recursive processing of links as follows:

```
if (depth > 0) {
  println(s"Processing links of $url, descending now")

  children = Set()
  answered = 0

  for { l <- links } dispatch(l, depth - 1, visited ++ buffer)
  context become processing
}
```

First, we are going to define an empty set of the child actors so that we can keep track of their processing and be able to control our own state depending on the state change of the child actors. For example, we must know when exactly to report to the requesting actor with the results of the job. That must be done only once all the child actors have finished their work.

Also, we set the `answered` variable to 0. This is a variable to keep track of the number of actors who have successfully replied to this actor with the result of their processing. The idea is that once this metric reaches the `children` size number, we are going to reply to the `replyTo` actor with the result of the processing. The most interesting method here is `dispatch`:

```
def dispatch(lnk: URL, depth: Int, visited: Set[URL]): Unit = {
  val child = context actorOf Worker.workerProps
  children += child
  child ! Job(lnk, depth, visited)
}
```

So, `dispatch` creates a new worker actor and adds it to the set of all the child actors, and finally, they are requested to perform a processing job on a given URL. A separate worker actor is initialized for a separate URL.

Finally, let's pay attention to `context become processing` line of the `Job` clause. Essentially, `context become` is a method that switches the implementation of this actor's `receive`. Previously, we had an implementation of `awaitingForTasks`. However, now we are switching it to `processing`, which we will be discussing further in this chapter.

But before discussing it, let's have a look at their `else` branch of our `if` statement:

```
else {
 println(s"Reached maximal depth on $url - returning its links only")
 sender ! Result(buffer)
 context stop self
}
```

So, as we can see, once you have reached a certain depth, we are going to return the links collected into a buffer to the requesting actor.

Now let's have a look at the `processing` state of the actor:

```
def processing: Receive = {
  case Result(urls) =>
    replyTo match {
      case Some(to) =>
        answered += 1
        println(s"$self: $answered actors responded of ${children.size}")
        buffer ++= urls
        if (answered == children.size) {
          to ! Result(buffer)
          context stop self
        }

      case None => println("replyTo actor is None, something went wrong")
    }
}
```

As you can see, once this actor becomes processing actor, it is going to react to the `Result` messages, and it will stop reacting to the `Job` messages. This means that once you have sent a `Job` message to the actor and it starts processing it, it will no longer accept any other job request.

In the body of `processing`, we make sure that the `replyTo` actor is set. In principle, it should be set at all times once we reach this point. However, `replyTo` is an `Option`, and a nice way to handle optionality would be to have a `match` statement that explicitly checks for this `Option` to be defined. You never know what bugs can occur in such a program, so it's better to be safe than sorry.

The logic of `processing` is as follows. The `Result` is a message that is supposed to arrive at this actor from its child actors. First, we are going to increment the number of actors that have answered this actor. We are doing that with `answered += 1`.

After some debugging output, we add the payload that was sent to this actor by the child actor to the set of all the links collected by this actor—buffer ++ = urls.

Finally, we check whether all of the child actors have replied. We do so by checking the answered counter to be equal to the size of all the children. If it is, then we respond to the requesting actor with the links that we have collected, to ! Result(buffer), and finally we stop this actor because it has nothing else to do, context stop self.

The result of running this actor system is as follows:

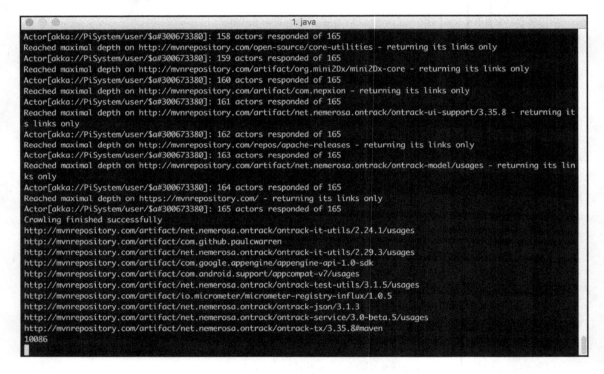

```
●  ●  ●                                    1. java
Actor[akka://PiSystem/user/$a#300673380]: 158 actors responded of 165
Reached maximal depth on http://mvnrepository.com/open-source/core-utilities - returning its links only
Actor[akka://PiSystem/user/$a#300673380]: 159 actors responded of 165
Reached maximal depth on http://mvnrepository.com/artifact/org.mini2Dx/mini2Dx-core - returning its links only
Actor[akka://PiSystem/user/$a#300673380]: 160 actors responded of 165
Reached maximal depth on http://mvnrepository.com/artifact/com.nepxion - returning its links only
Actor[akka://PiSystem/user/$a#300673380]: 161 actors responded of 165
Reached maximal depth on http://mvnrepository.com/artifact/net.nemerosa.ontrack/ontrack-ui-support/3.35.8 - returning it
s links only
Actor[akka://PiSystem/user/$a#300673380]: 162 actors responded of 165
Reached maximal depth on http://mvnrepository.com/repos/apache-releases - returning its links only
Actor[akka://PiSystem/user/$a#300673380]: 163 actors responded of 165
Reached maximal depth on http://mvnrepository.com/artifact/net.nemerosa.ontrack/ontrack-model/usages - returning its lin
ks only
Actor[akka://PiSystem/user/$a#300673380]: 164 actors responded of 165
Reached maximal depth on https://mvnrepository.com/ - returning its links only
Actor[akka://PiSystem/user/$a#300673380]: 165 actors responded of 165
Crawling finished successfully
http://mvnrepository.com/artifact/net.nemerosa.ontrack/ontrack-it-utils/2.24.1/usages
http://mvnrepository.com/artifact/com.github.paulcwarren
http://mvnrepository.com/artifact/net.nemerosa.ontrack/ontrack-it-utils/2.29.3/usages
http://mvnrepository.com/artifact/com.google.appengine/appengine-api-1.0-sdk
http://mvnrepository.com/artifact/com.android.support/appcompat-v7/usages
http://mvnrepository.com/artifact/net.nemerosa.ontrack/ontrack-test-utils/3.1.5/usages
http://mvnrepository.com/artifact/io.micrometer/micrometer-registry-influx/1.0.5
http://mvnrepository.com/artifact/net.nemerosa.ontrack/ontrack-json/3.1.3
http://mvnrepository.com/artifact/net.nemerosa.ontrack/ontrack-service/3.0-beta.5/usages
http://mvnrepository.com/artifact/net.nemerosa.ontrack/ontrack-tx/3.35.8#maven
10086
```

Caveats

Actor applications, although much more convenient to write and reason about compared to synchronization-based applications, are still much trickier than your ordinary sequential applications. In this section, we will discuss some caveats of the application.

Visited links

The caveat that has the most impact here is the partiality of tracking of the actors that this actor has already visited. If you remember, in the sequential example, we are using the `foldLeft` function to accumulate the results of every URL processing, and at all times we have a complete, up-to-date list of all the URLs collected by the entire application. This means the recursive crawling calls always have a full picture of what the application has collected so far.

In the diagram, we see a sequential example of processing with `foldLeft`:

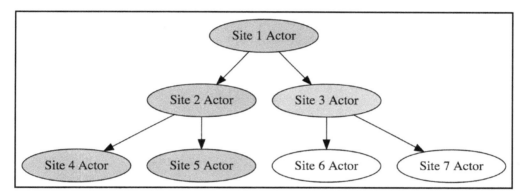

All the nodes that were already processed are highlighted in green, and the current URL is highlighted in blue. The current URL has the entire list of links that were collected previously. So, it is not going to process them. This situation is possible because the processing is done sequentially.

However, the situation is different for the parallel example described in the following diagram:

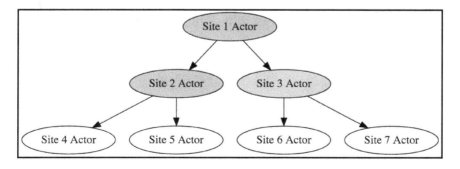

In the preceding diagram, in blue, you can see the current node. The green nodes are all the nodes the current node is aware of. Notice that although it is aware of its sibling nodes, it is not aware of the result of processing these sibling nodes. This is because the processing is done in parallel. In the sequential example, we had a depth-first tree-traversal from left to right. However, in the parallel example, the children are processed in parallel with each other. This means that one node may have information about its siblings. However, it will not have the information of the results collected from its siblings. This is because these results are collected in parallel with this node computing its own results. And we do not know which node will finish first. This means the preceding application is not ideal in terms of eliminating redundant work.

The problem of storing all the links the actors have visited is a classic problem of a shared mutable resource. A solution to this problem within an actor model would be to create a single actor that has a list of all the links already visited and that do not require further visiting. And so, before descending through the tree, every actor should consult that actor on the subject of whether or not to process certain links.

Another caveat that you should consider is fault tolerance.

Fault tolerance

To keep the example simple, in the parallel example we have used the `fetch` function from the sequential example to fetch the contents of a certain URL:

```
val links = fetch(url).getOrElse(Set()).filter(!visited(_))
```

The motivation for having this function return an `Option` was fault tolerance in the sequential example—if the result cannot be computed, we return a `None`. However, in an actor setting, Akka provides you with a framework to specify what to do if an actor has failed. So in principle, we could further refine our example with a dedicated `fetch` function that is perfectly capable of throwing exceptions. However, you might want to specify the actor-level logic on how to restart itself and how to keep its state through this kind of emergency.

Counting the responded actors

In the example, we counted the child actors that responded to an actor in order to determine when an actor is ready to respond to its parent actor:

```
answered += 1
// ...
if (answered == children.size) {
  to ! Result(buffer)
  context stop self
}
```

This scenario can give rise to certain undesirable outcomes. First of all, it means the time that it takes for the system to respond is equal to the time it takes for the deepest and slowest link to be resolved and processed.

The logic behind this reasoning is as follows. The `processing` callback determines when a node of a processing tree is considered completed:

```
if (answered == children.size)
```

So a node is completed whenever its slowest child is completed. However, we should remember that we are dealing with real-world processing, and we should not forget about all of the side effects that can happen in the real world. The first effect we've discussed is failures and errors. We address this side effect by engineering our application to be fault-tolerant. The other side effect is time. It can still be the case that some of the pages take unforgivably long to get fetched. So we must not forget that such a side effect can occur and might want to devise a strategy to tackle such side effects.

An intuitive strategy is timeouts. Just like in the case of fault tolerance, whenever a chunk of data takes too long to get processed, we can drop the chunk of data. The idea is that we still have enough data and for many applications, it is not crucial to have a 100% recall of all the target data.

Concretely, you might want to have a message scheduled to be sent to the current actor. Upon receiving this message, the actor will immediately send back all its results to the `replyTo` actor and terminate itself so that it doesn't react to any further messages. Also, the reaction to such a message may be to kill all the child actors recursively, because there is no longer a need for them to exist since they will not be able to report this error data through the parent actor. Another strategy may be to propagate this timeout message recursively to the child actors without killing them immediately. The child actors will then return whatever progress they have made at once and terminate.

Real-world side effects

In this subsection, we have already seen two instances of side effects—errors and time. The nature of the real world is such that often you don't know which side effects you will encounter.

Such side effects can include the necessity to limit the number of requests sent to a given domain because certain websites tend to block entities who send too many requests, or we might want to use proxy servers to access certain websites that are not accessible otherwise. Certain websites might have the data stored and fetched via Ajax, and ordinary techniques of scraping usually do not work.

All these scenarios can be modeled as their own side effects. The idea when working with a real-world application is always to have a look at the side effects that might arise in your particular scenario.

Once you have decided what you're going to encounter, you are able to decide how you are going to tackle and abstract the side effects. The tooling you can use includes the actor system's built-in capabilities or the capabilities of purely functional programming that we discussed in the first half of this book.

Summary

In this chapter, we looked at developing an application using Akka. First, we developed a sequential solution to the problem. Then, we determined the independent sub-tasks of this solution and discussed how to parallelize them. Finally, we devised a parallel solution using Akka.

Also, we discussed certain caveats that you might encounter when developing this kind of application. Most of them have to do with side effects that may occur, as well as actor-model-specific peculiarities when building parallel applications.

Introduction to Scala

This book uses Scala extensively as its primary example language. In this chapter, we will briefly overview the language basics. First, we will start from the motivation for using it as an example language.

Following are the topics covered in this chapter:

- Motivation for using Scala
- Variables and functions
- Control structures
- Inheritance model

This chapter is supposed to be a quick introduction for the rest of the book, and should not be regarded as a full-size tutorial on Scala.

Motivation for using Scala

The primary motivation for using Scala for examples in this book is as follows. First of all, Scala is a functional language. This means that it has support for almost all of the functional programming styles that have been developed so far. Another reason for choosing Scala is that it is designed explicitly with object-oriented programmers in mind. Scala positions itself as a mix between object-oriented and functional languages. This means that new programmers that come from the object-oriented world can use Scala as an object-oriented language. This facilitates the transition from the object-oriented style. In fact, Scala is often used as Java without semicolons, meaning that you can program your Scala programs similarly to how you used to program your Java programs. The preceding reasons facilitate transition for new programmers greatly. Also, Scala features a very powerful mechanics for functional programming. So, you can write functional programs just the way you would do in Haskell.

We can even say that Scala is more potent than Haskell because, in some circumstances, the object-oriented approach is absolutely necessary. You can access the entire JVM infrastructure, meaning that you can use any Java library from Scala easily. The infrastructure is very mature and industry-oriented. Unfortunately, you cannot say the same thing about Haskell, which is less production-ready than JVM languages. Purely functional languages such as Haskell are used in production. However, they do not possess as mature infrastructure, say, for dependency management or compile tools as does Scala. Even though you can use all of the object-oriented libraries from Java in Scala, there is an entire host of native libraries for Scala, which are also production-ready and can facilitate a purely functional programming style.

A final thing about Scala worth mentioning is that it is an experimental language. This means it is often used as a playground to test new features and research in computer science. This means that leading-edge research is available to you as a Scala programmer. Combine that with accessibility to JVM, and you get an ideal tool to advance your knowledge in computer science while developing real-world software.

In short, all of this means that while using Scala, you can use a wide spectrum of styles, from a conventional object-oriented approach all the way to leading edge functional programming research. This makes it a great language for examples in this books.

Scala infrastructure

First, let's have a look at the infrastructure developed for Scala. Let's have a look at the Scala interpreter first.

Scala interpreter

Although Scala is a compiled language, it has its own interpreter. It comes as part of the standard language distribution, and if you install Scala, you will have access to it. Please consult `https://www.scala-lang.org/` on the instructions to install Scala.

You can access the interpreter from the command line by simply typing `scala`.

In this interpreter, you can run Scala expressions and get evaluations of them in real time. Besides ordinary expressions, you can run interpreter-specific expressions to tune it up. This kind of expression usually starts with a colon followed by a keyword. To access the list of all the relevant Scala interpreter expressions, type the following command:

```
:help
```

The output of the preceding command looks as follows:

```
●  ●  ●                              1. java
Welcome to Scala 2.12.6 (Java HotSpot(TM) 64-Bit Server VM, Java 1.8.0_101).
Type in expressions for evaluation. Or try :help.

scala> :help
All commands can be abbreviated, e.g., :he instead of :help.
:completions <string>    output completions for the given string
:edit <id>|<line>        edit history
:help [command]          print this summary or command-specific help
:history [num]           show the history (optional num is commands to show)
:h? <string>             search the history
:imports [name name ...] show import history, identifying sources of names
:implicits [-v]          show the implicits in scope
:javap <path|class>      disassemble a file or class name
:line <id>|<line>        place line(s) at the end of history
:load <path>             interpret lines in a file
:paste [-raw] [path]     enter paste mode or paste a file
:power                   enable power user mode
:quit                    exit the interpreter
:replay [options]        reset the repl and replay all previous commands
:require <path>          add a jar to the classpath
:reset [options]         reset the repl to its initial state, forgetting all session entries
:save <path>             save replayable session to a file
:sh <command line>       run a shell command (result is implicitly => List[String])
:settings <options>      update compiler options, if possible; see reset
:silent                  disable/enable automatic printing of results
:type [-v] <expr>        display the type of an expression without evaluating it
:kind [-v] <type>        display the kind of a type. see also :help kind
:warnings                show the suppressed warnings from the most recent line which had any

scala>
```

SBT build tool

SBT is a build tool for Scala. It is a dedicated build tool developed specifically for Scala. It is possible to integrate Scala with Gradle or Maven, and in fact, this is an option that many teams prefer to do. SBT is supposed to be simple, but in fact, it is the precise opposite of simple. If you decide to use SBT as your Scala build tool, be advised that it possesses a complex infrastructure and is not well documented.

However, it is rather powerful. It allows you to write build descriptions in a subset of the Scala language. This means that your build scripts are Scala programs in themselves. This is not something you get with build tools, such as Gradle or Maven.

For this book, we do not need to be familiar with SBT. The GitHub repository with the examples for this books uses SBT, so you will need some basic familiarity with this software to run the examples. However, in this book, we do not feature SBT in parts that are crucial to functional programming. If you want to become more familiar with this tool, please see the official documentation of SBT.

Variables and functions

The backbone of the Scala language is variables and functions.

The variables are defined as follows:

```
scala> var foo = 3
foo: Int = 3
```

Variables are defined using the `var` keyword followed by the name of the variable, followed by the value you would like to assign to the variable.

Variables defined in the preceding manner are mutable. This means that once they are assigned, you can modify them:

```
scala> var foo = 3
foo: Int = 3

scala> foo = 20
foo: Int = 20
```

However, purely functional programming advocates against this style. Since Scala positions itself as a mixture of purely functional and object-oriented styles, it offers a way to define an immutable variable:

```
scala> val bar = 3
bar: Int = 3
```

Now, if you try to modify is this variable, you will get a compile-time error:

```
scala> val bar = 3
bar: Int = 3
```

```
scala> bar = 20
<console>:12: error: reassignment to val
       bar = 20
```

Besides all of these, Scala has a similar syntax for functions:

```
scala> def square(x: Int) = x * x
square: (x: Int)Int

scala> square(10)
res0: Int = 100

scala> square(2)
res1: Int = 4
```

So, a function is just like a value. However, it can be parameterized by arguments, and it will evaluate every time you call it. A normal value is evaluated only once.

Value can be modified with a `lazy` attribute to make it lazily evaluated:

```
scala> val x = { println("x value is evaluated now"); 10 }
x value is evaluated now
x: Int = 10

scala> lazy val x = { println("x value is evaluated now"); 10 }
x: Int = <lazy>

scala> x
x value is evaluated now
res2: Int = 10
```

When you do find this way, it is not evaluated right away but at the time when it is called for the first time. In a sense, it is similar to a function in this manner, because it is not evaluated right away. However, a function is evaluated every time we call it, and this can be not said of a value.

In the preceding code, all of their definitions are specified without the types they return. However, Scala is a strongly typed language. The compiler knows the types of all its variables. The compiler of Scala is powerful, and it can infer the types of its values and variables in a wide range of circumstances so that you do not need to provide them explicitly. So, in the preceding code, the compiler infers the types of the values, variables, and functions.

You can explicitly specify the type you would like a variable to have as follows:

```
scala> var x: Int = 5
x: Int = 5
```

```
scala> var x: String = 4
<console>:11: error: type mismatch;
 found : Int(4)
 required: String
       var x: String = 4
                       ^

scala> val x: Int = 5
x: Int = 5

scala> def square(x: Int): Int = x * x
square: (x: Int)Int
```

Also, notice that when you run the code without an explicit type specification through a Scala interpreter, the result will be aware of the type.

Control structures

Similarly to the majority of modern programming languages, the Scala language has a bunch of control structures; for example, for branching and looping. The control structures in question are `if`, `while`, `for`, and pattern matching.

If and While

`if` and `while` are implemented the same way as they are in any other programming language:

```
scala> val flag = true
flag: Boolean = true

scala> if (flag) {
     | println("Flag is true")
     | }
Flag is true

scala> if (!flag) {
     | println("Flag is false")
     | } else {
     | println("Flag is true")
     | }
Flag is true

scala> var x: Int = 0
x: Int = 0
```

```
scala> while (x < 5) {
     | x += 1
     | println(s"x = $x")
     | }
x = 1
x = 2
x = 3
x = 4
x = 5
```

Notice that in such constructs, you can optionally omit the curly braces if the body of the construct is a single expression:

```
scala> if (flag) println("Flag is true")
Flag is true
```

This is something you can do in many places in Scala. Wherever you have a body that consists of a single expression, you can omit the curly braces around this expression. There are certain exceptions to this rule, however.

For

The `for` statement is a little bit more unconventional. In fact, the `for` statement is syntactic sugar for an application of the `foreach`, `map`, and `flatMap` methods. For example, take a look at the following expression:

```
scala> val list = 0 to 3
list: scala.collection.immutable.Range.Inclusive = Range 0 to 3

scala> val result =
     | for {
     |   e <- list
     |   list2 = 0 to e
     |   e2 <- list2
     | } yield (e, e2)
result: scala.collection.immutable.IndexedSeq[(Int, Int)] = Vector((0,0),
(1,0), (1,1), (2,0), (2,1), (2,2), (3,0), (3,1), (3,2), (3,3))

scala> println(result.mkString("\n"))
(0,0)
(1,0)
(1,1)
(2,0)
(2,1)
(2,2)
(3,0)
```

```
(3,1)
(3,2)
(3,3)
```

The preceding `for` expression expands to the following method applications:

```
scala> val result = list.flatMap { e =>
     | val list2 = 0 to e
     | list2.map { e2 => (e, e2) }
     | }
result: scala.collection.immutable.IndexedSeq[(Int, Int)] = Vector((0,0),
(1,0), (1,1), (2,0), (2,1), (2,2), (3,0), (3,1), (3,2), (3,3))
```

So, basically, if a type defines the methods specified in the preceding code, you can write the application in terms of the `for` construct. For example, if you take an `Option` type that defines `map`, `flatMap`, and `foreach`, you can write a program as follows:

```
scala> val opt1 = Some(3)
opt1: Some[Int] = Some(3)

scala> val opt2 = Some(2)
opt2: Some[Int] = Some(2)

scala> val opt3: Option[Int] = None
opt3: Option[Int] = None

scala> val res1 =
     | for {
     |   e1 <- opt1
     |   e2 <- opt2
     | } yield e1 * e2
res1: Option[Int] = Some(6)

scala> val res2 =
     | for {
     |   e1 <- opt1
     |   e3 <- opt3
     | } yield e1 * e3
res2: Option[Int] = None
```

The `for` construct is not called a loop in Scala, but a Monadic flow. This is due to the special meaning of the `map` and `flatMap` functions in functional programming.

Pattern matching

Special constructs in Scala are partial functions and pattern matching. For example, you can write expressions as follows:

```
scala> val str = "Foo"
str: String = Foo

scala> str match {
     | case "Bar" => println("It is a bar")
     | case "Foo" => println("It is a foo")
     | }
It is a foo
```

More complex pattern matching is also possible. For example, given a list, we can match on its head and tail, or its head and its second argument and its tail:

```
scala> val list = List(1, 2, 3, 4, 5)
list: List[Int] = List(1, 2, 3, 4, 5)

scala> list match {
     | case e1 :: e2 :: rest => e1 + e2
     | }
<console>:13: warning: match may not be exhaustive.
It would fail on the following inputs: List(_), Nil
       list match {
       ^
res10: Int = 3
```

In fact, we can perform pattern matching on virtually anything with the help of so-called extractors. For example, it is possible to match on a custom data type as follows:

```
scala> class Dummy(x: Int) { val xSquared = x * x }
defined class Dummy

scala> object square {
     | def unapply(d: Dummy): Option[Int] = Some(d.xSquared)
     | }
defined object square

scala> new Dummy(3) match {
     | case square(s) => println(s"Square is $s")
     | }
Square is 9
```

The semantics of pattern matching is that on runtime, the environment will call the unapply function on the data type in question, and see whether this function returns some result or whether it is a None. If some result is returned in an option, the result is used to populate the variables in the pattern matching clause. Otherwise, the pattern is considered not matched.

Partial functions

The preceding pattern matching statements are very close to the notion of partial functions in Scala. The same way pattern matching statements have a certain domain of cases that they can handle and throw an exception in all other cases, partial functions are defined on a part of their input domain. For example, the preceding match statement can be converted into a partial function, as follows:

```scala
scala> val findSquare: PartialFunction[Any, Int] = {
     | case x: Int => x * x
     | case square(s) => s
     | }
findSquare: PartialFunction[Any,Int] = <function1>

scala> findSquare(2)
res12: Int = 4

scala> findSquare(new Dummy(3))
res13: Int = 9

scala> findSquare("Stuff")
scala.MatchError: Stuff (of class java.lang.String)
  at scala.PartialFunction$$anon$1.apply(PartialFunction.scala:255)
  at scala.PartialFunction$$anon$1.apply(PartialFunction.scala:253)
  at $anonfun$1.applyOrElse(<console>:13)
  at
scala.runtime.AbstractPartialFunction.apply(AbstractPartialFunction.scala:3
4)
  ... 28 elided
```

Inheritance model

Scala features a lot of object-oriented functionality. This means it supports inheritance concepts that are core to the object-oriented programming. Moreover, since Scala compiles to the Java Virtual Machine, it is essential that it supports the same model as Java for Java interoperability reasons.

Classes

Classes in Scala have similar semantics to their Java counterparts. They are defined as follows:

```
scala> :paste
// Entering paste mode (ctrl-D to finish)

class Dummy(constructorArgument: String) {
  var variable: Int = 0
  val value: String = constructorArgument * 2
  def method(x: Int): String = s"You gave me $x"
}

// Exiting paste mode, now interpreting.

defined class Dummy

scala> new Dummy("Foo")
res15: Dummy = Dummy@1a2f7e20

scala> res15.variable
res16: Int = 0

scala> res15.value
res17: String = FooFoo

scala> res15.method(2)
res18: String = You gave me 2
```

Also, it is possible to define so-called case classes in Scala. These classes are used to represent product types, that is, several types bound together in one datatype. For example, you can define a case class for the `User` domain object as follows:

```
scala> case class User(id: Int, name: String, passwordHash: String)
defined class User
```

As follows from their name, case classes are primarily used for pattern matching. When you are defining a case class, the compiler automatically generates extractors for this class, so that it can be used in pattern matching, as follows:

```
scala> val user = User(1, "dummyuser123",
"d8578edf8458ce06fbc5bb76a58c5ca4")
user: User = User(1,dummyuser123,d8578edf8458ce06fbc5bb76a58c5ca4)

scala> user match {
     |  case User(id, name, hash) => println(s"The user $name has id $id and
```

```
password hash $hash")
    | }
The user dummyuser123 has id 1 and password hash
d8578edf8458ce06fbc5bb76a58c5ca4
```

Also, the compiler generates convenient `toString`, `equals`, and `hashCode` methods for case classes:

```
scala> user.toString
res20: String = User(1,dummyuser123,d8578edf8458ce06fbc5bb76a58c5ca4)

scala> val user2 = User(user.id, user.name, user.passwordHash)
user2: User = User(1,dummyuser123,d8578edf8458ce06fbc5bb76a58c5ca4)

scala> user.equals(user2)
res21: Boolean = true

scala> user.hashCode
res22: Int = -363163489

scala> user2.hashCode
res23: Int = -363163489
```

Case classes are especially useful when modeling your domain.

Traits

The concept of an object-oriented interface is encapsulated in a trait in Scala. Similarly to an interface, a trait can have abstract members. However, unlike Java interfaces, traits may also have concrete members. These are injected into the implementing classes:

```
scala> :paste
// Entering paste mode (ctrl-D to finish)

trait Foo {
  def saySomething = println("I am inherited from Foo")
}

// Exiting paste mode, now interpreting.

defined trait Foo
```

Just like in Java, Scala classes can implement more than one trait. However, since traits in Scala can have concrete members, a new inheritance model that allows for that is required.

In Scala, a so-called linearization model is implemented. This means that whenever a class is inherited from multiple traits, they are organized into a clear sequence, which determines the priority of inheritance. For example, consider the following inheritance case:

```scala
scala> :paste
// Entering paste mode (ctrl-D to finish)

trait Foo {
  def saySomething = println("I am inherited from Foo")
}

trait Bar {
  def saySomething = println("I am inherited from Bar")
}

class Dummy extends Foo with Bar {
  override def saySomething = super.saySomething
}

// Exiting paste mode, now interpreting.

defined trait Foo
defined trait Bar
defined class Dummy

scala> new Dummy().saySomething
I am inherited from Bar
```

In this case, the `Bar` trait will get a priority over the `Foo` trait. This allows you to inherit from multiple traits and be aware of the precise sequence in which they will be applied.

Singleton objects

In Scala, it is impossible to make a class have static members. However, the concept of a static member is present in Java. Since Scala compiles to JVM, it needs a way to model this concept from Java. In Scala, a concept of a singleton object is used to model static members:

```scala
scala> :paste
// Entering paste mode (ctrl-D to finish)

object Foo {
  def say = println("I am Foo")
```

```
}

// Exiting paste mode, now interpreting.

defined object Foo

scala> Foo.say
I am Foo
```

In the preceding code, we can call the members of the singleton object without instantiating it or doing anything else with it, directly by its name. This is because it is a standalone fully fledged object that is constructed by our object statement. It exists in a single instance for the entire JVM.

The concept of a singleton object can be leveraged to model static members from Java. In Scala, there is a concept of a so-called companion object of a trait or a class. For any trait or class, if you define an object with the same name as the entity in question, it is considered a companion object to it. All of the static members of this class are defined as members of this singleton object. This allows you a clear separation between object and types. No longer can you call a member of a class without instantiating it.

Summary

In this chapter, we had a brief overview of the Scala programming language, in which the examples in this book are implemented. First of all, we have motivated the usage of Scala as an example language by the fact that it supports a wide range of programming styles.

Next, we had a look at what makes Scala different from other languages. Please keep in mind that this section is meant as a brief overview of the language, and you should use more comprehensive tutorials if you are interested in finding out more about Scala.

Assessments

Chapter 1

1. Specify what you want to do without specifying how exactly to do it.
2. Don't Repeat Yourself.
3. Goto is a lower-level primitive used to construct higher-level logic. All the logic that can be done with goto is doable with loops and other control structures. Declaring that you want to have a chunk of code looped excludes the possibility of bugs you would have if you tried to implement that loop by yourself, via goto.

Chapter 2

1. As behaviors of their objects.
2. As mathematical functions. Computations of a value based on some input values without side effects.
3. Functions that accept other functions as their inputs.
4. One application is to write control structures.

Chapter 3

1. You specify what needs to be done algorithmically, with the help of the low-level operations defined in the imperative collections.
2. You specify your program as an expression, with the help of high-level operations defined in the functional collections.
3. All the algorithms you may need are already implemented in the framework. You only need to call them by name when you need them. All the programs you may want to write can be expressed as a combination of the high-level operations implemented in the framework.

4. Understand the program as a mathematical expression rather than an algorithm. An expression is a structure that consists of operands (data) bound together by operators (behavior).

5. Lesser mental load on the programmer's mind. Algebraic programs usually remove side effects such as errors or time from the equation. So you do not need to think about them. This is in contrast to imperative programs where side effects occur freely and you need to keep them all in mind.

6. They reify side effects. Reification means turning phenomena into data. For example, instead of throwing an exception (phenomenon), we can return a data structure with that exception object from a method.

Chapter 4

1. For this book, side effects are defined as modifications and interactions with the environment outside the scope of the current unit of logic (function).

2. It is a data that can be changed by the program.

3. They cause extra mental load on your mind, which may lead to bugs. There are much more things to keep in mind with side effects and mutable state. The scope of your attention must extend much further than the piece of logic that you are working on at the moment.

4. It is a function that does not produce any side effects.

5. The ability to substitute a call to a function with the result of that call in code without changing the semantics of that code.

6. Decrease the mental load you face. Hence decrease the possibility of bugs.

7. Errors, an absence of a result, delayed competition, logging, input-output operations.

8. Yes, it is. Programming in the purely functional style is just a matter of understanding the concepts of side effects, understanding how they are harmful, being able to see the side effects and their harm in code, and knowledge on how to abstract them away. It is possible to write abstractions for side effects in modern imperative programming languages.

9. It is the presence of the infrastructure to support you. Most of the abstractions you may need are already present in the language. Most of the libraries are functional. The community is also likely to be oriented to the functional style.

Chapter 5

1. The first order reality is the reality of their business domain. The reality of the business domain is the reality in which the programming is solving their business task. The second-order reality is the reality of writing and running a program.
2. It provides a set of techniques to abstract away the phenomena of the second-order reality. First, you need to identify a repeating phenomenon. Then, you need to create a data structure to abstract away this phenomenon. The idea is to abstract away the phenomena by describing them, without actually making them happen.
3. The control over how the program runs and how its codebase is structured. If left without control, the complexity of the second-order reality can overwhelm you and cause mental load.

Chapter 6

1. Asynchronous computations.
2. Try represents the erroneous case as an exception. Exceptions may not always be desirable in a functional context since they make sense only when we want to throw them. Functional programming discourages throwing exceptions since they are side effects. Hence, we have a more general type called Either that is capable of representing an alternative between any two values.
3. One way of representing dependency injection in functional programming is via the Reader type. It is an abstraction of the fact that a computation depends on some value and cannot be executed without it. Reader is basically a function. However, it has a more concise signature, and the concept of continuation with flatmap is applied to it the same way as to any other effect type.
4. Flatmap allows you to sequentially compose side-effecting computations that use effect types to represent side effects.

Chapter 7

1. In Scala, Rich Wrapper is a pattern that allows you to simulate method injection into classes.
2. The pattern is implemented in Scala using the implicit conversions mechanism. Whenever you are trying to call a method on a class that doesn't have this method, the compiler tries to convert the instance of that class into another class that has this method.
3. See the explanation in the Intuition section in Chapter 7.
4. The motivation behind the type class pattern is to separate the effect types from their behaviour so that it is possible to define new behaviours and inject them into existing type classes based on different scenarios that arise when performing functional programming.
5. Yes, imperative languages do have type classes. However, in general, they lack mechanisms for their convenient usage.

Chapter 8

1. The type classes repeat from project to project. Hence, it makes sense to unify them into libraries.
2. `foldLeft, foldRight, traverse`.
3. Composition of a list of effectful computations.
4. `flatMap, pure, tailRecM`.
5. Sequential composition of two computations, one of which depends on the result of another.
6. Core package with type classes, `syntax` package with rich wrappers to inject syntax into effect types, `instances` package with the type class implementations for some effect types, `data` package with effect types for functional programming. Also, Cats has some auxiliary packages for more specific tasks not discussed in the book. Consult Cats documentation to learn about these.

Chapter 9

1. Blocking computations block the thread they are using in case they need to wait for some event to happen. Non-blocking computations release the thread if they don't need it. Released threads can be reused by other tasks.

2. You need asynchronous programming so that the threads are utilized doing useful work and not waiting upon an event to happen.

3. You can separate the business logic from the strategy of concurrent execution.

4. `IO` is an effect type which encapsulates the side effect of delayed computations. It uses the computation-as-a-value approach, and thus is a specification of the computation to be performed.

5. `start` to start `IO` asynchronously from a monadic flow. `flatMap` to compose `IO` with other `IO`s sequentially. Please see API documentation of `IO` for the full list.

Chapter 10

1. Monad Transformers are used to combine two effect types into one.

2. Tagless Final allows to delay the choice of an effect type and compose the program in terms of the capabilities this effect type must have.

3. Type-level computations allow to identify more errors on compile time, hence increasing compile-time safety.

Chapter 11

1. Whenever a thread needs to access a non-thread-safe resource, it takes a monitor on this resource. Monitor guarantees that only the thread that owns this monitor can work with his resource.

2. A Deadlock is a situation when two threads depend on the progress of one another, and neither of them can't progress until the other thread does. So both threads stagnate. See chapter 11 for an example of how a deadlock can occur.

3. An actor is a concurrency primitive. It has a mailbox where it can accept messages from other actors. It can send messages to other actors. It is defined in terms of reactions to the messages of other actors. Only one message can be processed at a time by a given actor. It is guaranteed that if an actor owns a non-thread-safe resource, no other actor is allowed to own it.

4. Since only one actor controls a non-thread safe resource, there is no danger of race conditions or deadlocks. Whenever other actors need access to the resource in question, they do so by asking the owner actor. The operation is performed indirectly by the owner actor of the resource, and the resource itself is never exposed to the outer world.

Chapter 12

1. Encapsulation with Actors—mutable state is only accessible from one actor, one thread. Actors are organized in hierarchies, and parents supervise children to achieve fault tolerance.

2. We do so by extending the `Actor` class and implementing the `receive` method.

3. We do so by calling the `actorOf` method on `ActorSystem` or `ActorContext`.

4. Using the `!` operator on an `ActorRef`—`targetActor ! message`.

5. The `!` operator implements a `fire-and-forget` type of message sending. It sends a message and returns immediately. Ask pattern involves sending a message using `?` operator instead, which returns a `Future[Any]` which will complete once the target actor responds—`val futureMessage: Future[Any] = targetActor ? message`.

6. The Pipe pattern instructs a `Future` to send a message to an actor upon completion of the `Future`'s computation—`future pipeTo targetActor`.

Other Books You May Enjoy

If you enjoyed this book, you may be interested in these other books by Packt:

Scala Reactive Programming
Rambabu Posa

ISBN: 9781787288645

- Understand the fundamental principles of Reactive and Functional programming
- Develop applications utilizing features of the Akka framework
- Explore techniques to integrate Scala, Akka, and Play together
- Learn about Reactive Streams with real-time use cases
- Develop Reactive Web Applications with Play, Scala, Akka, and Akka Streams
- Develop and deploy Reactive microservices using the Lagom framework and ConductR

Modern Scala Projects
Ilango Gurusamy

ISBN: 9781788624114

- Create pipelines to extract data or analytics and visualizations
- Automate your process pipeline with jobs that are reproducible
- Extract intelligent data efficiently from large, disparate datasets
- Automate the extraction, transformation, and loading of data
- Develop tools that collate, model, and analyze data
- Maintain the integrity of data as data flows become more complex
- Develop tools that predict outcomes based on "pattern discovery"
- Build really fast and accurate machine-learning models in Scala

Leave a review - let other readers know what you think

Please share your thoughts on this book with others by leaving a review on the site that you bought it from. If you purchased the book from Amazon, please leave us an honest review on this book's Amazon page. This is vital so that other potential readers can see and use your unbiased opinion to make purchasing decisions, we can understand what our customers think about our products, and our authors can see your feedback on the title that they have worked with Packt to create. It will only take a few minutes of your time, but is valuable to other potential customers, our authors, and Packt. Thank you!

Index

www.ingramcontent.com/pod-product-compliance
Lightning Source LLC
Chambersburg PA
CBHW080612060326
40690CB00021B/4665